Programming Bitcoin
Learn How to Program Bitcoin from Scratch

Jimmy Song

Beijing · Boston · Farnham · Sebastopol · Tokyo

Programming Bitcoin

by Jimmy Song

Published by O'Reilly Media, Inc., 1005 Gravenstein Highway North, Sebastopol, CA 95472.

O'Reilly books may be purchased for educational, business, or sales promotional use. Online editions are also available for most titles (*http://oreilly.com*). For more information, contact our corporate/institutional sales department: 800-998-9938 or *corporate@oreilly.com*.

Editors: Mike Loukides and Michele Cronin
Production Editor: Kristen Brown
Copyeditor: James Fraleigh
Proofreader: Rachel Head

Indexer: Judy McConville
Interior Designer: David Futato
Cover Designer: Karen Montgomery
Illustrator: Rebecca Demarest

March 2019:   First Edition

Revision History for the First Edition
2019-02-08:   First Release
2019-05-03:   Second Release

See *http://oreilly.com/catalog/errata.csp?isbn=9781492031499* for release details.

978-1-492-03149-9

[LSI]

Table of Contents

Foreword

It's fun to be a science fiction writer. To build a society where wealth is no longer a mirage erected on the empty promises of governments and manipulations of central banks, where exchanges of value can be completed among the trustless without paying a tax to middlemen, where code can be law, where collective decision making is not subject to the distortions of centralization…all I have to do is to open up a text editor and start making up stuff.

But compelling stories require more than imagination. They require knowledge of the world. "Worldbuilding" isn't about literary verisimilitude or strings of technobabble—it's about piercing through the superficial to ask "what if" questions that get at the heart of how the world works. The more a writer understands the mechanisms and codes that make up the world, the more interesting the questions they ask become.

Changing the real world is much, much harder than writing fiction, but it similarly requires knowledge. Beyond wisdom, idealism, grit, discipline, and single-minded determination in the face of doubt, a would-be world-changer needs understanding: of the available tools, their capabilities, and their limits.

The world of Bitcoin and blockchain today is still largely a world of fiction. Pundits selling hope and hype, with no understanding of the underlying reality, are far louder and more influential than those who are doing the hard work of bringing about change. Politically motivated screeds premised on fear and get-rich-quick schemes appealing to greed pass for knowledge with the help of a sprinkling of technobabble and trending hashtags.

But you can no more understand blockchain by reading whitepapers or thinkpieces than you can learn to build a company by going to business school and watching PowerPoints.

You have to code.

There is no better way to understand a technology than to build something useful to you in it. Until you've coded the fundamental building blocks of a blockchain application with your own hands, you will not be able to intuit the difference between empty hype and realizable possibility.

This book is the most efficient and comprehensive way to learn about Bitcoin and blockchain through coding. With great skill and insight, Jimmy Song has crafted a learning path that will take you from the basic math behind Bitcoin to the latest extensions and forks. Along the way, the exercises—refined through extensive work with live students—will not only teach you the mechanics of working with the blockchain, but also an intuition for the elegance and beauty of this technology.

The journey will not be easy. Even with a teacher as adept as Jimmy to guide you, this isn't a book to be flipped through when you're bored from bingeing on Netflix. It requires you to put in considerable work to get the most out of it. There is no shortcut, no CliffsNotes. But that is very much in line with the constitutive principle of Bitcoin: you must have skin in the game; you must demonstrate proof-of-work. Only then can you trust your knowledge.

Happy coding!

— Ken Liu

A winner of the Nebula, Hugo, and World Fantasy awards, Ken Liu (http://kenliu.name) is the author of The Dandelion Dynasty, *a silkpunk epic fantasy series in which the magic is engineering, and* The Paper Menagerie and Other Stories, *a collection. His SF story about blockchain, "Byzantine Empathy" (https://breakermag.com/kchain-science-fiction-premiere-byzantine-empathy/), was originally published by the MIT Press.*

Preface

This book will teach you the technology of Bitcoin at a fundamental level. It doesn't cover the monetary, economic, or social dynamics of Bitcoin, but knowing how Bitcoin works under the hood should give you greater insight into what's possible. There's a tendency to hype Bitcoin and blockchain without really understanding what's going on; this book is meant to be an antidote to that tendency.

After all, there are lots of books about Bitcoin, covering the history and the economic aspects and giving technical descriptions. The aim of this book is to get you to understand Bitcoin by coding all of the components necessary for a Bitcoin library. The library is not meant to be exhaustive or efficient. The aim of the library is to help you learn.

Who Is This Book For?

This book is for programmers who want to learn how Bitcoin works by coding it themselves. You will learn Bitcoin by coding the "bare metal" stuff in a Bitcoin library you will create from scratch. This is not a reference book where you can look up the specification for a particular feature.

The material from this book has been largely taken from my two-day seminar (*https://programmingblockchain.com*) where I teach developers all about Bitcoin. The material has been refined extensively, as I've taught this course more than 20 times, to over 400 people as of this writing.

By the time you're done with the book, you'll not only be able to create transactions, but also get all the data you need from peers and send the transactions over the network. It covers everything needed to accomplish this, including the math, parsing, network connectivity, and block validation.

What Do I Need to Know?

A prerequisite for this book is that you know programming—Python, in particular. The library itself is written in Python 3, and a lot of the exercises can be done in a controlled environment like a Jupyter notebook. An intermediate knowledge of Python is preferable, but even a beginning knowledge is probably sufficient to get a lot of the concepts.

Some knowledge of math is required, especially for Chapters 1 and 2. These chapters introduce mathematical concepts probably not familiar to those who didn't major in mathematics. Math knowledge around algebra level should suffice to understand the new concepts and to code the exercises covered in those chapters.

General computer science knowledge, for example, of hash functions, will come in handy but is not strictly necessary to complete the exercises in this book.

How Is the Book Arranged?

This book is split into 14 chapters. Each is meant to build on the previous one as the Bitcoin library gets built from scratch all the way to the end.

Roughly speaking, Chapters 1–4 establish the mathematical tools that we need; Chapters 5–8 cover transactions, which are the fundamental unit of Bitcoin; and Chapters 9–12 cover blocks and networking. The last two chapters cover some advanced topics but don't actually require you to write code.

Chapters 1 and 2 cover some math that we need. Finite fields and elliptic curves are needed to understand elliptic curve cryptography in Chapter 3. After we've established the public key cryptography at the end of Chapter 3, Chapter 4 adds parsing and serialization, which are how cryptographic primitives are stored and transmitted.

Chapter 5 covers the transaction structure. Chapter 6 goes into the smart contract language behind Bitcoin, called Script. Chapter 7 builds on all the previous chapters, showing how to validate and create transactions based on the elliptic curve cryptography from the first four chapters. Chapter 8 establishes how pay-to-script-hash (p2sh) works, which is a way to make more powerful smart contracts.

Chapter 9 covers blocks, which are groups of ordered transactions. Chapter 10 covers network communication in Bitcoin. Chapters 11 and 12 go into how a light client, or software without access to the entire blockchain, might request and broadcast data to and from nodes that store the entire blockchain.

Chapter 13 covers Segwit, a backward-compatible upgrade introduced in 2017, and Chapter 14 provides suggestions for further study. These chapters are not strictly necessary, but are included as a way to give you a taste of what more there is to learn.

Chapters 1–12 have exercises that require you to build up the library from scratch. The answers are in Appendix A and in the corresponding chapter directory in the GitHub repo (*https://github.com/jimmysong/programmingbitcoin*). You will be writing many Python classes and building toward not just validating transactions/blocks, but also creating your own transactions and broadcasting them on the network.

The last exercise in Chapter 12 specifically asks you to connect to another node on the testnet network, calculate what you can spend, construct and sign a transaction of your devising, and broadcast that on the network. The first 11 chapters essentially prepare you for this exercise.

There will be a lot of unit tests that your code will need to pass. The book has been designed this way so you can do the "fun" part of coding. To aid your progress, we will be looking at a lot of code and diagrams throughout.

Setting Up

To get the most out of this book, you'll want to create an environment where you can run the example code and do the exercises. Here are the steps required to set everything up:

1. Install Python 3.5 or higher on your machine:

   Windows

   https://www.python.org/ftp/python/3.6.2/python-3.6.2-amd64.exe

   macOS

   https://www.python.org/ftp/python/3.6.2/python-3.6.2-macosx10.6.pkg

   Linux

   See your distro docs (many Linux distributions, like Ubuntu, come with Python 3.5+ preinstalled)

2. Install pip by downloading this script: *https://bootstrap.pypa.io/get-pip.py*.

3. Run this script using Python 3:

   ```
   $ python3 get-pip.py
   ```

4. Install Git. The commands for downloading and installing it are at *https://git-scm.com/downloads*.

5. Download the source code for this book:

   ```
   $ git clone https://github.com/jimmysong/programmingbitcoin
   $ cd programmingbitcoin
   ```

6. Install virtualenv:

   ```
   $ pip install virtualenv --user
   ```

7. Install the requirements:

Linux/macOS

```
$ virtualenv -p python3 .venv
$ . .venv/bin/activate
(.venv) $ pip install -r requirements.txt
```

Windows

```
C:\programmingbitcoin> virtualenv -p
    C:\PathToYourPythonInstallation\Python.exe .venv
C:\programmingbitcoin> .venv\Scripts\activate.bat
C:\programmingbitcoin> pip install -r requirements.txt
```

8. Run Jupyter Notebook:

```
(.venv) $ jupyter notebook
[I 11:13:23.061 NotebookApp] Serving notebooks from local directory:
  /home/jimmy/programmingbitcoin
[I 11:13:23.061 NotebookApp] The Jupyter Notebook is running at:
[I 11:13:23.061 NotebookApp] http://localhost:8888/?token=
  f849627e4d9d07d2158e3fcde93590eff4a9a7a01f65a8e7
[I 11:13:23.061 NotebookApp] Use Control-C to stop this server and
  shut down all kernels (twice to skip confirmation).
[C 11:13:23.065 NotebookApp]

    Copy/paste this URL into your browser when you connect for
    the first time, to login with a token:
        http://localhost:8888/?token=
        f849627e4d9d07d2158e3fcde93590eff4a9a7a01f65a8e7
```

You should have a browser open up automatically, as shown in Figure P-1.

Figure P-1. Jupyter

From here, you can navigate to the chapter directories. To do the exercises from Chapter 1, you would navigate to *code-ch01* (Figure P-2).

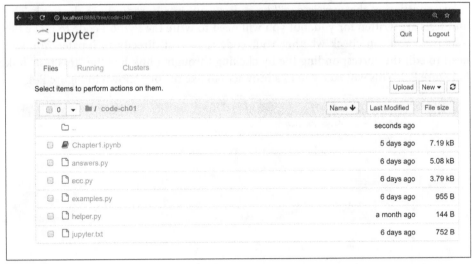

Figure P-2. Jupyter directory view

From here you can open *Chapter1.ipynb* (Figure P-3).

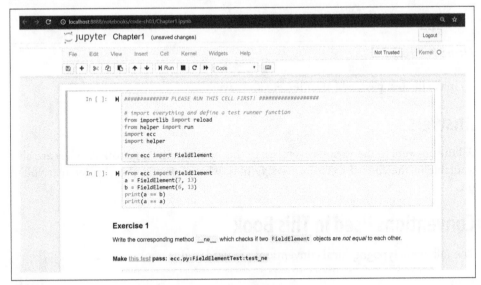

Figure P-3. Jupyter notebook

You may want to familiarize yourself with this interface if you haven't seen it before, but the gist of Jupyter is that it can run Python code from the browser in a way that makes experimenting easy. You can run each "cell" and see the results as if this were an interactive Python shell.

A large portion of the exercises will be coding concepts introduced in the book. The unit tests are written for you, but you will need to write the Python code to make the tests pass. You can check whether your code is correct directly in Jupyter. You will need to edit the corresponding file by clicking through a link like the "this test" link in Figure P-3. This will take you to a browser tab like the one shown in Figure P-4.

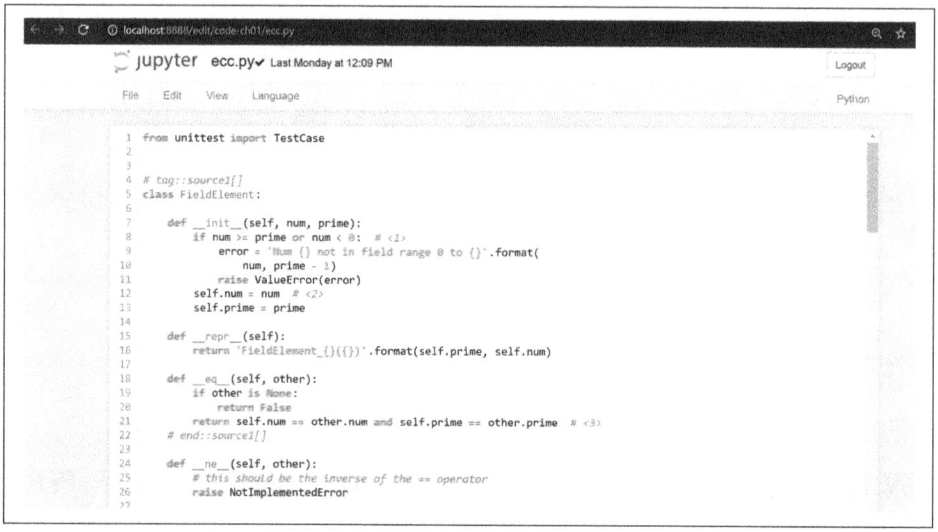

Figure P-4. ecc.py

To make the test pass, edit the file here and save.

Answers

All the answers to the various exercises in this book are in Appendix A. They are also available in the *code-ch<xx>/answers.py* files, where *<xx>* is the chapter that you're on.

Conventions Used in This Book

The following typographical conventions are used in this book:

Italic
> Indicates new terms, URLs, email addresses, filenames, and file extensions.

Constant width

Used for program listings, as well as within paragraphs to refer to program elements such as variable or function names, databases, data types, environment variables, statements, and keywords.

Constant width bold

Shows commands or other text that should be typed literally by the user.

Constant width italic

Shows text that should be replaced with user-supplied values or by values determined by context.

 This element signifies a tip or suggestion.

 This element signifies a general note.

 This element indicates a warning or caution.

Using Code Examples

Supplemental material (code examples, exercises, etc.) is available for download at *https://github.com/jimmysong/programmingbitcoin*.

This book is here to help you get your job done. In general, if example code is offered with this book, you may use it in your programs and documentation. You do not need to contact us for permission unless you're reproducing a significant portion of the code. For example, writing a program that uses several chunks of code from this book does not require permission. Selling or distributing a CD-ROM of examples from O'Reilly books does require permission. Answering a question by citing this book and quoting example code does not require permission. Incorporating a significant amount of example code from this book into your product's documentation does require permission.

We appreciate, but do not require, attribution. An attribution usually includes the title, author, publisher, and ISBN. For example: "*Programming Bitcoin* by Jimmy Song (O'Reilly). Copyright 2019 Jimmy Song, 978-1-492-03149-9."

If you feel your use of code examples falls outside fair use or the permission given above, feel free to contact us at *permissions@oreilly.com*.

O'Reilly Online Learning

 For almost 40 years, *O'Reilly Media* has provided technology and business training, knowledge, and insight to help companies succeed.

Our unique network of experts and innovators share their knowledge and expertise through books, articles, conferences, and our online learning platform. O'Reilly's online learning platform gives you on-demand access to live training courses, in-depth learning paths, interactive coding environments, and a vast collection of text and video from O'Reilly and 200+ other publishers. For more information, please visit *http://oreilly.com*.

How to Contact Us

Please address comments and questions concerning this book to the publisher:

O'Reilly Media, Inc.
1005 Gravenstein Highway North
Sebastopol, CA 95472
800-998-9938 (in the United States or Canada)
707-829-0515 (intenational or local)
707-829-0104 (fax)

We have a web page for this book, where we list errata, examples, and any additional information. You can access this page at *http://bit.ly/programmingBitcoin*.

To comment or ask technical questions about this book, send email to *bookquestions@oreilly.com*.

For more information about our books, courses, conferences, and news, see our website at *http://www.oreilly.com*.

Find us on Facebook: *http://facebook.com/oreilly*

Follow us on Twitter: *http://twitter.com/oreillymedia*

Watch us on YouTube: *http://www.youtube.com/oreillymedia*

Acknowledgments

The number of people that got me here is legion. The experiences and knowledge that an author draws from tend to have a lot of sources, and it's difficult to give them all their proper credit. This is my way of saying that I'm probably going to forget a significant number of people, and for that I sincerely apologize.

First, I want to thank my Lord Jesus Christ for putting me on this journey. If not for my faith, I would not have had the ethical conviction to blog about the importance of sound money in general and Bitcoin in particular, which ultimately led to the writing of this book.

My parents, Kathy and Kyung-Sup, had the courage to immigrate to America back when I was eight years old, which ultimately led to the opportunities I've had. My dad got me my first computers (a Commodore 16, a generic Hyundai 8086, and a 486 33-Mhz from a manufacturer I don't remember), and my mom got me private programming tutoring as a sixth- and seventh-grader from a woman whose name I can't remember. How she found her when I showed some proclivity for programming, I don't know. That teacher-whose-name-I-can't-remember stoked that natural tendency, and I hope this acknowledgment finds its way to her.

Speaking of which, I've had many teachers along the way, some of whom I hated at the time. Mr. Marain, Mrs. Edelman, and Mrs. Nelson taught me math and computer science back in high school. I'm not necessarily a fan of the current education system, but what I learned in those classes was instrumental to my love of math and programming.

My high school classmate Eric Silberstein gave me my first job out of college as a programmer at Idiom Technologies. I was slated to go down the consulting path before a fateful phone call back in 1998 that led me down the programmer/startup path instead. In a sense, I've never left.

At that first job, I met Ken Liu, and I'm amazed that we're where we are in our careers writing books. He not only gave me great advice about book publishing, but also wrote the wonderful foreword. He's also a great sounding board and an amazing friend, and I'm privileged to know him.

With regard to Bitcoin, the anonymous developer Satoshi Nakamoto invented what I thought before was impossible: decentralized digital scarcity. Bitcoin is a profound invention that the world hasn't fully grokked. The website Slashdot (*http://slash dot.org*) introduced me to Bitcoin in 2011, and Alex Mizrahi gave me my first work as a Bitcoin developer in 2013. I had no idea what I was doing, but I learned quite a bit about what Bitcoin was about through his direction.

The Austin Bitcoin Meetup in 2013 was where I met a lot of Bitcoiners, and at the subsequent Texas Bitcoin Conference in 2014 I met a ton of people that I still know today. Though this meetup and conference are not ones I attend anymore, I am grateful for the people I met there—among them Michael Goldstein, Daniel Krawisz, and Napoleon Cole.

Alan Reiner recruited me to Armory back in 2014, and I'm grateful I had the opportunity to contribute to such a significant project.

Paxos/itBit was where I worked next. Chad Cascarilla and Raj Nair were the CEO and VP of Engineering who stretched me while I was there. Raj, in particular, made me write some blog posts for Paxos, which I was surprised to find I enjoyed. This led to blog posts on my own site, which eventually led to my seminars, which finally led to this book.

Three colleagues I met at Paxos were particularly significant. Richard Kiss, creator of pycoin, was the impetus for my writing this book, as he proposed that we write one together. Somewhere along the way, that turned into just me writing a book, but I'm grateful to him for giving me the idea. Aaron Caswell is a great dev who has helped me out in my seminars and reviewed this book. He's a great programmer and mathematician, and a pretty good karate fighter from what I hear. Michael Flaxman has reviewed almost everything Bitcoin-related I've written, including my blog, many of my GitHub libraries, and this book. He's also helped me out on my seminars and is just a great person to talk to. He's one of those people who make others sharper, and I'm grateful for his significant friendship.

Vortex, Thomas Hunt, and Tone Vays brought me into the World Crypto Network back in 2017, which launched my YouTube career. Tone in particular has been an inspiration on working hard and being dedicated to a craft.

John Newbery was very helpful to me when I first contributed to Bitcoin Core, and he's just a really good person, period. He's become such a significant contributor in a relatively short time, which speaks to his talent and dedication. I'm grateful to other Core developers too, like Marco Falke, Wladimir van der Laan, Alex Morcos, Pieter Wuille, Matt Corallo, Suhas Daftuar, and Greg Maxwell, who have reviewed some of my code and blog posts.

David Harding was exceptional in his technical review of this book. He reviewed the text three times, with a lot of great comments. He'd better write a book about Bitcoin at some point, because he has an encyclopedic knowledge of nearly everything that's happend in Bitcoin's history.

Jim Calvin helped me get in contact with people at O'Reilly, and Mike Loukides was the intake editor who green-lighted the project. Andreas Antonopolous gave me some great pointers and recommended me to people at O'Reilly. Michele Cronin kept me on track during my year-long writing spree. Kristen Brown was the production editor who did a lot to get this book out on time. James Fraleigh did copyediting. I'm a big fan of this publisher, and Tim O'Reilly has done a great service to the tech community by making such great books available.

The crew of Bitcoiners in Austin have helped keep me on track. They include Bryan Bishop, Will Cole, Napoleon Cole, Tipton Cole, Tuur Demeester, Johnny Dilley, Michael Flaxman, Parker Lewis, Justin Moon, Alan Piscitello, and Andrew Poelstra. There's also a Slack channel (TAAS) where Saifedean Ammous announced that he was writing a book whose success inspired me.

Alumni of my course, Programming Blockchain, in addition to Bitcoiners on GitHub also did tech reviews of my book. Jeff Flowers, Brian Liotti, Casey Bowman, Johnson Lau, Albert Chen, Jason Les, Thomas Braunberger, Eduardo Cobain, and Spencer Hanson are among the people who found issues. Katrina Javier is my faithful assistant that helped me make a lot of the diagrams.

My subscribers on YouTube, my followers on Twitter, and my readers on Medium have been instrumental in helping me find my voice and setting me on my path as an entrepreneur.

Lastly, my wife, Julie, and my kids supported me throughout the past couple of years. If not for them, I doubt I'd have had the motivation to work as I have.

CHAPTER 1

Finite Fields

One of the most difficult things about learning how to program Bitcoin is knowing where to start. There are so many components that depend on each other that learning one thing may lead you to have to learn another, which in turn may lead you to need to learn something else before you can understand the original thing.

This chapter is going to get you off to a more manageable start. It may seem strange, but we'll start with the basic math that you need to understand elliptic curve cryptography. Elliptic curve cryptography, in turn, gives us the signing and verification algorithms. These are at the heart of how transactions work, and transactions are the atomic unit of value transfer in Bitcoin. By learning about finite fields and elliptic curves first, you'll get a firm grasp of concepts that you'll need to progress logically.

Be aware that this chapter and the next two chapters may feel a bit like you're eating vegetables, especially if you haven't done formal math in a long time. I would encourage you to get through them, though, as the concepts and code presented here will be used throughout the book.

Learning Higher-Level Math

Learning about new mathematical structures can be a bit intimidating, and in this chapter, I hope to dispel the myth that high-level math is difficult. Finite fields, in particular, don't require all that much more in terms of prior mathematical knowledge than, say, algebra.

Think of finite fields as something that you could have learned instead of trigonometry, except that the education system you're a part of decided that trigonometry was more important for you to learn. This is my way of telling you that finite fields are not that hard to learn and require no more background than algebra.

This chapter is required if you want to understand elliptic curve cryptography. Elliptic curve cryptography is required for understanding signing and verification, which is at the heart of Bitcoin itself. As I've said, this chapter and the next two may feel a bit unrelated, but I encourage you to endure. The fundamentals here will not only make understanding Bitcoin a lot easier, but also make understanding Schnorr signatures, confidential transactions, and other leading-edge Bitcoin technologies easier.

Finite Field Definition

Mathematically, a *finite field* is defined as a finite set of numbers and two operations + (addition) and • (multiplication) that satisfy the following:

1. If a and b are in the set, $a + b$ and $a • b$ are in the set. We call this property *closed*.

2. 0 exists and has the property $a + 0 = a$. We call this the *additive identity*.

3. 1 exists and has the property $a • 1 = a$. We call this the *multiplicative identity*.

4. If a is in the set, $-a$ is in the set, which is defined as the value that makes $a + (-a) = 0$. This is what we call the *additive inverse*.

5. If a is in the set and is not 0, a^{-1} is in the set, which is defined as the value that makes $a • a^{-1} = 1$. This is what we call the *multiplicative inverse*.

Let's unpack each of these criteria.

We have a set of numbers that's finite. Because the set is finite, we can designate a number p, which is how big the set is. This is what we call the *order* of the set.

#1 says we are closed under addition and multiplication. This means that we have to define addition and multiplication in a way that ensures the results stay in the set. For example, a set containing {0,1,2} is *not* closed under addition, since $1 + 2 = 3$ and 3 is not in the set; neither is $2 + 2 = 4$. Of course we can define addition a little differently to make this work, but using "normal" addition, this set is not closed. On the other hand, the set {−1,0,1} is closed under normal multiplication. Any two numbers can be multiplied (there are nine such combinations), and the result is always in the set.

The other option we have in mathematics is to define multiplication in a particular way to make these sets closed. We'll get to how exactly we define addition and multiplication later in this chapter, but the key concept here is that we can *define addition and subtraction differently than the addition and subtraction you are familiar with*.

#2 and #3 mean that we have the additive and multiplicative identities. That means 0 and 1 are in the set.

#4 means that we have the additive inverse. That is, if a is in the set, $-a$ is in the set. Using the additive inverse, we can define subtraction.

#5 means that multiplication has the same property. If a is in the set, a^{-1} is in the set. That is $a \cdot a^{-1} = 1$. Using the multiplicative inverse, we can define division. This will be the trickiest to define in a finite field.

Defining Finite Sets

If the order (or size) of the set is p, we can call the elements of the set, 0, 1, 2, ... $p - 1$. These numbers are what we call the *elements* of the set, not necessarily the traditional numbers 0, 1, 2, 3, etc. They behave in many ways like traditional numbers, but have some differences in how we add, subtract, multiply, and so forth.

In math notation the finite field set looks like this:

$$F_p = \{0, 1, 2, ... p-1\}$$

What's in the finite field set are the elements. F_p is a specific finite field called "field of p" or "field of 29" or whatever the size of it is (again, the size is what mathematicians call *order*). The numbers between the {}s represent what elements are in the field. We name the elements 0, 1, 2, etc. because these names are convenient for our purposes.

A finite field of order 11 looks like this:

$$F_{11} = \{0, 1, 2, 3, 4, 5, 6, 7, 8, 9, 10\}$$

A finite field of order 17 looks like this:

$$F_{17} = \{0, 1, 2, 3, 4, 5, 6, 7, 8, 9, 10, 11, 12, 13, 14, 15, 16\}$$

A finite field of order 983 looks like this:

$$F_{983} = \{0, 1, 2, ... 982\}$$

Notice the order of the field is always 1 more than the largest element. You might have noticed that the field has a prime order every time. For a variety of reasons that will become clear later, it turns out that fields *must* have an order that is a power of a prime, and that the finite fields whose order is prime are the ones we're interested in.

Constructing a Finite Field in Python

We want to represent each finite field element, so in Python, we'll be creating a class that represents a single finite field element. Naturally, we'll name the class `FieldElement`.

The class represents an element in a field F_{prime}. The bare bones of the class look like this:

```
class FieldElement:

    def __init__(self, num, prime):
        if num >= prime or num < 0:    ❶
            error = 'Num {} not in field range 0 to {}'.format(
                num, prime - 1)
            raise ValueError(error)
        self.num = num    ❷
        self.prime = prime

    def __repr__(self):
        return 'FieldElement_{}({})'.format(self.prime, self.num)

    def __eq__(self, other):
        if other is None:
            return False
        return self.num == other.num and self.prime == other.prime    ❸
```

❶ We first check that num is between 0 and prime-1 inclusive. If not, we get an invalid FieldElement and we raise a ValueError, which is what we should raise when we get an inappropriate value.

❷ The rest of the __init__ method assigns the initialization values to the object.

❸ The __eq__ method checks if two objects of class FieldElement are equal. This is only true when the num and prime properties are equal.

What we've defined already allows us to do this:

```
>>> from ecc import FieldElement
>>> a = FieldElement(7, 13)
>>> b = FieldElement(6, 13)
>>> print(a == b)
False
>>> print(a == a)
True
```

Python allows us to override the == operator on FieldElement with the __eq__ method, which is something we'll be taking advantage of going forward.

You can see this in action in the code that accompanies this book. Once you've set up Jupyter Notebook (see "Setting Up" on page xv), you can navigate to *code-ch01/Chapter1.ipynb* and run the code to see the results. For the next exercise, you'll want to open up *ecc.py* by clicking the link in the Exercise 1 box. If you get stuck, please remember that the answers to every exercise are in Appendix A.

Exercise 1

Write the corresponding method `__ne__`, which checks if two `FieldElement` objects are *not equal* to each other.

Modulo Arithmetic

One of the tools we can use to make a finite field closed under addition, subtraction, multiplication, and division is something called *modulo arithmetic.*

We can define addition on the finite set using modulo arithmetic, which is something you probably learned when you first learned division. Remember problems like the one in Figure 1-1?

$$\begin{array}{r} 2R1 \\ 3\overline{)7} \end{array}$$

Figure 1-1. Long division example 1

Whenever the division wasn't even, there was something called the "remainder," which is the amount left over from the actual division. We define modulo in the same way. We use the operator % for modulo:

$$7 \% 3 = 1$$

Figure 1-2 shows another example.

$$\begin{array}{r} 3R6 \\ 7\overline{)27} \end{array}$$

Figure 1-2. Long division example 2

Formally speaking, the modulo operation is the remainder after division of one number by another. Let's look at another example with larger numbers:

$$1747 \% 241 = 60$$

If it helps, you can think of modulo arithmetic as "wraparound" or "clock" math. Imagine a problem like this:

It is currently 3 o'clock. What hour will it be 47 hours from now?

The answer is 2 o'clock because (3 + 47) % 12 = 2 (see Figure 1-3).

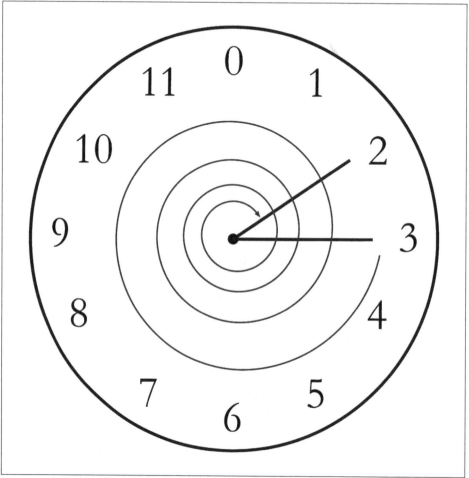

Figure 1-3. Clock going forward 47 hours

We can also see this as "wrapping around" in the sense that we go past 0 every time we move ahead 12 hours.

We can perform modulo on negative numbers. For example, you can ask:

It is currently 3 o'clock. What hour was it 16 hours ago?

The answer is 11 o'clock:

$(3 - 16) \% 12 = 11$

The minute hand is also a modulo operation. For example, you can ask:

It is currently 12 minutes past the hour. What minute will it be 843 minutes from now?

It will be 15 minutes past the hour:

$(12 + 843) \% 60 = 15$

Likewise, we can ask:

It is currently 23 minutes past the hour. What minute will it be 97 minutes from now?

In this case, the answer is 0:

$(23 + 97) \% 60 = 0$

0 is another way of saying there is no remainder.

The result of the modulo (%) operation for minutes is always between 0 and 59, inclusive. This happens to be a very useful property as even very large numbers can be brought down to a relatively small range with modulo:

$14738495684013 \% 60 = 33$

We'll be using modulo as we define field arithmetic. Most operations in finite fields use the modulo operator in some capacity.

Modulo Arithmetic in Python

Python uses the % operator for modulo arithmetic. Here is how the modulo operator is used:

```
>>> print(7 % 3)
1
```

We can also use the modulo operator on negative numbers, like this:

```
>>> print(-27 % 13)
12
```

Finite Field Addition and Subtraction

Remember that we need to define finite field addition such that we ensure the result is still in the set. That is, we want to make sure that addition in a finite field is *closed*.

We can use what we just learned, modulo arithmetic, to make addition closed. Let's say we have a finite field of 19:

$$F_{19} = \{0, 1, 2, \dots 18\}$$

where $a, b \in F_{19}$. Note that the symbol $\in$ means "is an element of." In our case, a and b are elements of F_{19}.

Addition being closed means:

$$a +_f b \in F_{19}$$

We denote finite field addition with $+_f$ to avoid confusion with normal integer addition, $+$.

If we utilize modulo arithmetic, we can guarantee this to be the case. We can define $a +_f b$ this way:

$$a +_f b = (a + b)\%19$$

For example:

$$7 +_f 8 = (7+8)\%19 = 15$$
$$11 +_f 17 = (11+17)\%19 = 9$$

and so on.

We take any two numbers in the set, add, and "wrap around" the end to get the sum. We are creating our own addition operator here and the result is a bit unintuitive. After all, $11 +_f 17 = 9$ just doesn't look right because we're not used to finite field addition.

More generally, we define field addition this way:

$$a +_f b = (a + b)\%p$$

where $a, b \in F_p$.

We also define the additive inverse this way. $a \in F_p$ implies that $-_f a \in F_p$:

$$-_f a = (-a) \% p$$

Again, for clarity, we use $-_f$ to distinguish field subtraction and negation from integer subtraction and negation.

In F_{19}:

$$-_f9 = (-9) \ \% \ 19 = 10$$

which means that:

$$9 +_f 10 = 0$$

And that turns out to be true.

Similarly, we can do field subtraction:

$$a -_f b = (a - b)\%p$$

where $a, b \in F_p$.

In F_{19}:

$$11 -_f 9 = (11-9)\%19 = 2$$
$$6 -_f 13 = (6-13)\%19 = 12$$

and so on.

Exercise 2

Solve these problems in F_{57} (assume all +'s here are $+_f$ and –'s here are $-_f$):

- $44 + 33$
- $9 - 29$
- $17 + 42 + 49$
- $52 - 30 - 38$

Coding Addition and Subtraction in Python

In the class `FieldElement` we can now define `__add__` and `__sub__` methods. The idea of these methods is that we want something like this to work:

```
>>> from ecc import FieldElement
>>> a = FieldElement(7, 13)
>>> b = FieldElement(12, 13)
>>> c = FieldElement(6, 13)
>>> print(a+b==c)
True
```

In Python we can define what addition (or the + operator) means for our class with the __add__ method. So how do we do this? We combine what we learned with modulo arithmetic and create a new method of the class FieldElement like so:

```
def __add__(self, other):
    if self.prime != other.prime:  ❶
        raise TypeError('Cannot add two numbers in different Fields')
    num = (self.num + other.num) % self.prime  ❷
    return self.__class__(num, self.prime)  ❸
```

❶ We have to ensure that the elements are from the same finite field, otherwise this calculation doesn't have any meaning.

❷ Addition in a finite field is defined with the modulo operator, as explained earlier.

❸ We have to return an instance of the class, which we can conveniently access with self.__class__. We pass the two initializing arguments, num and self.prime, for the __init__ method we saw earlier.

Note that we could use FieldElement instead of self.__class__, but this would not make the method easily inheritable. We will be subclassing FieldElement later, so making the method inheritable is important here.

Exercise 3

Write the corresponding __sub__ method that defines the subtraction of two FieldElement objects.

Finite Field Multiplication and Exponentiation

Just as we defined a new addition $(+_f)$ for finite fields that was closed, we can also define a new multiplication for finite fields that's closed. By multiplying the same number many times, we can also define exponentiation. In this section, we'll go through exactly how to define this using modulo arithmetic.

Multiplication is adding multiple times:

$$5 \cdot 3 = 5 + 5 + 5 = 15$$
$$8 \cdot 17 = 8 + 8 + 8 + \ldots (17 \text{ total 8's}) \ldots + 8 = 136$$

We can define multiplication on a finite field the same way. Operating in F_{19} once again:

$$5 \cdot_f 3 = 5 +_f 5 +_f 5$$
$$8 \cdot_f 17 = 8 +_f 8 +_f 8 +_f \ldots (17 \text{ total 8's}) \ldots +_f 8$$

We already know how to do the right side, and that yields a number within the F_{19} set:

$$5 \cdot_f 3 = 5 +_f 5 +_f 5 = 15 \% 19 = 15$$
$$8 \cdot_f 17 = 8 +_f 8 +_f 8 +_f ... \text{(17 total 8's)} ... +_f 8 = (8 \cdot 17) \% 19 = 136 \% 19 = 3$$

Note that the second result is pretty unintuitive. We don't normally think of $8 \cdot_f 17 = 3$, but that's part of what's necessary in order to define multiplication to be closed. That is, the result of field multiplication is always in the set $\{0, 1, ... p-1\}$.

Exponentiation is simply multiplying a number many times:

$$7^3 = 7 \cdot_f 7 \cdot_f 7 = 343$$

In a finite field, we can do exponentiation using modulo arithmetic.

In F_{19}:

$$7^3 = 343 \% 19 = 1$$
$$9^{12} = 7$$

Exponentiation again gives us counterintuitive results. We don't normally think $7^3 = 1$ or $9^{12} = 7$. Again, finite fields have to be defined so that the operations *always* result in a number within the field.

Exercise 4

Solve the following equations in F_{97} (again, assume $\cdot$ and exponentiation are field versions):

- $95 \cdot 45 \cdot 31$
- $17 \cdot 13 \cdot 19 \cdot 44$
- $12^7 \cdot 77^{49}$

Exercise 5

For $k = 1, 3, 7, 13, 18$, what is this set in F_{19}?

$$\{k \cdot 0, k \cdot 1, k \cdot 2, k \cdot 3, ... k \cdot 18\}$$

Do you notice anything about these sets?

Why Prime Fields are Useful

The answer to Exercise 5 is why we choose to use finite fields with a *prime* number of elements. No matter what k you choose, as long as it's greater than 0, multiplying the entire set by k will result in the same set as you started with.

Intuitively, the fact that we have a prime order results in every element of a finite field being equivalent. If the order of the set was a composite number, multiplying the set by one of the divisors would result in a smaller set.

Coding Multiplication in Python

Now that we understand what multiplication should be in FieldElement, we want to define the __mul__ method that overrides the * operator. We want this to work:

```
>>> from ecc import FieldElement
>>> a = FieldElement(3, 13)
>>> b = FieldElement(12, 13)
>>> c = FieldElement(10, 13)
>>> print(a*b==c)
True
```

As with addition and subtraction, the next exercise is to make multiplication work for our class by defining the __mul__ method.

Exercise 6

Write the corresponding __mul__ method that defines the multiplication of two finite field elements.

Coding Exponentiation in Python

We need to define the exponentiation for FieldElement, which in Python can be defined with the __pow__ method, overriding the ** operator. The difference here is that the exponent is *not* a FieldElement, so it has to be treated a bit differently. We want something like this to work:

```
>>> from ecc import FieldElement
>>> a = FieldElement(3, 13)
>>> b = FieldElement(1, 13)
>>> print(a**3==b)
True
```

Note that because the exponent is an integer, instead of another instance of FieldElement, the method receives the variable exponent as an integer. We can code it this way:

```
class FieldElement:
...
    def __pow__(self, exponent):
        num = (self.num ** exponent) % self.prime    ❶
        return self.__class__(num, self.prime)       ❷
```

❶ This is a perfectly fine way to do it, but pow(self.num, exponent, self.prime) is more efficient.

❷ We have to return an instance of the class as before.

Why don't we force the exponent to be a FieldElement object? It turns out that the exponent doesn't have to be a member of the finite field for the math to work. In fact, if it were, the exponents wouldn't display the intuitive behavior we expect, like being able to add the exponents when we multiply with the same base.

Some of what we're doing now may seem slow for large numbers, but we'll use some clever tricks to improve the performance of these algorithms.

Exercise 7

For $p = 7, 11, 17, 31$, what is this set in F_p?

$$\{1^{(p-1)}, 2^{(p-1)}, 3^{(p-1)}, 4^{(p-1)}, \ldots (p-1)^{(p-1)}\}$$

Finite Field Division

The intuition that helps us with addition, subtraction, multiplication, and perhaps even exponentiation unfortunately doesn't help us quite as much with division. Because division is the hardest operation to make sense of, we'll start with something that should make sense.

In normal math, division is the inverse of multiplication:

- $7 \cdot 8 = 56$ implies that $56/8 = 7$
- $12 \cdot 2 = 24$ implies that $24/12 = 2$

And so on. We can use this as the definition of division to help us. Note that like in normal math, you cannot divide by 0.

In F_{19}, we know that:

$3 \cdot_f 7 = 21\%19 = 2$ implies that $2/_f 7 = 3$
$9 \cdot_f 5 = 45\%19 = 7$ implies that $7/_f 5 = 9$

This is very unintuitive, as we generally think of $2/7$ or $7/5$ as fractions, not nice finite field elements. Yet that is one of the remarkable things about finite fields: finite fields are *closed* under division. That is, dividing any two numbers where the denominator is not 0 will result in another finite field element.

The question you might be asking yourself is, how do I calculate $2/7$ if I don't know beforehand that $3 \cdot 7 = 2$? This is indeed a very good question; to answer it, we'll have to use the result from Exercise 7.

In case you didn't get it, the answer is that $n^{(p-1)}$ is always 1 for every p that is prime and every $n > 0$. This is a beautiful result from number theory called Fermat's little theorem. Essentially, the theorem says:

$$n^{(p-1)} \% p = 1$$

where p is prime.

Since we are operating in prime fields, this will always be true.

Fermat's Little Theorem

There are many proofs of this theorem, but perhaps the simplest is using what we saw in Exercise 5—namely, that these sets are equal:

$$\{1, 2, 3, \dots p-2, p-1\} = \{n\%p, 2n\%p, 3n\%p\ (p-2)n\%p, (p-1)n\%p\}$$

The resulting numbers might not be in the right order, but the same numbers are in both sets. We can then multiply every element in both sets to get this equality:

$$1 \cdot 2 \cdot 3 \cdot \dots \cdot (p-2) \cdot (p-1) \% p = n \cdot 2n \cdot 3n \cdot \dots \cdot (p-2)n \cdot (p-1)n \% p$$

The left side is the same as $(p-1)! \% p$ where ! is the factorial (e.g., $5! = 5 \cdot 4 \cdot 3 \cdot 2 \cdot 1$). On the right side, we can gather up all the n`'s and get:

$$(p-1)! \cdot n^{(p-1)} \% p$$

Thus:

$$(p-1)! \% p = (p-1)! \cdot n^{(p-1)} \% p$$

The $(p-1)!$ on both sides cancel, giving us:

$$1 = n^{(p-1)} \% p$$

This proves Fermat's little theorem.

Because division is the inverse of multiplication, we know:

$$a/b = a \cdot (1/b) = a \cdot b^{-1}$$

We can reduce the division problem to a multiplication problem as long as we can figure out what b^{-1} is. This is where Fermat's little theorem comes into play. We know:

$$b^{(p-1)} = 1$$

because p is prime. Thus:

$$b^{-1} = b^{-1} \cdot 1 = b^{-1} \cdot b^{(p-1)} = b^{(p-2)}$$

or:

$$b^{-1} = b^{(p-2)}$$

In F_{19}, this means practically that $b^{18} = 1$, which means that $b^{-1} = b^{17}$ for all $b > 0$.

So in other words, we can calculate the inverse using the exponentiation operator. In F_{19}:

$$2/7 = 2 \cdot 7^{(19-2)} = 2 \cdot 7^{17} = 465261027974414 \% 19 = 3$$
$$7/5 = 7 \cdot 5^{(19-2)} = 7 \cdot 5^{17} = 5340576171875 \% 19 = 9$$

This is a relatively expensive calculation as exponentiating grows very fast. Division is the most expensive operation for that reason. To lessen the expense, we can use the pow function in Python, which does exponentiation. In Python, pow(7,17) does the same thing as 7**17. The pow function, however, has an optional third argument that makes our calculation more efficient. Specifically, pow will modulo by the third argument. Thus, pow(7,17,19) will give the same result as 7**17%19 but do so faster because the modulo function is done after each round of multiplication.

Exercise 8

Solve the following equations in F_{31}:

- $3 / 24$
- 17^{-3}
- $4^{-4} \cdot 11$

Exercise 9

Write the corresponding __truediv__ method that defines the division of two field elements.

Note that in Python 3, division is separated into __truediv__ and __floordiv__. The first does normal division and the second does integer division.

Redefining Exponentiation

One last thing that we need to take care of before we leave this chapter is the __pow__ method, which needs to handle negative exponents. For example, a^{-3} needs to be a finite field element, but the current code does not take care of this case. We want, for example, something like this to work:

```
>>> from ecc import FieldElement
>>> a = FieldElement(7, 13)
>>> b = FieldElement(8, 13)
>>> print(a**-3==b)
True
```

Unfortunately, the way we've defined __pow__ simply doesn't handle negative exponents, because the second parameter of the built-in Python function pow is required to be positive.

Thankfully, we can use some math we already know to solve this. We know from Fermat's little theorem that:

$$a^{p-1} = 1$$

This fact means that we can multiply by a^{p-1} as many times as we want. So, for a^{-3}, we can do:

$$a^{-3} = a^{-3} \cdot a^{p-1} = a^{p-4}$$

This is a way we can do negative exponents. A naive implementation would do something like this:

```
class FieldElement:
...
    def __pow__(self, exponent):
        n = exponent
        while n < 0:
            n += self.prime - 1  ❶
        num = pow(self.num, n, self.prime)  ❷
        return self.__class__(num, self.prime)
```

❶ We add until we get a positive exponent.

---

❷ We use the Python built-in pow to make this more efficient.

Thankfully, we can do even better. We already know how to force a number out of being negative, using our familiar friend %! As a bonus, we can also reduce very large exponents at the same time given that $a^{p-1} = 1$. This will make the pow function not work as hard:

```
class FieldElement:
...
    def __pow__(self, exponent):
        n = exponent % (self.prime - 1)  ❶
        num = pow(self.num, n, self.prime)
        return self.__class__(num, self.prime)
```

❶ Make the exponent into something within the 0 to $p-2$ range, inclusive.

Conclusion

In this chapter we learned about finite fields and how to implement them in Python. We'll be using finite fields in Chapter 3 for elliptic curve cryptography. We turn next to the other mathematical component that we need for elliptic curve cryptography: elliptic curves.

CHAPTER 2

Elliptic Curves

In this chapter we're going to learn about elliptic curves. In Chapter 3, we will combine elliptic curves with finite fields to make elliptic curve cryptography.

Like finite fields, elliptic curves can look intimidating if you haven't seen them before. But again, the actual math isn't very difficult. Most of what you need to know about elliptic curves could have been taught to you after algebra. In this chapter, we'll explore what these curves are and what we can do with them.

Definition

Elliptic curves are like many equations you've seen since pre-algebra. They have y on one side and x on the other, in some form. elliptic curves have a form like this:

$$y^2 = x^3 + ax + b$$

You've worked with other equations that look similar. For example, you probably learned the linear equation back in pre-algebra:

$$y = mx + b$$

You may even remember that m here has the name *slope* and b is the *y-intercept*. You can also graph linear equations, as shown in Figure 2-1.

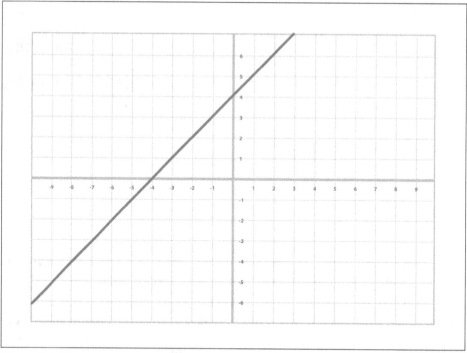

Figure 2-1. Linear equation

Similarly, you're probably familiar with the quadratic equation and its graph (Figure 2-2):

$$y = ax^2 + bx + c$$

And sometime around algebra, you did even higher orders of x—something called the cubic equation and its graph (Figure 2-3):

$$y = ax^3 + bx^2 + cx + d$$

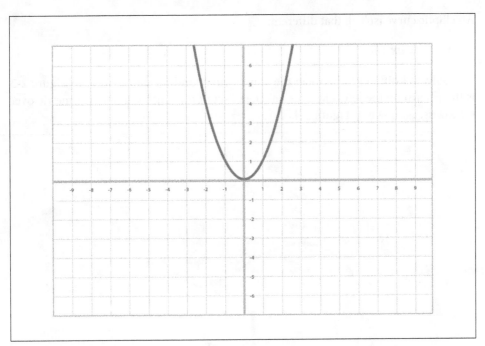

Figure 2-2. Quadratic equation

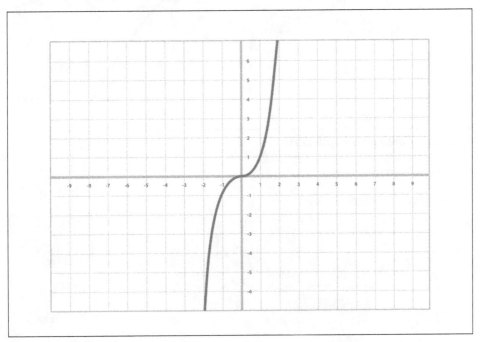

Figure 2-3. Cubic equation

An elliptic curve isn't all that different:

$$y^2 = x^3 + ax + b$$

The only real difference between the elliptic curve and the cubic curve in Figure 2-3 is the y^2 term on the left side. This has the effect of making the graph symmetric over the x-axis, as shown in Figure 2-4.

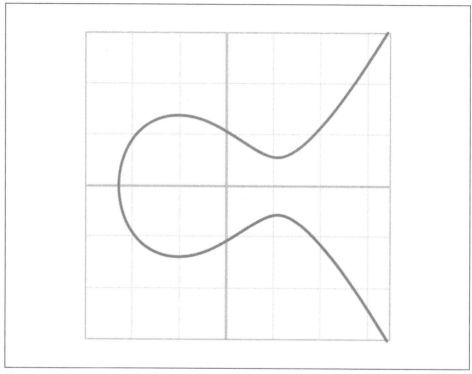

Figure 2-4. Continuous elliptic curve

The elliptic curve is also less steep than the cubic curve. Again, this is because of the y^2 term on the left side. At times, the curve may even be disjoint, as in Figure 2-5.

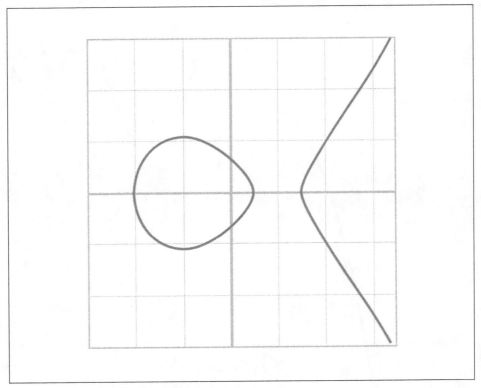

Figure 2-5. Disjoint elliptic curve

If it helps, an elliptic curve can be thought of as taking a cubic equation graph (Figure 2-6), flattening out the part above the x-axis (Figure 2-7), and then mirroring that part below the x-axis (Figure 2-8).

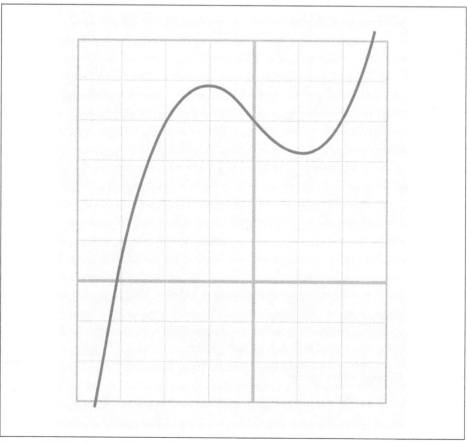

Figure 2-6. Step 1: A cubic equation

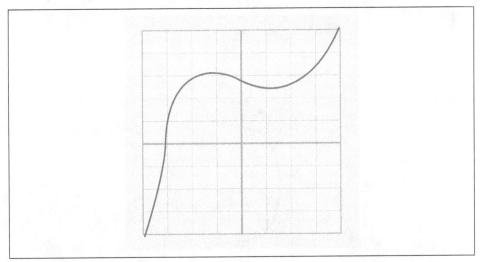

Figure 2-7. Step 2: Stretched cubic equation

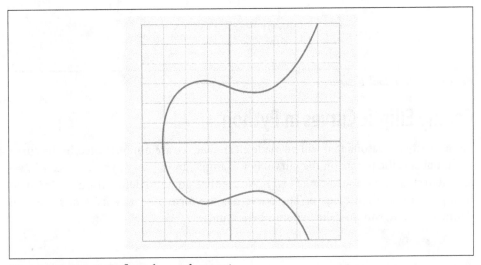

Figure 2-8. Step 3: Reflected over the x-axis

Specifically, the elliptic curve used in Bitcoin is called *secp256k1* and it uses this particular equation:

$$y^2 = x^3 + 7$$

The canonical form is $y^2 = x^3 + ax + b$, so the curve is defined by the constants $a = 0$, $b = 7$. It looks like Figure 2-9.

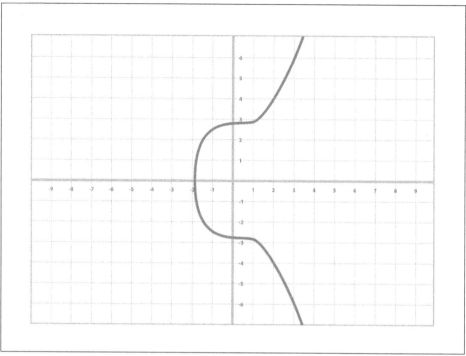

Figure 2-9. secp256k1 curve

Coding Elliptic Curves in Python

For a variety of reasons that will be made clear later, we are not interested in the curve itself, but specific points on the curve. For example, in the curve $y^2 = x^3 + 5x + 7$, we are interested in the coordinate $(-1,1)$. We are thus going to define the class `Point` to be a *point* on a specific curve. The curve has the form $y^2 = x^3 + ax + b$, so we can define the curve with just the two numbers a and b:

```python
class Point:

    def __init__(self, x, y, a, b):
        self.a = a
        self.b = b
        self.x = x
        self.y = y
        if self.y**2 != self.x**3 + a * x + b:  ❶
            raise ValueError('({}, {}) is not on the curve'.format(x, y))

    def __eq__(self, other):  ❷
        return self.x == other.x and self.y == other.y \
            and self.a == other.a and self.b == other.b
```

❶ We check here that the point is actually on the curve.

❷ Points are equal if and only if they are on the same curve and have the same coordinates.

We can now create `Point` objects, and we will get an error if the point is not on the curve:

```
>>> from ecc import Point
>>> p1 = Point(-1, -1, 5, 7)
>>> p2 = Point(-1, -2, 5, 7)
Traceback (most recent call last):
  File "<stdin>", line 1, in <module>
  File "ecc.py", line 143, in __init__
    raise ValueError('({}, {}) is not on the curve'.format(self.x, self.y))
ValueError: (-1, -2) is not on the curve
```

In other words, __init__ will raise an exception when the point is not on the curve.

Exercise 1

Determine which of these points are on the curve $y^2 = x^3 + 5x + 7$:

(2,4), (−1,−1), (18,77), (5,7)

Exercise 2

Write the __ne__ method for `Point`.

Point Addition

Elliptic curves are useful because of something called *point addition*. Point addition is where we can do an operation on two of the points on the curve and get a third point, also on the curve. This is called *addition* because the operation has a lot of the intuitions we associate with the mathematical operation of addition. For example, point addition is commutative. That is, adding point A to point B is the same as adding point B to point A.

The way we define point addition is as follows. It turns out that for every elliptic curve, a line will intersect it at either one point (Figure 2-10) or three points (Figure 2-11), except in a couple of special cases.

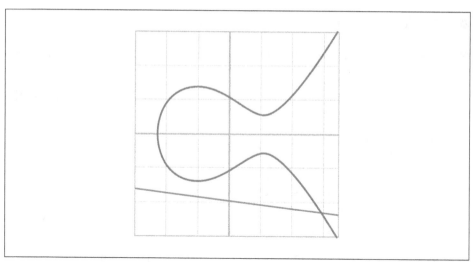

Figure 2-10. Line intersects at only one point

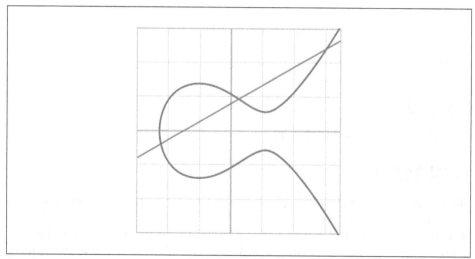

Figure 2-11. Line intersects at three points

The two exceptions are when a line is exactly vertical (Figure 2-12) and when a line is *tangent* to the curve (Figure 2-13).

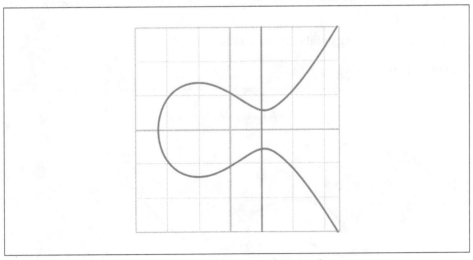

Figure 2-12. Line intersects at two points because it's vertical

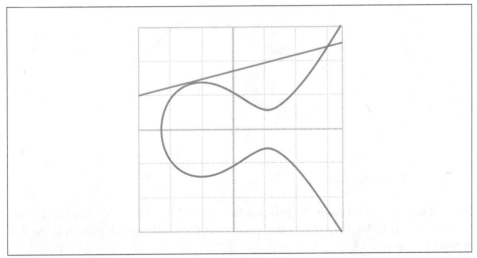

Figure 2-13. Line intersects at two points because it's tangent to the curve

We will come back to these two cases later.

We can define point addition using the fact that lines intersect one or three times with the elliptic curve. Two points define a line, so since that line must intersect the curve one more time, that third point reflected over the x-axis is the result of the point addition.

So, for any two points $P_1 = (x_1, y_1)$ and $P_2 = (x_2, y_2)$, we get $P_1 + P_2$ as follows:

- Find the point intersecting the elliptic curve a third time by drawing a line through P_1 and P_2.
- Reflect the resulting point over the x-axis.

Visually, it looks like Figure 2-14.

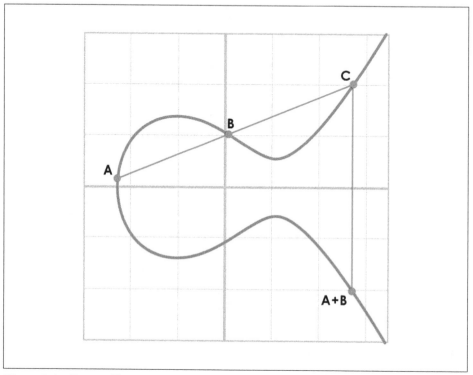

Figure 2-14. Point addition

We first draw a line through the two points we're adding (A and B). The third intersection point is C. We then reflect that point over the x-axis, which puts us at the $A + B$ point in Figure 2-14.

One of the properties that we are going to use is that point addition is not easily predictable. We can calculate point addition easily enough with a formula, but intuitively, the result of point addition can be almost anywhere given two points on the curve. Going back to Figure 2-14, $A + B$ is to the right of both points, $A + C$ would be somewhere between A and C on the x-axis, and $B + C$ would be to the left of both points. In mathematics parlance, point addition is *nonlinear*.

Math of Point Addition

Point addition satisfies certain properties that we associate with addition, such as:

- Identity
- Commutativity
- Associativity
- Invertibility

Identity here means that there's a zero. That is, there exists some point I that, when added to a point A, results in A:

$I + A = A$

We'll call this point the *point at infinity* (reasons for this will become clear in a moment).

This is related to *invertibility*. For some point A, there's some other point $-A$ that results in the identity point. That is:

$A + (-A) = I$

Visually, these points are opposite one another over the x-axis on the curve (see Figure 2-15).

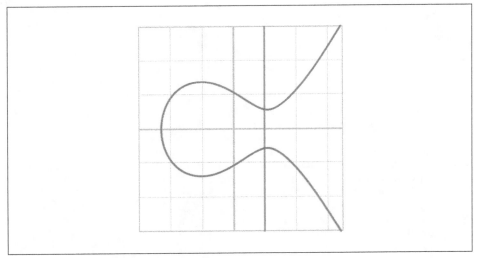

Figure 2-15. Vertical line intersection

This is why we call this point the point at infinity. We have one extra point in the elliptic curve, which makes the vertical line intersect the curve a third time.

Commutativity means that $A + B = B + A$. This is obvious since the line going through A and B will intersect the curve a third time in the same place, no matter the order.

Associativity means that $(A + B) + C = A + (B + C)$. This isn't obvious and is the reason for flipping over the x-axis. This is shown in Figures 2-16 and 2-17.

You can see that in both Figure 2-16 and Figure 2-17, the final point is the same. In other words, we have good reason to believe that $(A + B) + C = A + (B + C)$. While this doesn't prove the associativity of point addition, the visual should at least give you the intuition that this is true.

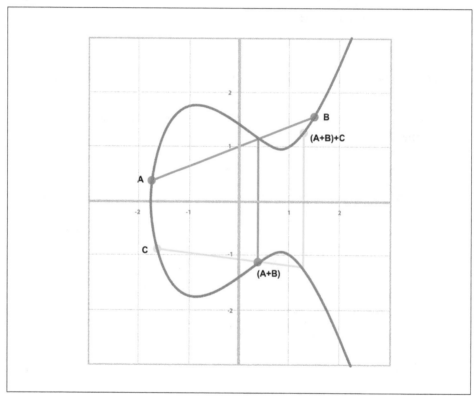

Figure 2-16. (A + B) + C

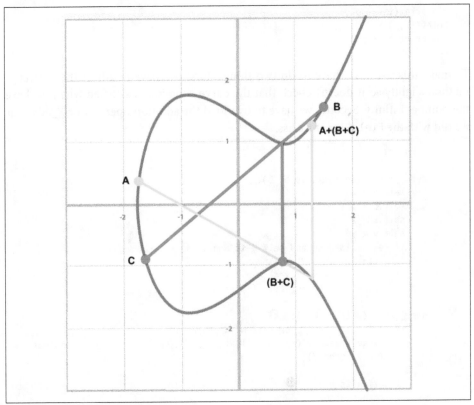

Figure 2-17. A + (B + C)

To code point addition, we're going to split it up into three steps:

1. Where the points are in a vertical line or using the identity point
2. Where the points are not in a vertical line, but are different
3. Where the two points are the same

Coding Point Addition

We first handle the identity point, or point at infinity. Since we can't easily use infinity in Python, we'll use the None value instead. What we want is this to work:

```
>>> from ecc import Point
>>> p1 = Point(-1, -1, 5, 7)
>>> p2 = Point(-1, 1, 5, 7)
>>> inf = Point(None, None, 5, 7)
>>> print(p1 + inf)
Point(-1,-1)_5_7
```

```
>>> print(inf + p2)
Point(-1,1)_5_7
>>> print(p1 + p2)
Point(infinity)
```

To make this work, we have to do two things. First, we have to adjust the __init__ method slightly so it doesn't check that the curve equation is satisfied when we have the point at infinity. Second, we have to overload the addition operator or __add__ as we did with the FieldElement class:

```
class Point:

    def __init__(self, x, y, a, b):
        self.a = a
        self.b = b
        self.x = x
        self.y = y
        if self.x is None and self.y is None:  ❶
            return
        if self.y**2 != self.x**3 + a * x + b:
            raise ValueError('({}, {}) is not on the curve'.format(x, y))

    def __add__(self, other):  ❷
        if self.a != other.a or self.b != other.b:
            raise TypeError('Points {}, {} are not on the same curve'.format
            (self, other))

        if self.x is None:  ❸
            return other
        if other.x is None:  ❹
            return self
```

❶ The *x* coordinate and *y* coordinate being None is how we signify the point at infinity. Note that the next if statement will fail if we don't return here.

❷ We overload the + operator here.

❸ self.x being None means that self is the point at infinity, or the additive identity. Thus, we return other.

❹ other.x being None means that other is the point at infinity, or the additive identity. Thus, we return self.

Exercise 3

Handle the case where the two points are additive inverses (that is, they have the same x but a different y, causing a vertical line). This should return the point at infinity.

Point Addition for When $x_1 \neq x_2$

Now that we've covered the vertical line, let's examine when the points are different. When we have points where the x's differ, we can add using a fairly simple formula. To help with intuition, we'll first find the slope created by the two points. We can figure this out using a formula from pre-algebra:

$$P_1 = (x_1, y_1), P_2 = (x_2, y_2), P_3 = (x_3, y_3)$$
$$P_1 + P_2 = P_3$$
$$s = (y_2 - y_1)/(x_2 - x_1)$$

This is the *slope*, and we can use the slope to calculate x_3. Once we know x_3, we can calculate y_3. P_3 can be derived using this formula:

$$x_3 = s^2 - x_1 - x_2$$
$$y_3 = s(x_1 - x_3) - y_1$$

Remember that y_3 is the reflection over the x-axis.

Deriving the Point Addition Formula

Supposing:

$$P_1 = (x_1, y_1), P_2 = (x_2, y_2), P_3 = (x_3, y_3)$$
$$P_1 + P_2 = P_3$$

We want to know what P_3 is.

Let's start with the fact that the line goes through P_1 and P_2, and has this formula:

$$s = (y_2 - y_1)/(x_2 - x_1)$$
$$y = s(x - x_1) + y_1$$

The second formula is the equation of the line that intersects at both P_1 and P_2. Using this formula and plugging it into the elliptic curve equation, we get:

$$y^2 = x^3 + ax + b$$
$$y^2 = (s(x - x_1) + y_1)^2 = x^3 + ax + b$$

Gathering all the terms, we have this polynomial equation:

$$x^3 - s^2x^2 + (a + 2s^2x_1 - 2sy_1)x + b - s^2x_1^2 + 2sx_1y_1 - y_1^2 = 0$$

We also know that x_1, x_2, and x_3 are solutions to this equation, thus:

$$(x - x_1)(x - x_2)(x - x_3) = 0$$

$$x^3 - (x_1 + x_2 + x_3)x^2 + (x_1x_2 + x_1x_3 + x_2x_3)x - x_1x_2x_3 = 0$$

From earlier, we know that:

$$x^3 - s^2x^2 + (a + 2s^2x_1 - 2sy_1)x + b - s^2x_1{}^2 + 2sx_1y_1 - y_1{}^2 = 0$$

There's a result from what's called Vieta's formula (*http://bit.ly/2HXJtMp*), which states that the coefficients have to equal each other if the roots are the same. The first coefficient that's interesting is the coefficient in front of x^2:

$$-s^2 = -(x_1 + x_2 + x_3)$$

We can use this to derive the formula for x_3:

$$x_3 = s^2 - x_1 - x_2$$

We can plug this into the formula for the line above:

$$y = s(x - x_1) + y_1$$

But we have to reflect over the x-axis, so the right side has to be negated:

$$y_3 = -(s(x_3 - x_1) + y_1) = s(x_1 - x_3) - y_1$$

QED.

Exercise 4

For the curve $y^2 = x^3 + 5x + 7$, what is $(2,5) + (-1,-1)$?

Coding Point Addition for When $x_1 \neq x_2$

We now code this into our library. That means we have to adjust the __add__ method to handle the case where $x_1 \neq x_2$. We have the formulas:

$$s = (y_2 - y_1)/(x_2 - x_1)$$
$$x_3 = s^2 - x_1 - x_2$$
$$y_3 = s(x_1 - x_3) - y_1$$

At the end of the method, we return an instance of the class Point using self.__class__ to make subclassing easier.

Exercise 5

Write the __add__ method where $x_1 \neq x_2$.

Point Addition for When $P_1 = P_2$

When the x coordinates are the same and the y coordinate is different, we have the situation where the points are opposite each other over the x-axis. We know that this means:

$P_1 = -P_2$ or $P_1 + P_2 = I$

We've already handled this in Exercise 3.

What happens when $P_1 = P_2$? Visually, we have to calculate the line that's *tangent* to the curve at P_1 and find the point at which the line intersects the curve. The situation looks like Figure 2-18, as we saw before.

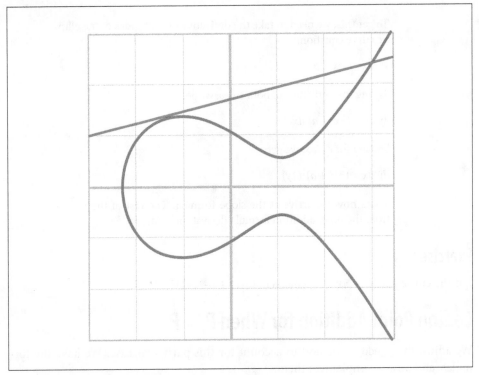

Figure 2-18. Line that's tangent to the curve

Once again, we'll find the slope of the tangent point:

$P_1 = (x_1, y_1), P_3 = (x_3, y_3)$
$P_1 + P_1 = P_3$
$s = (3x_1{}^2 + a)/(2y_1)$

The rest of the formula goes through as before, except $x_1 = x_2$, so we can combine them:

$$x_3 = s^2 - 2x_1$$
$$y_3 = s(x_1 - x_3) - y_1$$

Deriving the Slope Tangent to the Curve

We can derive the slope of the tangent line using some slightly more advanced math: calculus. We know that the slope at a given point is:

dy/dx

To get this, we need to take the derivative of both sides of the elliptic curve equation:

$y^2 = x^3 + ax + b$

Taking the derivative of both sides, we get:

$2y\,dy = (3x^2 + a)\,dx$

Solving for dy/dx, we get:

$dy/dx = (3x^2 + a)/(2y)$

That's how we arrive at the slope formula. The rest of the results from the point addition formula derivation hold.

Exercise 6

For the curve $y^2 = x^3 + 5x + 7$, what is $(-1,-1) + (-1,-1)$?

Coding Point Addition for When $P_1 = P_2$

We adjust the __add__ method to account for this particular case. We have the formulas, and now we implement them:

$$s = (3x_1^2 + a)/(2y_1)$$
$$x_3 = s^2 - 2x_1$$
$$y_3 = s(x_1 - x_3) - y_1$$

Exercise 7

Write the __add__ method when $P_1 = P_2$.

Coding One More Exception

There is one more exception, and this involves the case where the tangent line is vertical (Figure 2-19).

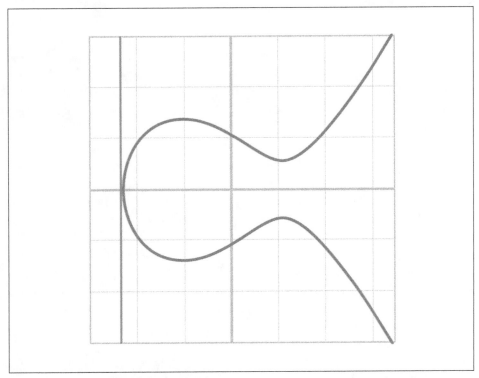

Figure 2-19. Vertical and tangent to the curve

This can only happen if $P_1 = P_2$ and the y coordinate is 0, in which case the slope calculation will end up with a 0 in the denominator.

We handle this with a special case:

```
class Point:
    ...
    def __add__(self, other):
        ...
        if self == other and self.y == 0 * self.x:  ❶
            return self.__class__(None, None, self.a, self.b)
```

❶ If the two points are equal and the *y* coordinate is 0, we return the point at infinity.

Conclusion

We've covered what elliptic curves are, how they work, and how to do point addition. We'll now combine the concepts from the first two chapters to learn elliptic curve cryptography in Chapter 3.

CHAPTER 3

Elliptic Curve Cryptography

The previous two chapters covered some fundamental math. We learned how finite fields work and what an elliptic curve is. In this chapter, we're going to combine the two concepts to learn elliptic curve cryptography. Specifically, we're going to build the primitives needed to sign and verify messages, which is at the heart of what Bitcoin does.

Elliptic Curves over Reals

We discussed in Chapter 2 what an elliptic curve looks like visually because we were plotting the curve over *real* numbers. Specifically, it's not just integers or even rational numbers, but all real numbers. Pi, *sqrt*(2), *e*+7th root of 19, and the like are all real numbers.

This worked because real numbers are also a field. Unlike a *finite* field, there are an *infinite* number of real numbers, but otherwise the same properties hold:

1. If a and b are in the set, $a + b$ and $a \cdot b$ are in the set.
2. 0 exists and has the property $a + 0 = a$.
3. 1 exists and has the property $a \cdot 1 = a$.
4. If a is in the set, $-a$ is in the set, which is defined as the value that makes $a + (-a) = 0$.
5. If a is in the set and is not 0, a^{-1} is in the set, which is defined as the value that makes $a \cdot a^{-1} = 1$.

Clearly, all of these are true: normal addition and multiplication apply for the first part, the additive and multiplicative identities 0 and 1 exist, $-x$ is the additive inverse, and $1/x$ is the multiplicative inverse.

Real numbers are easy to plot on a graph. For example, $y^2 = x^3 + 7$ can be plotted like Figure 3-1.

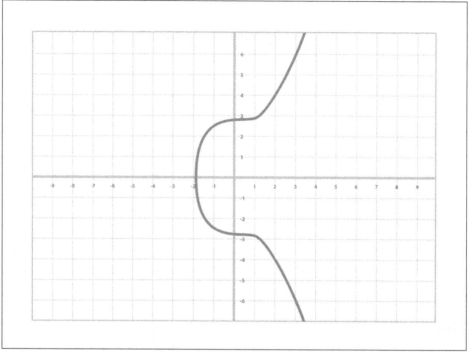

Figure 3-1. secp256k1 over real numbers

It turns out we can use the point addition equations over any field, including the finite fields we learned about in Chapter 1. The only difference is that we have to use the addition/subtraction/multiplication/division as defined in Chapter 1, not the "normal" versions that the real numbers use.

Elliptic Curves over Finite Fields

So what does an elliptic curve over a finite field look like? Let's look at the equation $y^2 = x^3 + 7$ over F_{103}. We can verify that the point (17,64) is on the curve by calculating both sides of the equation:

$$y^2 = 64^2 \,\%\, 103 = 79$$
$$x^3 + 7 = (17^3 + 7) \,\%\, 103 = 79$$

We've verified that the point is on the curve using finite field math.

Because we're evaluating the equation over a finite field, the plot of the equation looks vastly different (Figure 3-2).

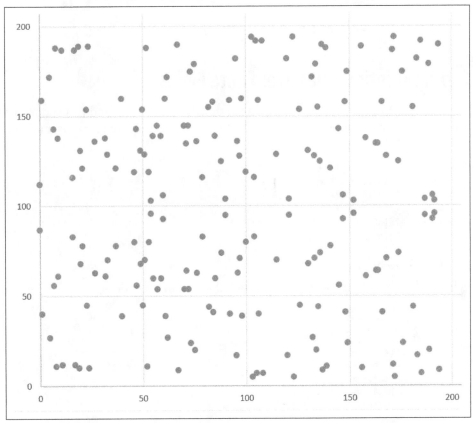

Figure 3-2. Elliptic curve over a finite field

As you can see, it's very much a scattershot of points and there's no smooth curve here. This is not surprising since the points are discrete. About the only pattern is that the curve is symmetric right around the middle, because of the y^2 term. The graph is not symmetric over the x-axis as in the curve over reals, but about halfway up the y-axis due to there not being negative numbers in a finite field.

What's amazing is that we can use the same point addition equations with the addition, subtraction, multiplication, division, and exponentiation as we defined them for finite fields, and everything still works. This may seem surprising, but abstract math has regularities like this despite being different from the traditional modes of calculation you may be familiar with.

Exercise 1

Evaluate whether these points are on the curve $y^2 = x^3 + 7$ over F_{223}:

(192,105), (17,56), (200,119), (1,193), (42,99)

Coding Elliptic Curves over Finite Fields

Because we defined an elliptic curve point and defined the +, - ,* and / operators for finite fields, we can combine the two classes to create elliptic curve points over a finite field:

```
>>> from ecc import FieldElement, Point
>>> a = FieldElement(num=0, prime=223)
>>> b = FieldElement(num=7, prime=223)
>>> x = FieldElement(num=192, prime=223)
>>> y = FieldElement(num=105, prime=223)
>>> p1 = Point(x, y, a, b)
>>> print(p1)
Point(192,105)_0_7 FieldElement(223)
```

When initializing `Point`, we will run through this part of the code:

```
class Point:

    def __init__(self, x, y, a, b):
        self.a = a
        self.b = b
        self.x = x
        self.y = y
        if self.x is None and self.y is None:
            return
        if self.y**2 != self.x**3 + a * x + b:
            raise ValueError('({}, {}) is not on the curve'.format(x, y))
```

The addition (+), multiplication (*), exponentiation (**), and not equals (!=) opera-tors here use the __add__, __mul__, __pow__, and __ne__ methods from Finite Field, respectively, and *not* the integer equivalents. Being able to do the same equation but with different definitions for the basic arithmetic operators is how we construct an elliptic curve cryptography library.

We've already coded the two classes that we need to implement elliptic curve points over a finite field. However, to check our work, it will be useful to create a test suite. We will do this using the results of Exercise 1:

```
class ECCTest(TestCase):

    def test_on_curve(self):
        prime = 223
        a = FieldElement(0, prime)
```

```
        b = FieldElement(7, prime)
        valid_points = ((192, 105), (17, 56), (1, 193))
        invalid_points = ((200, 119), (42, 99))
        for x_raw, y_raw in valid_points:
            x = FieldElement(x_raw, prime)
            y = FieldElement(y_raw, prime)
            Point(x, y, a, b)  ❶
        for x_raw, y_raw in invalid_points:
            x = FieldElement(x_raw, prime)
            y = FieldElement(y_raw, prime)
            with self.assertRaises(ValueError):
                Point(x, y, a, b)  ❶
```

❶ We pass in `FieldElement` objects to the `Point` class for initialization. This will, in turn, use all the overloaded math operations in `FieldElement`.

We can now run this test like so:

```
>>> import ecc
>>> from helper import run  ❶
>>> run(ecc.ECCTest('test_on_curve'))
.
----------------------------------------------------------------------
Ran 1 test in 0.001s

OK
```

❶ `helper` is a module with some very useful utility functions, including the ability to run unit tests individually.

Point Addition over Finite Fields

We can use all the same equations over finite fields, including the linear equation:

$$y = mx + b$$

It turns out that a "line" in a finite field is not quite what you'd expect (Figure 3-3).

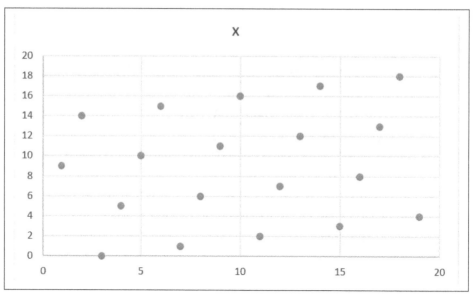

Figure 3-3. Line over a finite field

The equation nevertheless works, and we can calculate what y should be for a given x.

Remarkably, point addition works over finite fields as well. This is because elliptic curve point addition works over all fields! The same exact formulas we used to calculate point addition over reals work over finite fields. Specifically, when $x_1 \neq x_2$:

$$P_1 = (x_1, y_1), P_2 = (x_2, y_2), P_3 = (x_3, y_3)$$
$$P_1 + P_2 = P_3$$
$$s = (y_2 - y_1)/(x_2 - x_1)$$
$$x_3 = s^2 - x_1 - x_2$$
$$y_3 = s(x_1 - x_3) - y_1$$

And when $P_1 = P_2$:

$$P_1 = (x_1, y_1), P_3 = (x_3, y_3)$$
$$P_1 + P_1 = P_3$$
$$s = (3x_1^2 + a)/(2y_1)$$
$$x_3 = s^2 - 2x_1$$
$$y_3 = s(x_1 - x_3) - y_1$$

All of the equations for elliptic curves work over finite fields, which sets us up to create some cryptographic primitives.

Coding Point Addition over Finite Fields

Because we coded `FieldElement` in such a way as to define `__add__`, `__sub__`, `__mul__`, `__truediv__`, `__pow__`, `__eq__`, and `__ne__`, we can simply initialize `Point` with `FieldElement` objects and point addition will work:

```
>>> from ecc import FieldElement, Point
>>> prime = 223
>>> a = FieldElement(num=0, prime=prime)
>>> b = FieldElement(num=7, prime=prime)
>>> x1 = FieldElement(num=192, prime=prime)
>>> y1 = FieldElement(num=105, prime=prime)
>>> x2 = FieldElement(num=17, prime=prime)
>>> y2 = FieldElement(num=56, prime=prime)
>>> p1 = Point(x1, y1, a, b)
>>> p2 = Point(x2, y2, a, b)
>>> print(p1+p2)
Point(170,142)_0_7 FieldElement(223)
```

Exercise 2

For the curve $y^2 = x^3 + 7$ over F_{223}, find:

- $(170,142) + (60,139)$
- $(47,71) + (17,56)$
- $(143,98) + (76,66)$

Exercise 3

Extend `ECCTest` to test for the additions from the previous exercise. Call this `test_add`.

Scalar Multiplication for Elliptic Curves

Because we can add a point to itself, we can introduce some new notation:

$$(170,142) + (170,142) = 2 \cdot (170,142)$$

Similarly, because we have associativity, we can actually add the point again:

$$2 \cdot (170,142) + (170,142) = 3 \cdot (170, 142)$$

We can do this as many times as we want. This is what we call *scalar multiplication*. That is, we have a *scalar* number in front of the point. We can do this because we have defined point addition and point addition is associative.

One property of scalar multiplication is that it's really hard to predict without calculating (see Figure 3-4).

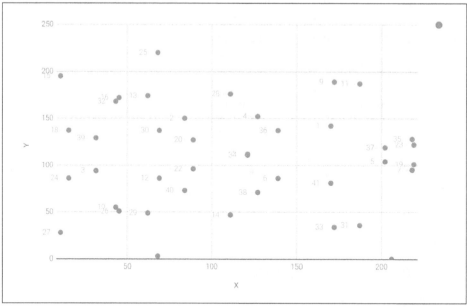

Figure 3-4. Scalar multiplication results for $y^2 = x^3 + 7$ over F_{223} for point (170,142)

Each point is labeled by how many times we've added the point. You can see that this is a complete scattershot. This is because point addition is nonlinear and not easy to calculate. Performing scalar multiplication is straightforward, but doing the opposite, point division, is not.

This is called the *discrete log problem* and is the basis of elliptic curve cryptography.

Another property of scalar multiplication is that at a certain multiple, we get to the point at infinity (remember, the point at infinity is the additive identity or 0). If we imagine a point G and scalar-multiply until we get the point at infinity, we end up with a set:

{ $G, 2G, 3G, 4G, ... nG$ } where $nG = 0$

It turns out that this set is called a *group*, and because n is finite, we have a *finite group* (or more specifically, a *finite cyclic group*). Groups are interesting mathematically because they behave well with respect to addition:

$G + 4G = 5G$ or $aG + bG = (a + b)G$

When we combine the fact that scalar multiplication is easy to do in one direction but hard in the other and the mathematical properties of a group, we have exactly what we need for elliptic curve cryptography.

Why Is This Called the Discrete Log Problem?

You may be wondering why the problem of reversing scalar *multiplication* is referred to as the discrete *log* problem.

We called the operation between the points "addition," but we could easily have called it a point "operation." Typically, a new operation that you define in math is denoted with the dot operator (·). The dot operator is also used for multiplication, and it sometimes helps to think that way:

$$P_1 \cdot P_2 = P_3$$

When you do lots of multiplying, that's the same as exponentiation. Scalar multiplication when we called it "point addition" becomes scalar exponentiation when thinking "point multiplication":

$$P^7 = Q$$

The discrete log problem in this context is the ability to reverse this equation, which ends up being:

$$\log_P Q = 7$$

The log equation on the left has no analytically calculable algorithm. That is, there is no known formula that you can plug in to get the answer generally. This is all a bit confusing, but it's fair to say that we could call the problem the "discrete point division" problem instead of the discrete log problem.

Exercise 4

For the curve $y^2 = x^3 + 7$ over F_{223}, find:

- $2 \cdot (192,105)$
- $2 \cdot (143,98)$
- $2 \cdot (47,71)$
- $4 \cdot (47,71)$
- $8 \cdot (47,71)$
- $21 \cdot (47,71)$

Scalar Multiplication Redux

Scalar multiplication is adding the same point to itself some number of times. The key to making scalar multiplication into public key cryptography is using the fact that scalar multiplication on elliptic curves is very hard to reverse. Note the previous exercise. Most likely, you calculated the point $s \cdot (47,71)$ in F_{223} for s from 1 until 21. Here are the results:

```
>>> from ecc import FieldElement, Point
>>> prime = 223
>>> a = FieldElement(0, prime)
>>> b = FieldElement(7, prime)
>>> x = FieldElement(47, prime)
>>> y = FieldElement(71, prime)
>>> p = Point(x, y, a, b)
>>> for s in range(1,21):
...     result = s*p
...     print('{}*(47,71)=({},{})'.format(s,result.x.num,result.y.num))
1*(47,71)=(47,71)
2*(47,71)=(36,111)
3*(47,71)=(15,137)
4*(47,71)=(194,51)
5*(47,71)=(126,96)
6*(47,71)=(139,137)
7*(47,71)=(92,47)
8*(47,71)=(116,55)
9*(47,71)=(69,86)
10*(47,71)=(154,150)
11*(47,71)=(154,73)
12*(47,71)=(69,137)
13*(47,71)=(116,168)
14*(47,71)=(92,176)
15*(47,71)=(139,86)
16*(47,71)=(126,127)
17*(47,71)=(194,172)
18*(47,71)=(15,86)
19*(47,71)=(36,112)
20*(47,71)=(47,152)
```

If you look closely at the numbers, there's no real discernible pattern to the scalar multiplication. The x coordinates don't always increase or decrease, and neither do the y coordinates. About the only pattern is that between 10 and 11, the x coordinates are equal (10 and 11 have the same x, as do 9 and 12, 8 and 13, and so on). This is due to the fact that $21 \cdot (47,71) = 0$.

Scalar multiplication looks really random, and that's what gives this equation *asymmetry*. An *asymmetric* problem is one that's easy to calculate in one direction, but hard to reverse. For example, it's easy enough to calculate 12 · (47,71). But if we were presented with this:

$$s \cdot (47,71) = (194,172)$$

would we be able to solve for s? We can look up the results shown earlier, but that's because we have a small group. We'll see in "Defining the Curve for Bitcoin" on page 58 that when we have numbers that are a lot larger, discrete log becomes an intractable problem.

Mathematical Groups

The preceding math (finite fields, elliptic curves, combining the two) was really to bring us to this point. What we actually want to generate for the purposes of public key cryptography are finite cyclic groups, and it turns out that if we take a generator point from an elliptic curve over a finite field, we can generate a finite cyclic group.

Unlike fields, groups have only a single operation. In our case, point addition is the operation. Groups also have a few other properties, like closure, invertibility, commutativity, and associativity. Lastly, we need the identity.

Let's look at each property, starting with that last one.

Identity

If you haven't guessed by now, the identity is defined as the point at infinity, which is guaranteed to be in the group since we generate the group when we get to the point at infinity. So:

$$0 + A = A$$

We call 0 the point at infinity because visually, it's the point that exists to help the math work out (Figure 3-5).

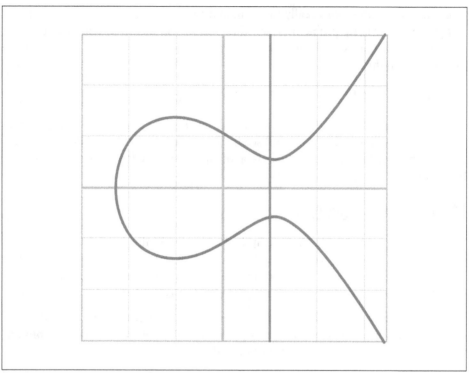

Figure 3-5. Vertical line "intersects" a third time at the point at infinity

Closure

This is perhaps the easiest property to prove since we generated the group in the first place by adding G over and over. Thus, if we have two different elements that look like this:

$aG + bG$

We know that the result is going to be:

$(a + b)G$

How do we know if this element is in the group? If $a+b < n$ (where n is the order of the group), then we know it's in the group by definition. If $a+b >= n$, then we know $a < n$ and $b < n$, so $a+b < 2n$, so $a+b-n < n$:

$(a + b - n)G = aG + bG - nG = aG + bG - 0 = aG + bG$

More generally, $(a + b)G = ((a + b) \% n)G$, where n is the order of the group.

So we know that this element is in the group, proving closure.

Invertibility

Invertibility is easy to depict (Figure 3-6).

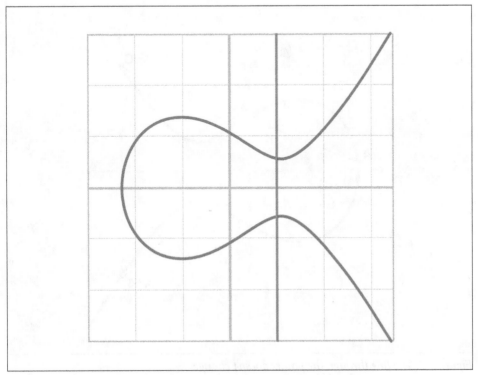

Figure 3-6. Each point is invertible by taking the reflection over the x-axis

Mathematically, we know that if aG is in the group, $(n - a)G$ is also in the group. You can add them together to get $aG + (n - a)G = (a + n - a)G = nG = 0$.

Commutativity

We know from point addition that $A + B = B + A$ (Figure 3-7).

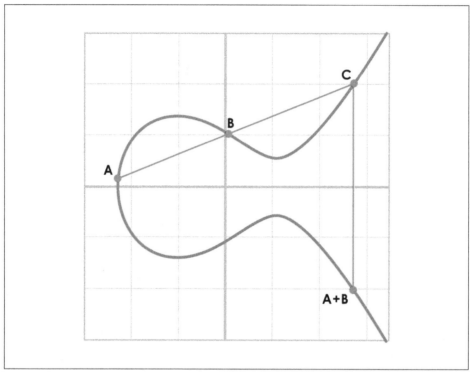

Figure 3-7. The line through the points doesn't change

This means that $aG + bG = bG + aG$, which proves commutativity.

Associativity

We know from point addition that $A + (B + C) = (A + B) + C$ (see Figures 3-8 and 3-9).

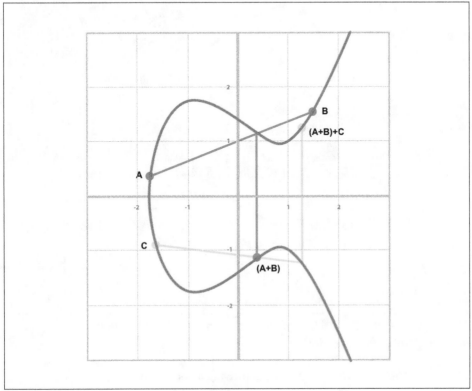

Figure 3-8. $(A + B) + C$: $A + B$ is computed first before C is added

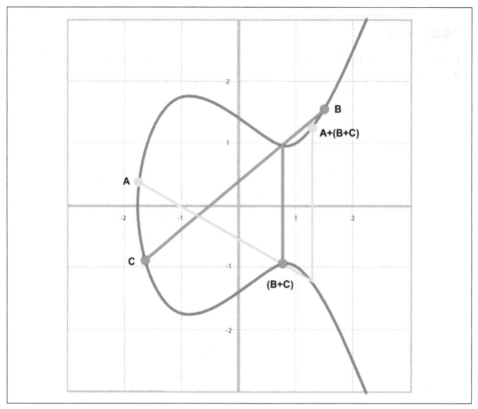

Figure 3-9. A + (B + C): B + C is added first before adding A (note that this results in the same point as in Figure 3-8)

Thus, $aG + (bG + cG) = (aG + bG) + cG$, proving associativity.

Exercise 5

For the curve $y^2 = x^3 + 7$ over F_{223}, find the order of the group generated by (15,86).

Coding Scalar Multiplication

What we're trying to do with Exercise 5 is this:

```
>>> from ecc import FieldElement, Point
>>> prime = 223
>>> a = FieldElement(0, prime)
>>> b = FieldElement(7, prime)
>>> x = FieldElement(15, prime)
>>> y = FieldElement(86, prime)
>>> p = Point(x, y, a, b)
>>> print(7*p)
Point(infinity)
```

We want to be able to scalar-multiply the point with some number. Thankfully, there's a method in Python called __rmul__ that can be used to override the front multiplication. A naive implementation looks something like this:

```
class Point:
    ...
    def __rmul__(self, coefficient):
        product = self.__class__(None, None, self.a, self.b)  ❶
        for _ in range(coefficient):  ❷
            product += self
        return product
```

❶ We start the product at 0, which in the case of point addition is the point at infinity.

❷ We loop coefficient times and add the point each time.

This is fine for small coefficients, but what if we have a very large coefficient—that is, a number that's so large that we won't be able to get out of this loop in a reasonable amount of time? For example, a coefficient of 1 trillion is going to take a really long time.

There's a cool technique called *binary expansion* that allows us to perform multiplication in $\log_2(n)$ loops, which dramatically reduces the calculation time for large numbers. For example, 1 trillion is 40 bits in binary, so we only have to loop 40 times for a number that's generally considered very large:

```
class Point:
    ...
    def __rmul__(self, coefficient):
        coef = coefficient
        current = self  ❶
        result = self.__class__(None, None, self.a, self.b)  ❷
        while coef:
            if coef & 1:  ❸
```

```
            result += current
    current += current    ❹
    coef >>= 1    ❺
return result
```

❶ `current` represents the point that's at the current bit. The first time through the loop it represents 1 × `self`; the second time it will be 2 × `self`, the third time 4 × `self`, then 8 × `self`, and so on. We double the point each time. In binary the coefficients are 1, 10, 100, 1000, 10000, etc.

❷ We start the result at 0, or the point at infinity.

❸ We are looking at whether the rightmost bit is a 1. If it is, then we add the value of the current bit.

❹ We need to double the point until we're past how big the coefficient can be.

❺ We bit-shift the coefficient to the right.

This is an advanced technique. If you don't understand bitwise operators, think of representing the coefficient in binary and only adding the point where there are 1's.

With `__add__` and `__rmul__`, we can start defining some more complicated elliptic curves.

Defining the Curve for Bitcoin

While we've been using relatively small primes for the sake of examples, we are not restricted to such small numbers. Small primes mean that we can use a computer to search through the entire group. If the group has a size of 301, the computer can easily do 301 computations to reverse scalar multiplication or break discrete log.

But what if we made the prime larger? It turns out that we can choose much larger primes than we've been using. The security of elliptic curve cryptography depends on computers *not* being able to go through an appreciable fraction of the group.

An elliptic curve for public key cryptography is defined with the following parameters:

- We specify the a and b of the curve $y^2 = x^3 + ax + b$.
- We specify the prime of the finite field, p.
- We specify the x and y coordinates of the generator point G.
- We specify the order of the group generated by G, n.

These numbers are known publicly and together form the cryptographic curve. There are many cryptographic curves and they have different security/convenience trade-offs, but the one we're most interested in is the one Bitcoin uses: secp256k1. The parameters for secp256k1 are these:

- $a = 0$, $b = 7$, making the equation $y^2 = x^3 + 7$
- $p = 2^{256} - 2^{32} - 977$
- $G_x = $
  0x79be667ef9dcbbac55a06295ce870b07029bfcdb2dce28d959f2815b16f81798
- $G_y = $
  0x483ada7726a3c4655da4fbfc0e1108a8fd17b448a68554199c47d08ffb10d4b8
- $n = $ 0xfffffffffffffffffffffffffffffffffebaaedce6af48a03bbfd25e8cd0364141

G_x refers to the x coordinate of the point G and G_y the y coordinate. The numbers starting with 0x are hexadecimal numbers.

There are a few things to notice about this curve. First, the equation is relatively simple. Many curves have a and b values that are much bigger.

Second, p is extremely close to 2^{256}. This means that most numbers under 2^{256} are in the prime field, and thus any point on the curve has x and y coordinates that are expressible in 256 bits each. n is also very close to 2^{256}. This means any scalar multiple can also be expressed in 256 bits.

Third, 2^{256} is a huge number (see sidebar). Amazingly, any number below 2^{256} can be stored in 32 bytes. This means that we can store the private key relatively easily.

How Big is 2^{256}?

2^{256} doesn't seem that big because we can express it succinctly, but in reality, it is an enormous number. To give you an idea, here are some relative scales:

$2^{256} \sim 10^{77}$
- Number of atoms in and on Earth $\sim 10^{50}$
- Number of atoms in the solar system $\sim 10^{57}$
- Number of atoms in the Milky Way $\sim 10^{68}$
- Number of atoms in the universe $\sim 10^{80}$

A trillion (10^{12}) computers doing a trillion computations every trillionth (10^{-12}) of a second for a trillion years is still less than 10^{56} computations.

Think of finding a private key this way: there are as many possible private keys in Bitcoin as there are atoms in a billion galaxies.

Working with secp256k1

Since we know all of the parameters for secp256k1, we can verify in Python whether the generator point, G, is on the curve $y^2 = x^3 + 7$:

```
>>> gx = 0x79be667ef9dcbbac55a06295ce870b07029bfcdb2dce28d959f2815b16f81798
>>> gy = 0x483ada7726a3c4655da4fbfc0e1108a8fd17b448a68554199c47d08ffb10d4b8
>>> p = 2**256 - 2**32 - 977
>>> print(gy**2 % p == (gx**3 + 7) % p)
True
```

Furthermore, we can verify in Python whether the generator point, G, has the order n:

```
>>> from ecc import FieldElement, Point
>>> gx = 0x79be667ef9dcbbac55a06295ce870b07029bfcdb2dce28d959f2815b16f81798
>>> gy = 0x483ada7726a3c4655da4fbfc0e1108a8fd17b448a68554199c47d08ffb10d4b8
>>> p = 2**256 - 2**32 - 977
>>> n = 0xfffffffffffffffffffffffffffffffebaaedce6af48a03bbfd25e8cd0364141
>>> x = FieldElement(gx, p)
>>> y = FieldElement(gy, p)
>>> seven = FieldElement(7, p)
>>> zero = FieldElement(0, p)
>>> G = Point(x, y, zero, seven)
>>> print(n*G)
Point(infinity)
```

Since we know the curve we will work in, this is a good time to create a subclass in Python to work exclusively with the parameters for secp256k1. We'll define the equivalent FieldElement and Point objects, but specific to the secp256k1 curve. Let's start by defining the field we'll be working in:

```
P = 2**256 - 2**32 - 977
...
class S256Field(FieldElement):

    def __init__(self, num, prime=None):
        super().__init__(num=num, prime=P)

    def __repr__(self):
        return '{:x}'.format(self.num).zfill(64)
```

We're subclassing the FieldElement class so we don't have to pass in P all the time. We also want to display a 256-bit number consistently by filling 64 characters so we can see any leading zeros.

Similarly, we can define a point on the secp256k1 curve and call it S256Point:

```
A = 0
B = 7
...
class S256Point(Point):
```

```
def __init__(self, x, y, a=None, b=None):
    a, b = S256Field(A), S256Field(B)
    if type(x) == int:
        super().__init__(x=S256Field(x), y=S256Field(y), a=a, b=b)
    else:
        super().__init__(x=x, y=y, a=a, b=b)   ❶
```

❶ In case we initialize with the point at infinity, we need to let x and y through directly instead of using the S256Field class.

We now have an easier way to initialize a point on the secp256k1 curve, without having to define a and b every time like we have to with the Point class.

We can also define __rmul__ a bit more efficiently, since we know the order of the group, n. Since we're coding Python, we'll name this with a capital N to make it clear that N is a constant:

```
N = 0xfffffffffffffffffffffffffffffffebaaedce6af48a03bbfd25e8cd0364141
...
class S256Point(Point):
    ...
    def __rmul__(self, coefficient):
        coef = coefficient % N   ❶
        return super().__rmul__(coef)
```

❶ We can mod by n because $nG = 0$. That is, every n times we cycle back to zero or the point at infinity.

We can now define G directly and keep it around since we'll be using it a lot going forward:

```
G = S256Point(
    0x79be667ef9dcbbac55a06295ce870b07029bfcdb2dce28d959f2815b16f81798,
    0x483ada7726a3c4655da4fbfc0e1108a8fd17b448a68554199c47d08ffb10d4b8)
```

Now checking that the order of G is n is trivial:

```
>>> from ecc import G, N
>>> print(N*G)
S256Point(infinity)
```

Public Key Cryptography

At last, we have the tools that we need to do public key cryptography operations. The key operation that we need is $P = eG$, which is an asymmetric equation. We can easily compute P when we know e and G, but we cannot easily compute e when we know P and G. This is the discrete log problem described earlier.

The difficulty of discrete log will be essential to understanding signing and verification algorithms.

Generally, we call e the *private key* and P the *public key*. Note here that the private key is a single 256-bit number and the public key is a coordinate (x,y), where x and y are *each* 256-bit numbers.

Signing and Verification

To set up the motivation for why signing and verification exists, imagine this scenario. You want to prove that you are a really good archer, like at the level where you can hit any target you want within 500 yards as opposed to being able to hit any particular target.

Now, if someone could observe you and interact with you, proving this would be easy. Perhaps they would position your son 400 yards away with an apple on his head and challenge you to hit that apple with an arrow. You, being a very good archer, could do this and prove your expertise. The target, if specified by the challenger, makes your archery skill easy to verify.

Unfortunately, this doesn't scale very well. If, for example you wanted to prove this to 10 people, you would have to shoot 10 different arrows at 10 different targets from 10 different challenges. You could try to do something like have 10 people watch you shoot a single arrow, but since they can't all choose the target, they can never be sure that you're not just good at hitting one particular target instead of an arbitrary target. What we want is something that you can do once, that requires no interaction back and forth with the verifiers, but that still proves that you are indeed, a good archer that can hit *any* target.

If, for example, you simply shot an arrow into a target of your choosing, the people observing afterward wouldn't necessarily be convinced. After all, you might have painted the target around wherever your arrow happened to land. So what can you do?

Here's a very clever thing you can do. Inscribe the tip of the arrow with the position of the target that you're hitting ("apple on top of my son's head") and then hit that target with your arrow. Now anyone seeing the target can take an X-ray machine and look at the tip of the embedded arrow and see that the tip indeed says exactly where it was going to hit. The tip clearly had to be inscribed before the arrow was shot, so this can prove you are actually a good archer (provided the actual target isn't just one that you've practiced hitting over and over).

This is the same technique we're using with signing and verification, except what we're proving isn't that we're good archers, but that we know a secret number. We want to prove possession of the secret without revealing the secret itself. We do this by putting the target into our calculation and hitting that target.

Ultimately this is going to be used in transactions, which will prove that the rightful owners of the secrets are spending the bitcoins.

Inscribing the Target

The inscribing of the target depends on the *signature algorithm*, and in our case that algorithm is called the Elliptic Curve Digital Signature Algorithm, or ECDSA for short.

The secret in our case is e satisfying the following:

$$eG = P$$

where P is the public key and e is the private key.

The target that we're going to aim at is a random 256-bit number, k. We then do this:

$$kG = R$$

R is now the target that we're aiming for. In fact, we're only going to care about the x coordinate of R, which we'll call r. You may have guessed already that r here stands for *random*.

We claim at this point that the following equation is equivalent to the discrete log problem:

$$uG + vP = kG$$

where k was chosen randomly, $u,v \neq 0$ can be chosen by the signer, and G and P are known. This is due to the fact that:

$$uG + vP = kG \text{ implies } vP = (k - u)G$$

Since $v \neq 0$, we can divide by the scalar multiple v:

$$P = ((k - u)/v)G$$

If we know e, we have:

$$eG = ((k - u)/v)G \text{ or } e = (k - u)/v$$

This means that any (u,v) combination that satisfies the preceding equation will suffice.

Now suppose we don't know e, but we can solve $uG + vP = kG$ with some (u,v) combination. Then $e = (k-u)/v$ gives a solution to $P = eG$ while knowing only P and G. In other words, we'd have broken the discrete log problem.

This means to provide a correct u and v, we either have to break the discrete log problem or know the secret e. Since we assume discrete log is hard, we can say e is assumed to be known by the one who came up with u and v.

One subtle thing that we haven't talked about is that we have to incorporate the purpose of our shooting. This is a contract that gets fulfilled as a result of shooting at the target. William Tell, for example, was shooting so that he could save his son (shoot the target and you get to save your son). You can imagine there would be other reasons to hit the target and other "rewards" that the person hitting the target would receive. This has to be incorporated into our equations.

In signature/verification parlance, this is called the *signature hash*. A hash is a deterministic function that takes arbitrary data into data of fixed size. This is a fingerprint of the message containing the intent of the shooter, which anyone verifying the message already knows. We denote this with the letter z. This is incorporated into our $uG + vP$ calculation this way:

$$u = z/s, v = r/s$$

Since r is used in the calculation of v, we now have the tip of the arrow inscribed. We also have the intent of the shooter incorporated into u, so both the reason for shooting and the target that is being aimed at are now part of the equation.

To make the equation work, we can calculate s:

$$uG + vP = R = kG$$
$$uG + veG = kG$$
$$u + ve = k$$
$$z/s + re/s = k$$
$$(z + re)/s = k$$
$$s = (z + re)/k$$

This is the basis of the signature algorithm, and the two numbers in a signature are r and s.

Verification is straightforward:

$$uG + vP \text{ where } u,v \neq 0$$
$$uG + vP = (z/s)G + (re/s)G = ((z + re)/s)G = ((z + re)/((z + re)/k))G = kG = (r,y)$$

Why We Don't Reveal k

At this point, you might be wondering why we don't reveal k and instead reveal the x coordinate of R, or r. If we were to reveal k, then:

$uG + vP = R$
$uG + veG = kG$
$kG - uG = veG$
$(k - u)G = veG$
$(k - u) = ve$
$(k - u)/v = e$

means that our secret would be revealed, which would defeat the whole purpose of the signature. We can, however, reveal R.

It's worth mentioning again: make sure you're using truly random numbers for k, as even accidentally revealing k for a known signature is the equivalent of revealing your secret and losing your funds!

Verification in Depth

Signatures sign some fixed-length value (our "contract")—in our case, something that's 32 bytes. The fact that 32 bytes is 256 bits is not a coincidence, as the thing we're signing will be a scalar for G.

To guarantee that the thing we're signing is 32 bytes, we hash the document first. In Bitcoin, the hashing function is hash256, or two rounds of sha256. This guarantees the thing that we're signing is exactly 32 bytes. We will call the result of the hash the *signature hash*, or z.

The signature that we are verifying has two components, (r,s). r is the x coordinate of some point R that we'll come back to. The formula for s is as above:

$s = (z+re)/k$

Keep in mind that we know e ($P = eG$, or what we're proving we know in the first place), we know k ($kG = R$, remember?), and we know z.

We will now construct $R = uG + vP$ by defining u and v this way:

$u = z/s$
$v = r/s$

Thus:

$$uG + vP = (z/s)G + (r/s)P = (z/s)G + (re/s)G = ((z + re)/s)G$$

We know $s = (z + re)/k$, so:

$$uG + vP = ((z + re) / ((z + re)/k))G = kG = R$$

We've successfully chosen u and v in such a way as to generate R as we intended. Furthermore, we used r in the calculation of v, proving we knew what R would be. The only way we can know the details of R beforehand is if we know e.

To wit, here are the steps:

1. We are given (r,s) as the signature, z as the hash of the thing being signed, and P as the public key (or public point) of the signer.
2. We calculate $u = z/s$, $v = r/s$.
3. We calculate $uG + vP = R$.
4. If R's x coordinate equals r, the signature is valid.

Why Two Rounds of sha256?

The calculation of z requires two rounds of sha256, or hash256. You may be wondering why there are two rounds when only one is necessary to get a 256-bit number. The reason is for security.

There is a well-known hash collision attack on SHA-1 called a *birthday attack* that makes finding collisions much easier. Google found a SHA-1 collision (*https://security.googleblog.com/2017/02/announcing-first-sha1-collision.html*) using some modifications of a birthday attack and a lot of other things in 2017. Using SHA-1 twice, or *double SHA-1*, is the way to defeat or slow down some forms of this attack.

Two rounds of sha256 don't necessarily prevent all possible attacks, but doing two rounds is a defense against some potential weaknesses.

Verifying a Signature

We can now verify a signature using some of the primitives that we have:

```
>>> from ecc import S256Point, G, N
>>> z = 0xbc62d4b80d9e36da29c16c5d4d9f11731f36052c72401a76c23c0fb5a9b74423
>>> r = 0x37206a0610995c58074999cb9767b87af4c4978db68c06e8e6e81d282047a7c6
>>> s = 0x8ca63759c1157ebeaec0d03cecca119fc9a75bf8e6d0fa65c841c8e2738cdaec
>>> px = 0x04519fac3d910ca7e7138f7013706f619fa8f033e6ec6e09370ea38cee6a7574
>>> py = 0x82b51eab8c27c66e26c858a079bcdf4f1ada34cec420cafc7eac1a42216fb6c4
```

```
>>> point = S256Point(px, py)
>>> s_inv = pow(s, N-2, N)    ❶
>>> u = z * s_inv % N         ❷
>>> v = r * s_inv % N         ❸
>>> print((u*G + v*point).x.num == r)    ❹
True
```

❶ Note that we use Fermat's little theorem for $1/s$, since n is prime.

❷ $u = z/s$.

❸ $v = r/s$.

❹ $uG + vP = (r,y)$. We need to check that the x coordinate is r.

Exercise 6

Verify whether these signatures are valid:

```
P = (0x887387e452b8eacc4acfde10d9aaf7f6d9a0f975aabb10d006e4da568744d06c,
     0x61de6d95231cd89026e286df3b6ae4a894a3378e393e93a0f45b666329a0ae34)

# signature 1
z = 0xec208baa0fc1c19f708a9ca96fdeff3ac3f230bb4a7ba4aede4942ad003c0f60
r = 0xac8d1c87e51d0d441be8b3dd5b05c8795b48875dffe00b7ffcfac23010d3a395
s = 0x68342ceff8935ededd102dd876ffd6ba72d6a427a3edb13d26eb0781cb423c4

# signature 2
z = 0x7c076ff316692a3d7eb3c3bb0f8b1488cf72e1afcd929e29307032997a838a3d
r = 0xeff69ef2b1bd93a66ed5219add4fb51e11a840f404876325a1e8ffe0529a2c
s = 0xc7207fee197d27c618aea621406f6bf5ef6fca38681d82b2f06fddbdce6feab6
```

Programming Signature Verification

We already have a class S256Point, which is the public point for the private key. We create a Signature class that houses the r and s values:

```
class Signature:

    def __init__(self, r, s):
        self.r = r
        self.s = s

    def __repr__(self):
        return 'Signature({:x},{:x})'.format(self.r, self.s)
```

We will be doing more with this class in Chapter 4.

We can now write the verify method on S256Point based on this:

```
class S256Point(Point):
    ...
    def verify(self, z, sig):
        s_inv = pow(sig.s, N - 2, N)   ❶
        u = z * s_inv % N   ❷
        v = sig.r * s_inv % N   ❸
        total = u * G + v * self   ❹
        return total.x.num == sig.r   ❺
```

❶ s_inv ($1/s$) is calculated using Fermat's little theorem on the order of the group, n, which is prime.

❷ $u = z/s$. Note that we can mod by n as that's the order of the group.

❸ $v = r/s$. Note that we can mod by n as that's the order of the group.

❹ $uG + vP$ should be R.

❺ We check that the x coordinate is r.

So, given a public key that is a point on the secp256k1 curve and a signature hash, z, we can verify whether a signature is valid or not.

Signing in Depth

Given that we know how verification should work, signing is straightforward. The only missing step is figuring out what k, and thus $R = kG$, to use. We do this by choosing a random k.

The signing procedure is as follows:

1. We are given z and know e such that $eG = P$.
2. Choose a random k.
3. Calculate $R = kG$ and $r = x$ coordinate of R.
4. Calculate $s = (z + re)/k$.
5. Signature is (r,s).

Note that the public key (pubkey) P has to be transmitted to whoever wants to verify it, and z must be known by the verifier. We'll see later that z is computed and P is sent along with the signature.

Creating a Signature

We can now create a signature.

Be Careful with Random Number Generation

Note that using something like the random library from Python to do cryptography is generally not a good idea. This library is for teaching purposes only, so please don't use any of the code explained to you here for production purposes.

We do this using some of the primitives that we have:

```
>>> from ecc import S256Point, G, N
>>> from helper import hash256
>>> e = int.from_bytes(hash256(b'my secret'), 'big')   ❶
>>> z = int.from_bytes(hash256(b'my message'), 'big')  ❷
>>> k = 1234567890   ❸
>>> r = (k*G).x.num   ❹
>>> k_inv = pow(k, N-2, N)
>>> s = (z+r*e) * k_inv % N   ❺
>>> point = e*G   ❻
>>> print(point)
S256Point(028d003eab2e428d11983f3e97c3fa0addf3b42740df0d211795ffb3be2f6c52, \
0ae987b9ec6ea159c78cb2a937ed89096fb218d9e7594f02b547526d8cd309e2)
>>> print(hex(z))
0x231c6f3d980a6b0fb7152f85cee7eb52bf92433d9919b9c5218cb08e79cce78
>>> print(hex(r))
0x2b698a0f0a4041b77e63488ad48c23e8e8838dd1fb7520408b121697b782ef22
>>> print(hex(s))
0xbb14e602ef9e3f872e25fad328466b34e6734b7a0fcd58b1eb635447ffae8cb9
```

❶ This is an example of a "brain wallet," which is a way to keep the private key in your head without having to memorize something too difficult. Please don't use this for a real secret.

❷ This is the signature hash, or hash of the message that we're signing.

❸ We're going to use a fixed k here for demonstration purposes.

❹ $kG = (r,y)$, so we take the x coordinate only.

❺ $s = (z + re)/k$. We can mod by n because we know this is a cyclical group of order n.

❻ The public point needs to be known by the verifier.

Exercise 7

Sign the following message with the secret:

```
e = 12345
z = int.from_bytes(hash256('Programming Bitcoin!'), 'big')
```

Programming Message Signing

To program message signing, we now create a `PrivateKey` class, which will house our secret:

```
class PrivateKey:

    def __init__(self, secret):
        self.secret = secret
        self.point = secret * G    ❶

    def hex(self):
        return '{:x}'.format(self.secret).zfill(64)
```

❶ We keep around the public key, `self.point`, for convenience.

We then create the `sign` method:

```
from random import randint
...
class PrivateKey:
...
    def sign(self, z):
        k = randint(0, N)    ❶
        r = (k*G).x.num    ❷
        k_inv = pow(k, N-2, N)    ❸
        s = (z + r*self.secret) * k_inv % N    ❹
        if s > N/2:    ❺
            s = N - s
        return Signature(r, s)    ❻
```

❶ `randint` chooses a random integer from $[0,n)$. Please don't use this function in production, because the random number from this library is not nearly random enough.

❷ r is the x coordinate of kG.

❸ We use Fermat's little theorem again, and n, which is prime.

❹ $s = (z + re)/k$.

❺ It turns out that using the low-s value will get nodes to relay our transactions. This is for malleability reasons.

❻ We return a `Signature` object from the class defined earlier.

Importance of a Unique k

There's an important rule in signatures that utilize a random component like we have here: the k needs to be unique per signature. That is, it cannot get reused. In fact, a k that's reused will result in you revealing your secret! Why?

If our secret is e and we are reusing k to sign z_1 and z_2:

$kG = (r,y)$
$s_1 = (z_1 + re) / k, s_2 = (z_2 + re) / k$
$s_1/s_2 = (z_1 + re) / (z_2 + re)$
$s_1(z_2 + re) = s_2(z_1 + re)$
$s_1z_2 + s_1re = s_2z_1 + s_2re$
$s_1re - s_2re = s_2z_1 - s_1z_2$
$e = (s_2z_1 - s_1z_2) / (rs_1 - rs_2)$

If anyone sees both signatures, they can use this formula and find our secret! The PlayStation 3 hack (*https://arstechnica.com/gaming/2010/12/ps3-hacked-through-poor-implementation-of-cryptography/*) back in 2010 was due to the reuse of the k value in multiple signatures.

To combat this, there is a deterministic k generation standard that uses the secret and z to create a unique, deterministic k every time. The specification is in RFC 6979 (*https://tools.ietf.org/html/rfc6979*) and the code changes to look like this:

```
class PrivateKey:
...
    def sign(self, z):
        k = self.deterministic_k(z)   ❶
        r = (k * G).x.num
        k_inv = pow(k, N - 2, N)
        s = (z + r * self.secret) * k_inv % N
        if s > N / 2:
            s = N - s
        return Signature(r, s)

    def deterministic_k(self, z):
        k = b'\x00' * 32
        v = b'\x01' * 32
        if z > N:
            z -= N
        z_bytes = z.to_bytes(32, 'big')
        secret_bytes = self.secret.to_bytes(32, 'big')
        s256 = hashlib.sha256
        k = hmac.new(k, v + b'\x00' + secret_bytes + z_bytes, s256).digest()
        v = hmac.new(k, v, s256).digest()
        k = hmac.new(k, v + b'\x01' + secret_bytes + z_bytes, s256).digest()
        v = hmac.new(k, v, s256).digest()
        while True:
```

```
v = hmac.new(k, v, s256).digest()
candidate = int.from_bytes(v, 'big')
if candidate >= 1 and candidate < N:
    return candidate  ❷
k = hmac.new(k, v + b'\x00', s256).digest()
v = hmac.new(k, v, s256).digest()
```

❶ We are using the deterministic *k* instead of a random one. Everything else about `sign` remains the same.

❷ This algorithm returns a candidate that's suitable.

A deterministic *k* will be unique with very high probability. This is because sha256 is collision-resistant, and no collisions have been found to date.

Another benefit from a testing perspective is that the signature for a given *z* and the same private key will be the same every time. This makes debugging much easier and unit tests a lot easier to write. In addition, transactions that use deterministic *k* will create the same transaction every time, as the signature will not change. This makes transactions less malleable (more on that in Chapter 13).

Conclusion

We've covered elliptic curve cryptography and can now prove that we know a secret by signing something. We can also verify that the person with the secret actually signed a message. Even if you don't read another page in this book, you've learned to implement what was once considered "weapons-grade munitions" (*https://en.wikipedia.org/wiki/Export_of_cryptography_from_the_United_States*). This is a major step in your journey and will be essential for the rest of the book!

We now turn to serializing a lot of these structures so that we can store them on disk and send them over the network.

CHAPTER 4

Serialization

We've created a lot of classes thus far, including `PrivateKey`, `S256Point`, and `Signature`. We now need to start thinking about how to transmit these objects to other computers on the network, or even to disk. This is where serialization comes into play. We want to communicate or store a `S256Point` or a `Signature` or a `PrivateKey`. Ideally, we want to do this efficiently, for reasons we'll see in Chapter 10.

Uncompressed SEC Format

We'll start with the `S256Point` class, which is the public key class. Recall that the public key in elliptic curve cryptography is really a coordinate in the form of (x,y). How can we serialize this data?

It turns out there's already a standard for serializing ECDSA public keys, called *Standards for Efficient Cryptography* (SEC)—and as the word "Efficient" in the name suggests, it has minimal overhead. There are two forms of SEC format that we need to be concerned with: uncompressed and compressed. We'll begin with the former, and look at the compressed format in the next section.

Here is how the uncompressed SEC format for a given point $P = (x,y)$ is generated:

1. Start with the prefix byte, which is `0x04`.
2. Next, append the x coordinate in 32 bytes as a big-endian integer.
3. Next, append the y coordinate in 32 bytes as a big-endian integer.

The uncompressed SEC format is shown in Figure 4-1.

```
047211a824f55b505228e4c3d5194c1fcfaa15a456abdf37f9b9d97a4040afc073dee6c8906498
4f03385237d92167c13e236446b417ab79a0fcae412ae3316b77

    - 04 - Marker
    - x coordinate - 32 bytes
    - y coordinate - 32 bytes
```

Figure 4-1. Uncompressed SEC format

Big- and Little-Endian

The motivation for big- and little-endian encodings is storing a number on disk. A number under 256 is easy enough to encode, as a single byte (2^8) is enough to hold it. When it's bigger than 256, how do we serialize the number to bytes?

Arabic numerals are read left to right. A number like 123 is 100 + 20 + 3 and not 1 + 20 + 300. This is what we call big-endian, because the "big end" starts first.

Computers can sometimes be more efficient using the opposite order, or little-endian—that is, starting with the little end first.

Since computers work in bytes, which have 8 bits, we have to think in base 256. This means that a number like 500 looks like 01f4 in big-endian—that is, 500 = 1 × 256 + 244 (f4 in hexadecimal). The same number looks like f401 in little-endian.

Unfortunately, some serializations in Bitcoin (like the SEC format x and y coordinates) are big-endian, while others (like the transaction version number in Chapter 5) are little-endian. This book will let you know which ones are big- versus little-endian.

Creating the uncompressed SEC format serialization is pretty straightforward. The trickiest part is converting a 256-bit number into 32 bytes, big-endian. Here's how this is done in code:

```
class S256Point(Point):
...
    def sec(self):
        '''returns the binary version of the SEC format'''
        return b'\x04' + self.x.num.to_bytes(32, 'big') \
            + self.y.num.to_bytes(32, 'big')  ❶
```

❶ In Python 3, you can convert a number to bytes using the to_bytes method. The first argument is how many bytes it should take up and the second argument is the endianness (see the preceding note).

Exercise 1

Find the uncompressed SEC format for the public key where the private key secrets are:

- 5,000
- $2,018^5$
- 0xdeadbeef12345

Compressed SEC Format

Recall that for any x coordinate, there are at most two y coordinates due to the y^2 term in the elliptic curve equation (Figure 4-2).

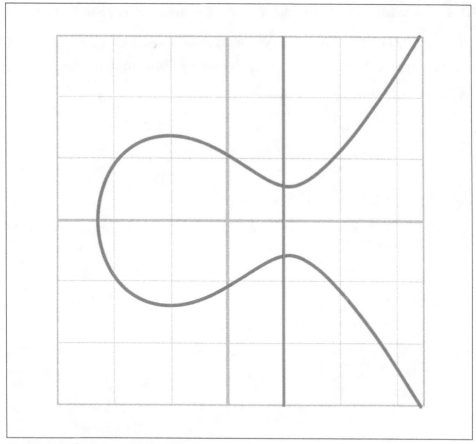

Figure 4-2. The two possible values for y are where this vertical line intersects the curve

It turns out that even over a finite field, we have the same symmetry.

This is because for any (x,y) that satisfies $y^2 = x^3 + ax + b$, $(x,-y)$ also satisfies the equation. Furthermore, in a finite field, $-y \% p = (p - y) \% p$. Or, more accurately, if (x,y) satisfies the elliptic curve equation, $(x,p - y)$ also satisfies the equation. These are the only two solutions for a given x, as shown, so if we know x, we know the y coordinate has to be either y or $p - y$.

Since p is a prime number greater than 2, we know that p is odd. Thus, if y is even, $p - y$ (odd minus even) will be odd. If y is odd, $p - y$ will be even. In other words, between y and $p - y$, exactly one will be even and one will be odd. This is something we can use to our advantage to shorten the uncompressed SEC format: we can provide the x coordinate and the evenness of the y coordinate. We call this the *compressed SEC format* because of how the y coordinate is compressed into a single byte (namely, whether it's even or odd).

Here is the serialization of the compressed SEC format for a given point $P = (x,y)$:

1. Start with the prefix byte. If y is even, it's 0x02; otherwise, it's 0x03.

2. Next, append the x coordinate in 32 bytes as a big-endian integer.

The compressed SEC format is shown in Figure 4-3.

```
0349fc4e631e3624a545de3f89f5d8684c7b8138bd94bdd531d2e213bf016b278a

    - 02 if y is even, 03 if odd - Marker
    - x coordinate - 32 bytes
```

Figure 4-3. Compressed SEC format

Again, the procedure is pretty straightforward. We can update the sec method to handle compressed SEC keys:

```python
class S256Point(Point):
...
    def sec(self, compressed=True):
        '''returns the binary version of the SEC format'''
        if compressed:
            if self.y.num % 2 == 0:
                return b'\x02' + self.x.num.to_bytes(32, 'big')
            else:
                return b'\x03' + self.x.num.to_bytes(32, 'big')
        else:
            return b'\x04' + self.x.num.to_bytes(32, 'big') + \
                self.y.num.to_bytes(32, 'big')
```

The big advantage of the compressed SEC format is that it only takes up 33 bytes instead of 65 bytes. This is a big savings when amortized over millions of transactions.

At this point, you may be wondering how you can analytically calculate y given the x coordinate. This requires us to calculate a square root in a finite field.

Stated mathematically:

Find w such that $w^2 = v$ when we know v.

It turns out that if the finite field prime $p \% 4 = 3$, we can do this rather easily. Here's how.

First, we know:

$$p \% 4 = 3$$

which implies:

$$(p + 1) \% 4 = 0$$

That is, $(p + 1)/4$ is an integer.

By definition:

$$w^2 = v$$

We are looking for a formula to calculate w. From Fermat's little theorem:

$$w^{p-1} \% p = 1$$

which means:

$$w^2 = w^2 \cdot 1 = w^2 \cdot w^{p-1} = w^{(p+1)}$$

Since p is odd (recall p is prime), we know we can divide $(p+1)$ by 2 and still get an integer, implying:

$$w = w^{(p+1)/2}$$

Now we can use $(p+1)/4$ being an integer this way:

$$w = w^{(p+1)/2} = w^{2(p+1)/4} = (w^2)^{(p+1)/4} = v^{(p+1)/4}$$

So our formula for finding the square root becomes:

if $w^2 = v$ and p % 4 = 3, $w = v^{(p+1)/4}$

It turns out that the p used in secp256k1 is such that p % 4 == 3, so we can use this formula:

$$w^2 = v$$
$$w = v^{(p+1)/4}$$

That will be one of the two possible w's; the other will be $p - w$. This is due to taking the square root means that both the positive and negative will work.

We can add this as a general method in the S256Field class:

```
class S256Field(FieldElement):
    ...
    def sqrt(self):
        return self**((P + 1) // 4)
```

When we get a serialized SEC pubkey, we can write a parse method to figure out which y we need:

```
class S256Point:
    ...
    @classmethod
    def parse(self, sec_bin):
        '''returns a Point object from a SEC binary (not hex)'''
        if sec_bin[0] == 4:  ❶
            x = int.from_bytes(sec_bin[1:33], 'big')
            y = int.from_bytes(sec_bin[33:65], 'big')
            return S256Point(x=x, y=y)
        is_even = sec_bin[0] == 2  ❷
        x = S256Field(int.from_bytes(sec_bin[1:], 'big'))
        # right side of the equation y^2 = x^3 + 7
        alpha = x**3 + S256Field(B)
        # solve for left side
        beta = alpha.sqrt()  ❸
        if beta.num % 2 == 0:  ❹
            even_beta = beta
            odd_beta = S256Field(P - beta.num)
        else:
            even_beta = S256Field(P - beta.num)
            odd_beta = beta
        if is_even:
            return S256Point(x, even_beta)
        else:
            return S256Point(x, odd_beta)
```

❶ The uncompressed SEC format is pretty straightforward.

❷ The evenness of the y coordinate is given in the first byte.

❸ We take the square root of the right side of the elliptic curve equation to get y.

❹ We determine evenness and return the correct point.

Exercise 2

Find the compressed SEC format for the public key where the private key secrets are:

- 5,001
- $2,019^5$
- 0xdeadbeef54321

DER Signatures

Another class that we need to learn to serialize is `Signature`. Much like the SEC format, it needs to encode two different numbers, `r` and `s`. Unfortunately, unlike `S256Point`, `Signature` cannot be compressed as `s` cannot be derived solely from `r`.

The standard for serializing signatures (and lots of other things, for that matter) is called Distinguished Encoding Rules (DER) format. DER format was used by Satoshi to serialize signatures. This was most likely because the standard was already defined in 2008, was supported in the OpenSSL library (used in Bitcoin at the time), and was easy enough to adopt, rather than creating a new standard.

DER signature format is defined like this:

1. Start with the `0x30` byte.
2. Encode the length of the rest of the signature (usually `0x44` or `0x45`) and append.
3. Append the marker byte, `0x02`.
4. Encode `r` as a big-endian integer, but prepend it with the `0x00` byte if `r`'s first byte ≥ `0x80`. Prepend the resulting length to `r`. Add this to the result.
5. Append the marker byte, `0x02`.
6. Encode `s` as a big-endian integer, but prepend with the `0x00` byte if `s`'s first byte ≥ `0x80`. Prepend the resulting length to `s`. Add this to the result.

The rules for #4 and #6 with the first byte starting with something greater than or equal to `0x80` are because DER is a general encoding and allows for negative numbers to be encoded. The first bit being 1 means that the number is negative. All numbers in an ECDSA signature are positive, so we have to prepend with `0x00` if the first bit is 1, which is equivalent to first byte ≥ `0x80`.

The DER format is shown in Figure 4-4.

```
3045022100ed81ff192e75a3fd2304004dcadb746fa5e24c5031ccfcf213
20b0277457c98f02207a986d955c6e0cb35d446a89d3f56100f4d7f67801
c31967743a9c8e10615bed

                    - 30 - Marker
                    - 45 - Length of sig
                    - 02 - Marker for r value
                    - 21 - r value lenth
                    - 00ed...8f - r value
                    - 02 - Marker for s value
                    - 20 - s value length
                    - 7a98...ed - s value
```

Figure 4-4. DER format

Because we know r is a 256-bit integer, r will be at most 32 bytes expressed as big-endian. It's also possible the first byte could be ≥ 0x80, so #4 can be at most 33 bytes. However, if r is a relatively small number, it could be less than 32 bytes. The same goes for s and #6.

Here's how this is coded in Python:

```python
class Signature:
...
    def der(self):
        rbin = self.r.to_bytes(32, byteorder='big')
        # remove all null bytes at the beginning
        rbin = rbin.lstrip(b'\x00')
        # if rbin has a high bit, add a \x00
        if rbin[0] & 0x80:
            rbin = b'\x00' + rbin
        result = bytes([2, len(rbin)]) + rbin    ❶
        sbin = self.s.to_bytes(32, byteorder='big')
        # remove all null bytes at the beginning
        sbin = sbin.lstrip(b'\x00')
        # if sbin has a high bit, add a \x00
        if sbin[0] & 0x80:
            sbin = b'\x00' + sbin
        result += bytes([2, len(sbin)]) + sbin
        return bytes([0x30, len(result)]) + result
```

❶ In Python 3, you can convert a list of numbers to the byte equivalents using bytes([some_integer1, some_integer2]).

Overall, this is an inefficient way to encode r and s as there are at least 6 bytes that aren't strictly necessary.

Exercise 3

Find the DER format for a signature whose r and s values are:

```
r = 0x37206a0610995c58074999cb9767b87af4c4978db68c06e8e6e81d282047a7c6

s = 0x8ca63759c1157ebeaec0d03cecca119fc9a75bf8e6d0fa65c841c8e2738cdaec
```

Base58

In the early days of Bitcoin, bitcoins were assigned to public keys specified in SEC format (uncompressed) and then were redeemed using DER signatures. For reasons we'll get to in Chapter 6, using this particular very simple script turned out to be both wasteful for storing unspent transaction outputs (UTXOs) and a little less secure than the scripts in more prominent use now. For now, we'll go through what addresses are and how they are encoded.

Transmitting Your Public Key

In order for Alice to pay Bob, she has to know where to send the money. This is true not just in Bitcoin, but for any method of payment. Since Bitcoin is a digital bearer instrument, the address can be something like a public key in a public key cryptography scheme. Unfortunately, SEC format, especially uncompressed, is a bit long (65 or 33 bytes). Furthermore, the 65 or 33 bytes are in binary format—not something that's easy to read, at least raw.

There are three major considerations. The first is that the public key be readable (easy to hand-write and not too difficult to mistake, say, over the phone). The second is that it's short (not so long that it's cumbersome). The third is that it's secure (so it's harder to make mistakes).

So how do we get readability, compression, and security? If we express the SEC format in hexadecimal (4 bits per character), it's double the length (130 or 66 characters). Can we do better?

We can use something like Base64, which can express 6 bits per character. This results in 87 characters for uncompressed SEC and 44 characters for compressed SEC. Unfortunately, Base64 is prone to mistakes, as a lot of letters and numbers look similar (0 and O, l and I, - and _). If we remove these characters, we can achieve a result that has good readability and decent compression (around 5.86 bits per character). Lastly, we can add a checksum at the end to ensure that mistakes are easy to detect.

This construction is called *Base58*. Instead of hexadecimal (base 16) or Base64, we're encoding numbers in Base58.

The actual mechanics of doing the Base58 encoding are as follows.

All numbers, uppercase letters, and lowercase letters are utilized, except for the afore-mentioned 0/O and l/I. That leaves us with 10 + 26 + 26 – 4 = 58. Each of these characters represents a digit in Base58. We can encode with a function that does exactly this:

```python
BASE58_ALPHABET = '123456789ABCDEFGHJKLMNPQRSTUVWXYZabcdefghijkmnopqrstuvwxyz'
...
def encode_base58(s):
    count = 0
    for c in s:    ❶
        if c == 0:
            count += 1
        else:
            break
    num = int.from_bytes(s, 'big')
    prefix = '1' * count
    result = ''
    while num > 0:    ❷
        num, mod = divmod(num, 58)
        result = BASE58_ALPHABET[mod] + result
    return prefix + result    ❸
```

❶ The purpose of this loop is to determine how many of the bytes at the front are 0 bytes. We want to add them back at the end.

❷ This is the loop that figures out what Base58 digit to use.

❸ Finally, we prepend all the zeros that we counted at the front, because otherwise they wouldn't show up as prefixed ones. This annoyingly happens with pay-to-pubkey-hash (p2pkh); more on that in Chapter 6.

This function will take any bytes in Python 3 and convert them to Base58.

Why Base58 Is on the Way Out

Base58 has been used for a long time, and while it does make it somewhat easier than something like Base64 to communicate, it's not really that convenient. Most people prefer to copy and paste the addresses, and if you've ever tried to communicate a Base58 address vocally, you know it can be a nightmare.

What's much better is the new Bech32 standard, which is defined in BIP0173. Bech32 uses a 32-character alphabet that's just numbers and lowercase letters, except 1, b, i, and o. Thus far, it's only used for Segwit (Chapter 13).

Exercise 4

Convert the following hex values to binary and then to Base58:

- 7c076ff316692a3d7eb3c3bb0f8b1488cf72e1afcd929e29307032997a838a3d

- eff69ef2b1bd93a66ed5219add4fb51e11a840f404876325a1e8ffe0529a2c

- c7207fee197d27c618aea621406f6bf5ef6fca38681d82b2f06fddbdce6feab6

Address Format

The 264 bits from compressed SEC format are still a bit too long, not to mention a bit less secure (see Chapter 6). To both shorten the address and increase security, we can use the ripemd160 hash.

By not using the SEC format directly, we can go from 33 bytes to 20 bytes, shortening the address significantly. Here is how a Bitcoin address is created:

1. For mainnet addresses, start with the prefix 0x00, for testnet 0x6f.

2. Take the SEC format (compressed or uncompressed) and do a sha256 operation followed by the ripemd160 hash operation, the combination of which is called a hash160 operation.

3. Combine the prefix from #1 and resulting hash from #2.

4. Do a hash256 of the result from #3 and get the first 4 bytes.

5. Take the combination of #3 and #4 and encode it in Base58.

The result of step 4 of this process is called the *checksum*. We can do steps 4 and 5 in one go this way:

```
def encode_base58_checksum(b):
    return encode_base58(b + hash256(b)[:4])
```

 What Is Testnet?

Testnet is a parallel Bitcoin network that's meant to be used by developers. The coins on there are not worth anything and the proof-of-work required to find a block is relatively easy. The mainnet chain as of this writing has around 550,000 blocks, while testnet has significantly more (around 1,450,000 blocks).

We can implement the hash160 operation in *helper.py*:

```
def hash160(s):
    '''sha256 followed by ripemd160'''
    return hashlib.new('ripemd160', hashlib.sha256(s).digest()).digest()  ❶
```

❶ Note that `hashlib.sha256(s).digest` does the sha256 and the wrapper around it does the ripemd160.

We can also update `S256Point` with `hash160` and `address` methods:

```
class S256Point:
...
    def hash160(self, compressed=True):
        return hash160(self.sec(compressed))

    def address(self, compressed=True, testnet=False):
        '''Returns the address string'''
        h160 = self.hash160(compressed)
        if testnet:
            prefix = b'\x6f'
        else:
            prefix = b'\x00'
        return encode_base58_checksum(prefix + h160)
```

Exercise 5

Find the addresses corresponding to the public keys whose private key secrets are:

- 5002 (use uncompressed SEC on testnet)
- 2020^5 (use compressed SEC on testnet)
- 0x12345deadbeef (use compressed SEC on mainnet)

WIF Format

The private key in our case is a 256-bit number. Generally, we are not going to need to serialize our secret that often, as it doesn't get broadcast (that would be a bad idea!). That said, there are instances where you may want to transfer your private key from one wallet to another—for example, from a paper wallet to a software wallet.

For this purpose, you can use Wallet Import Format (WIF). WIF is a serialization of the private key that's meant to be human-readable. WIF uses the same Base58 encoding that addresses use.

Here is how the WIF format is created:

1. For mainnet private keys, start with the prefix 0x80, for testnet 0xef.
2. Encode the secret in 32-byte big-endian.

3. If the SEC format used for the public key address was compressed, add a suffix of 0x01.

4. Combine the prefix from #1, serialized secret from #2, and suffix from #3.

5. Do a hash256 of the result from #4 and get the first 4 bytes.

6. Take the combination of #4 and #5 and encode it in Base58.

We can now create the `wif` method on the `PrivateKey` class:

```python
class PrivateKey
...
    def wif(self, compressed=True, testnet=False):
        secret_bytes = self.secret.to_bytes(32, 'big')
        if testnet:
            prefix = b'\xef'
        else:
            prefix = b'\x80'
        if compressed:
            suffix = b'\x01'
        else:
            suffix = b''
        return encode_base58_checksum(prefix + secret_bytes + suffix)
```

Exercise 6

Find the WIF for the private key whose secrets are:

- 5003 (compressed, testnet)
- 2021^5 (uncompressed, testnet)
- 0x54321deadbeef (compressed, mainnet)

Big- and Little-Endian Redux

It will be very useful to know how big- and little-endian are done in Python, as the next few chapters will be parsing and serializing numbers to and from big-/little-endian quite a bit. In particular, Satoshi used a lot of little-endian for Bitcoin and unfortunately, there's no easy-to-learn rule for where little-endian is used and where big-endian is used. Recall that SEC format uses big-endian encoding, as do addresses and WIF. From Chapter 5 onward, we will use little-endian encoding a lot more. For this reason, we turn to the next two exercises. The last exercise of this section is to create a testnet address for yourself.

Exercise 7

Write a function `little_endian_to_int` that takes Python bytes, interprets those bytes in little-endian, and returns the number.

Exercise 8

Write a function `int_to_little_endian` that does the reverse of the last exercise.

Exercise 9

Create a testnet address for yourself using a long secret that only you know. This is important as there are bots on testnet trying to steal testnet coins. Make sure you write this secret down somewhere! You will be using it later to sign transactions.

Go to a testnet faucet (*https://faucet.programmingbitcoin.com*) and send some testnet coins to that address (it should start with m or n, or else something is wrong). If you succeeded, congrats! You're now the proud owner of some testnet coins!

Conclusion

In this chapter we learned how to serialize a lot of different structures that we created in the previous chapters. We now turn to parsing and understanding transactions.

CHAPTER 5

Transactions

Transactions are at the heart of Bitcoin. Transactions, simply put, are value transfers from one entity to another. We'll see in Chapter 6 how "entities" in this case are really smart contracts—but we're getting ahead of ourselves. Let's first look at what transactions in Bitcoin are, what they look like, and how they are parsed.

Transaction Components

At a high level, a transaction really only has four components. They are:

1. Version
2. Inputs
3. Outputs
4. Locktime

A general overview of these fields might be helpful. The version indicates what additional features the transaction uses, inputs define what bitcoins are being spent, outputs define where the bitcoins are going, and locktime defines when this transaction starts being valid. We'll go through each component in depth.

Figure 5-1 shows a hexadecimal dump of a typical transaction that shows which parts are which.

```
0100000001813f79011acb80925dfe69b3def355fe914bd1d96a3f5f71bf8303c6a989c7d10000000
06b483045022100ed81ff192e75a3fd2304004dcadb746fa5e24c5031ccfcf21320b0277457c98f02
207a986d955c6e0cb35d446a89d3f56100f4d7f67801c31967743a9c8e10615bed01210349fc4e631
e3624a545de3f89f5d8684c7b8138bd94bdd531d2e213bf016b278afefffffff02a135ef0100000000
1976a914bc3b654dca7e56b04dca18f2566cdaf02e8d9ada88ac99c39800000000001976a9141c4bc
762dd5423e332166702cb75f40df79fea1288ac19430600
```

Figure 5-1. Transaction components: version, inputs, outputs, and locktime

The differently highlighted parts represent the version, inputs, outputs, and locktime, respectively.

With this in mind, we can start constructing the transaction class, which we'll call Tx:

```python
class Tx:

    def __init__(self, version, tx_ins, tx_outs, locktime, testnet=False):
        self.version = version
        self.tx_ins = tx_ins        ❶
        self.tx_outs = tx_outs
        self.locktime = locktime
        self.testnet = testnet      ❷

    def __repr__(self):
        tx_ins = ''
        for tx_in in self.tx_ins:
            tx_ins += tx_in.__repr__() + '\n'
        tx_outs = ''
        for tx_out in self.tx_outs:
            tx_outs += tx_out.__repr__() + '\n'
        return 'tx: {}\nversion: {}\ntx_ins:\n{}tx_outs:\n{}locktime: {}'.format(
            self.id(),
            self.version,
            tx_ins,
            tx_outs,
            self.locktime,
        )

    def id(self):       ❸
        '''Human-readable hexadecimal of the transaction hash'''
        return self.hash().hex()

    def hash(self):     ❹
        '''Binary hash of the legacy serialization'''
        return hash256(self.serialize())[::-1]
```

❶ Input and output are very generic terms, so we specify what kind of inputs they are. We'll define the specific object types later.

❷ We need to know which network this transaction is on to be able to validate it fully.

❸ The id is what block explorers use for looking up transactions. It's the hash256 of the transaction in hexadecimal format.

❹ The hash is the hash256 of the serialization in little-endian. Note we don't have the serialize method yet; so until we do, this won't work.

The rest of this chapter will be concerned with parsing transactions. We could, at this point, write code like this:

```
class Tx:
    ...

    @classmethod  ❶
    def parse(cls, serialization):
        version = serialization[0:4]  ❷
        ...
```

❶ This method has to be a class method as the serialization will return a new instance of a Tx object.

❷ We assume here that the variable serialization is a byte array.

This could definitely work, but the transaction may be very large. Ideally, we want to be able to parse from a *stream* instead. This will allow us to not need the entire serialized transaction before we start parsing, and that allows us to fail early and be more efficient. Thus, the code for parsing a transaction will look more like this:

```
class Tx:
    ...

    @classmethod
    def parse(cls, stream):
        serialized_version = stream.read(4)  ❶
        ...
```

❶ The read method will allow us to parse on the fly as we won't have to wait on I/O.

This is advantageous from an engineering perspective as the stream can be a socket connection on the network or a file handle. We can start parsing the stream right away instead of waiting for the whole thing to be transmitted or read first. Our method will be able to handle any sort of stream and return the Tx object that we need.

Version

When you see a version number in something (Figure 5-2 shows an example), it's meant to give the receiver information about what the versioned thing is supposed to represent. If, for example, you are running Windows 3.1, that's a version number that's very different than Windows 8 or Windows 10. You could specify just "Windows," but specifying the version number after the operating system helps you know what features it has and what APIs you can program against.

```
0100000001813f79011acb80925dfe69b3def355fe914bd1d96a3f5f71bf8303c6a989c7d10000000
06b483045022100ed81ff192e75a3fd2304004dcadb746fa5e24c5031ccfcf21320b0277457c98f02
207a986d955c6e0cb35d446a89d3f56100f4d7f67801c31967743a9c8e10615bed01210349fc4e631
e3624a545de3f89f5d8684c7b8138bd94bdd531d2e213bf016b278afefffffff02a135ef0100000000
1976a914bc3b654dca7e56b04dca18f2566cdaf02e8d9ada88ac99c39800000000001976a9141c4bc
762dd5423e332166702cb75f40df79fea1288ac19430600
```

Figure 5-2. Version

Similarly, Bitcoin transactions have version numbers. In Bitcoin's case, the transaction version is generally 1, but there are cases where it can be 2 (transactions using an opcode called OP_CHECKSEQUENCEVERIFY as defined in BIP0112 require use of version > 1).

You may notice here that the actual value in hexadecimal is `01000000`, which doesn't look like 1. Interpreted as a little-endian integer, however, this number is actually 1 (recall the discussion from Chapter 4).

Exercise 1

Write the version parsing part of the `parse` method that we've defined. To do this properly, you'll have to convert 4 bytes into a little-endian integer.

Inputs

Each input points to an output of a previous transaction (see Figure 5-3). This fact requires more explanation, as it's not intuitively obvious at first.

```
0100000001813f79011acb80925dfe69b3def355fe914bd1d96a3f5f71bf8303c6a989c7d10000000
06b483045022100ed81ff192e75a3fd2304004dcadb746fa5e24c5031ccfcf21320b0277457c98f02
207a986d955c6e0cb35d446a89d3f56100f4d7f67801c31967743a9c8e10615bed01210349fc4e631
e3624a545de3f89f5d8684c7b8138bd94bdd531d2e213bf016b278afefffffff02a135ef0100000000
1976a914bc3b654dca7e56b04dca18f2566cdaf02e8d9ada88ac99c39800000000001976a9141c4bc
762dd5423e332166702cb75f40df79fea1288ac19430600
```

Figure 5-3. Inputs

Bitcoin's inputs are spending outputs of a previous transaction. That is, you need to have received bitcoins first to spend something. This makes intuitive sense. You cannot spend money unless you've received money first. The inputs refer to bitcoins that belong to you. Each input needs two things:

- A reference to bitcoins you received previously
- Proof that these are yours to spend

The second part uses ECDSA (Chapter 3). You don't want people to be able to forge this, so most inputs contain signatures that only the owner(s) of the private key(s) can produce.

The inputs field can contain more than one input. This is analogous to using either a single $100 bill to pay for a $70 meal, or a $50 and a $20. The former only requires one input ("bill"); the latter requires two. There are situations where there could be even more inputs. In our analogy, we could pay for a $70 meal with 14 $5 bills, or even 7,000 pennies. This would be analogous to 14 inputs or 7,000 inputs.

The number of inputs is the next part of the transaction, as highlighted in Figure 5-4.

```
0100000001813f79011acb80925dfe69b3def355fe914bd1d96a3f5f71bf8303c6a989c7d10000000
06b483045022100ed81ff192e75a3fd2304004dcadb746fa5e24c5031ccfcf21320b0277457c98f02
207a986d955c6e0cb35d446a89d3f56100f4d7f67801c31967743a9c8e10615bed01210349fc4e631
e3624a545de3f89f5d8684c7b8138bd94bdd531d2e213bf016b278afeffffff02a135ef0100000000
1976a914bc3b654dca7e56b04dca18f2566cdaf02e8d9ada88ac99c39800000000001976a9141c4bc
762dd5423e332166702cb75f40df79fea1288ac19430600
```

Figure 5-4. Number of inputs

We can see that the byte is actually 01, which means that this transaction has one input. It may be tempting here to assume that it's always a single byte, but it's not. A single byte has 8 bits, so anything over 255 inputs will not be expressible in a single byte.

This is where *varints* come in. Varint is shorthand for *variable integer*, which is a way to encode an integer into bytes that range from 0 to $2^{64} - 1$. We could, of course, always reserve 8 bytes for the number of inputs, but that would be a lot of wasted space if we expect the number of inputs to be relatively small (say, under 200). This is the case with the number of inputs in a normal transaction, so using varints helps to save space. You can see how they work in the following sidebar.

Varints

Variable integers work by these rules:

- If the number is below 253, encode that number as a single byte (e.g., 100 → 0x64).
- If the number is between 253 and $2^{16} - 1$, start with the 253 byte (fd) and then encode the number in 2 bytes in little-endian (e.g., 255 → 0xfdff00, 555 → 0xfd2b02).
- If the number is between 2^{16} and $2^{32} - 1$, start with the 254 byte (fe) and then encode the number in 4 bytes in little-endian (e.g., 70015 → 0xfe7f110100).
- If the number is between 2^{32} and $2^{64} - 1$, start with the 255 byte (ff) and then encode the number in 8 bytes in little-endian (e.g., 18005558675309 → 0xff6dc7ed3e60100000).

Two functions from *helper.py* will be used to parse and serialize varint fields:

```python
def read_varint(s):
    '''read_varint reads a variable integer from a stream'''
    i = s.read(1)[0]
    if i == 0xfd:
        # 0xfd means the next two bytes are the number
        return little_endian_to_int(s.read(2))
    elif i == 0xfe:
        # 0xfe means the next four bytes are the number
        return little_endian_to_int(s.read(4))
    elif i == 0xff:
        # 0xff means the next eight bytes are the number
        return little_endian_to_int(s.read(8))
    else:
        # anything else is just the integer
        return i


def encode_varint(i):
    '''encodes an integer as a varint'''
    if i < 0xfd:
        return bytes([i])
    elif i < 0x10000:
        return b'\xfd' + int_to_little_endian(i, 2)
    elif i < 0x100000000:
        return b'\xfe' + int_to_little_endian(i, 4)
    elif i < 0x10000000000000000:
        return b'\xff' + int_to_little_endian(i, 8)
    else:
        raise ValueError('integer too large: {}'.format(i))
```

> `read_varint` will read from a stream and return the integer that was encoded. `encode_varint` will do the opposite, which is to take an integer and return the varint byte representation.

Each input contains four fields. The first two fields point to the previous transaction output and the last two fields define how the previous transaction output can be spent. The fields are as follows:

- Previous transaction ID
- Previous transaction index
- ScriptSig
- Sequence

As just explained, each input has a reference to a previous transaction's output. The previous transaction ID is the hash256 of the previous transaction's contents. This uniquely defines the previous transaction, as the probability of a hash collision is impossibly low.

As we'll see, each transaction has to have at least one output, but may have many. Thus, we need to define exactly which output *within a transaction* we're spending, which is captured in the previous transaction index.

Note that the previous transaction ID is 32 bytes and that the previous transaction index is 4 bytes. Both are in little-endian.

The ScriptSig has to do with Bitcoin's smart contract language, Script, discussed more thoroughly in Chapter 6. For now, think of the ScriptSig as opening a locked box—something that can only be done by the owner of the transaction output. The ScriptSig field is a variable-length field, not a fixed-length field like most of what we've seen so far. A variable-length field requires us to define exactly how long the field will be, which is why the field is preceded by a varint telling us how long it is.

The sequence was originally intended as a way to do what Satoshi called "high-frequency trades" with the locktime field (see "Sequence and Locktime" on page 94), but is currently used with Replace-By-Fee (RBF) and `OP_CHECKSEQUENCEVERIFY`. The sequence is also in little-endian and takes up 4 bytes.

The fields of the input look like Figure 5-5.

```
0100000001813f79011acb80925dfe69b3def355fe914bd1d96a3f5f71bf8303c6a989c7d10000000
06b483045022100ed81ff192e75a3fd2304004dcadb746fa5e24c5031ccfcf21320b0277457c98f02
207a986d955c6e0cb35d446a89d3f56100f4d7f67801c31967743a9c8e10615bed01210349fc4e631
e3624a545de3f89f5d8684c7b8138bd94bdd531d2e213bf016b278afefffffff02a135ef0100000000
1976a914bc3b654dca7e56b04dca18f2566cdaf02e8d9ada88ac99c39800000000001976a9141c4bc
762dd5423e332166702cb75f40df79fea1288ac19430600
```

Figure 5-5. The fields of an input: previous transaction ID, previous index, ScriptSig, and sequence

Sequence and Locktime

Originally, Satoshi wanted the sequence and locktime fields to be used for something called "high-frequency trades." What Satoshi envisioned was a way to do payments back and forth with another party without making lots of on-chain transactions. For example, if Alice pays Bob x bitcoins for something and then Bob pays Alice y bitcoins for something else (say, if $x > y$), then Alice can just pay Bob $x - y$, instead of there being two separate transactions on-chain. We could do the same thing if Alice and Bob had 100 transactions between them—that is, compress a bunch of transactions into a single transaction.

That's the idea that Satoshi had: a continuously updating mini-ledger between the two parties involved that gets settled on-chain. Satoshi's intent was to use the sequence and locktime fields to update the high-frequency trade transaction every time a new payment between the two parties occurred. The trade transaction would have two inputs (one from Alice and one from Bob) and two outputs (one to Alice and one to Bob). The trade transaction would start with sequence at 0 and with a far-away locktime (say, 500 blocks from now, so valid in 500 blocks). This would be the base transaction where Alice and Bob get the same amounts as they put in.

After the first transaction, where Alice pays Bob x bitcoins, the sequence of each input would be 1. After the second transaction, where Bob pays Alice y bitcoins, the sequence of each input would be 2. Using this method, we could have lots of payments compressed into a single on-chain transaction as long as they happened before the locktime became valid.

Unfortunately, as clever as this is, it turns out that it's quite easy for a miner to cheat. In our example, Bob could be a miner; he could ignore the updated trade transaction with sequence number 2 and mine the trade transaction with sequence number 1, cheating Alice out of y bitcoins.

A much better design was created later with "payment channels," which is the basis for the Lightning Network.

Now that we know what the fields are, we can start creating a `TxIn` class in Python:

```python
class TxIn:
    def __init__(self, prev_tx, prev_index, script_sig=None, sequence=0xffffffff):
        self.prev_tx = prev_tx
        self.prev_index = prev_index
        if script_sig is None:  ❶
            self.script_sig = Script()
        else:
            self.script_sig = script_sig
        self.sequence = sequence

    def __repr__(self):
        return '{}:{}'.format(
            self.prev_tx.hex(),
            self.prev_index,
        )
```

❶ We default to an empty ScriptSig.

There are a couple things to note here. First, the amount of each input is not specified. We have no idea how much is being spent unless we look it up in the blockchain for the transaction(s) that we're spending. Furthermore, we don't even know if the transaction is unlocking the right box, so to speak, without knowing about the previous transaction. Every node must verify that this transaction unlocks the right box and that it doesn't spend nonexistent bitcoins. How we do that is further discussed in Chapter 7.

Parsing Script

We'll delve more deeply into how Script is parsed in Chapter 6, but for now, here's how you get a `Script` object from hexadecimal in Python:

```python
>>> from io import BytesIO
>>> from script import Script  ❶
>>> script_hex = ('6b483045022100ed81ff192e75a3fd2304004dcadb746fa5e24c5031ccf\
cf21320b0277457c98f02207a986d955c6e0cb35d446a89d3f56100f4d7f67801c31967743a9c8\
e10615bed01210349fc4e631e3624a545de3f89f5d8684c7b8138bd94bdd531d2e213bf016b278\
a')
>>> stream = BytesIO(bytes.fromhex(script_hex))
>>> script_sig = Script.parse(stream)
>>> print(script_sig)
3045022100ed81ff192e75a3fd2304004dcadb746fa5e24c5031ccfcf21320b0277457c98f0220\
7a986d955c6e0cb35d446a89d3f56100f4d7f67801c31967743a9c8e10615bed01 0349fc4e631\
e3624a545de3f89f5d8684c7b8138bd94bdd531d2e213bf016b278a
```

❶ The `Script` class will be more thoroughly explored in Chapter 6. For now, please trust that the `Script.parse` method will create the object that we need.

Exercise 2

Write the inputs parsing part of the `parse` method in `Tx` and the `parse` method for `TxIn`.

Outputs

As hinted in the previous section, outputs define where the bitcoins are going. Each transaction must have one or more outputs. Why would anyone have more than one output? An exchange may batch transactions, for example, and pay out to a lot of people at once instead of generating a single transaction for every single person that requests bitcoins.

Like with inputs, output serialization starts with how many outputs there are as a varint, as shown in Figure 5-6.

```
0100000001813f79011acb80925dfe69b3def355fe914bd1d96a3f5f71bf8303c6a989c7d10000000
06b483045022100ed81ff192e75a3fd2304004dcadb746fa5e24c5031ccfcf21320b0277457c98f02
207a986d955c6e0cb35d446a89d3f56100f4d7f67801c31967743a9c8e10615bed01210349fc4e631
e3624a545de3f89f5d8684c7b8138bd94bdd531d2e213bf016b278afefffffff02a135ef0100000000
1976a914bc3b654dca7e56b04dca18f2566cdaf02e8d9ada88ac99c398000000000001976a9141c4bc
762dd5423e332166702cb75f40df79fea1288ac19430600
```

Figure 5-6. Number of outputs

Each output has two fields: amount and ScriptPubKey. The amount is the amount of bitcoins being assigned and is specified in satoshis, or 1/100,000,000ths of a bitcoin. This allows us to divide bitcoins very finely, down to 1/300th of a penny in USD terms as of this writing. The absolute maximum for the amount is the asymptotic limit of 21 million bitcoins in satoshis, which is 2,100,000,000,000,000 (2,100 trillion) satoshis. This number is greater than 2^{32} (4.3 billion or so) and is thus stored in 64 bits, or 8 bytes. The amount is serialized in little-endian.

The ScriptPubKey, like the ScriptSig, has to do with Bitcoin's smart contract language, Script. Think of the ScriptPubKey as the locked box that can only be opened by the holder of the key. It's like a one-way safe that can receive deposits from anyone, but can only be opened by the owner of the safe. We'll explore this in more detail in Chapter 6. Like ScriptSig, ScriptPubKey is a variable-length field and is preceded by the length of the field in a varint.

A complete output looks like Figure 5-7.

```
0100000001813f79011acb80925dfe69b3def355fe914bd1d96a3f5f71bf8303c6a989c7d10000000
06b483045022100ed81ff192e75a3fd2304004dcadb746fa5e24c5031ccfcf21320b0277457c98f02
207a986d955c6e0cb35d446a89d3f56100f4d7f67801c31967743a9c8e10615bed01210349fc4e631
e3624a545de3f89f5d8684c7b8138bd94bdd531d2e213bf016b278afeffffff02a135ef0100000000
1976a914bc3b654dca7e56b04dca18f2566cdaf02e8d9ada88ac99c398000000000001976a9141c4bc
762dd5423e332166702cb75f40df79fea1288ac19430600
```

Figure 5-7. A complete output field, showing the amount and ScriptPubKey—this one is at index 0

UTXO Set

UTXO stands for *unspent transaction output*. The entire set of unspent transaction outputs at any given moment is called the *UTXO set*. The reason why UTXOs are important is because at any moment in time, they represent all the bitcoins that are available to be spent. In other words, these are the bitcoins that are in circulation. Full nodes on the network must keep track of the UTXO set, and keeping the UTXO set indexed makes validating new transactions much faster.

For example, it's easy to enforce a no-double-spending rule by looking up the previous transaction output in the UTXO set. If the input of a new transaction is using a transaction output that's not in the UTXO set, that's an attempt at a double-spend or a nonexistent output and thus invalid. Keeping the UTXO set handy is also very useful for validating transactions. As we'll see in Chapter 6, we need to look up the amount and ScriptPubKey from the previous transaction output to validate transactions, so having these UTXOs handy can speed up transaction validation.

We can now start coding the TxOut class:

```
class TxOut:

    def __init__(self, amount, script_pubkey):
        self.amount = amount
        self.script_pubkey = script_pubkey

    def __repr__(self):
        return '{}:{}'.format(self.amount, self.script_pubkey)
```

Exercise 3

Write the outputs parsing part of the parse method in Tx and the parse method for TxOut.

Locktime

Locktime is a way to time-delay a transaction. A transaction with a locktime of 600,000 cannot go into the blockchain until block 600,001. This was originally construed as a way to do high-frequency trades (see "Sequence and Locktime" on page 94), which turned out to be insecure. If the locktime is greater than or equal to 500,000,000, it's a Unix timestamp. If it's less than 500,000,000, it's a block number. This way, transactions can be signed but unspendable until a certain point in Unix time or block height is reached.

When Locktime Is Ignored

Note that locktime is ignored if the sequence numbers for every input are ffffffff.

The serialization is in little-endian and 4 bytes (Figure 5-8).

```
0100000001813f79011acb80925dfe69b3def355fe914bd1d96a3f5f71bf8303c6a989c7d10000000
06b483045022100ed81ff192e75a3fd2304004dcadb746fa5e24c5031ccfcf21320b0277457c98f02
207a986d955c6e0cb35d446a89d3f56100f4d7f67801c31967743a9c8e10615bed01210349fc4e631
e3624a545de3f89f5d8684c7b8138bd94bdd531d2e213bf016b278afeffffff02a135ef0100000000
1976a914bc3b654dca7e56b04dca18f2566cdaf02e8d9ada88ac99c398000000000001976a9141c4bc
762dd5423e332166702cb75f40df79fea1288ac19430600
```

Figure 5-8. Locktime

The main problem with using locktime is that the recipient of the transaction has no certainty that the transaction will be good when the locktime comes. This is similar to a postdated bank check, which has the possibility of bouncing. The sender can spend the inputs prior to the locktime transaction getting into the blockchain, thus invalidating the transaction at locktime.

The uses before BIP0065 were limited. BIP0065 introduced OP_CHECKLOCKTIMEVERIFY, which makes locktime more useful by making an output unspendable until a certain locktime.

Exercise 4

Write the locktime parsing part of the parse method in Tx.

Exercise 5

What are the ScriptSig of the second input, the ScriptPubKey of the first output, and the amount of the second output for this transaction?

010000000456919960ac691763688d3d3bcea9ad6ecaf875df5339e148a1fc61c6ed7a069e0100
00006a47304402204585bcdef85e6b1c6af5c2669d4830ff86e42dd205c0e089bc2a821657e951
c002201024a10366077f87d6bce1f7100ad8cfa8a064b39d4e8fe4ea13a7b71aa8180f012102f0
da57e85eec2934a82a585ea337ce2f4998b50ae699dd79f5880e253dafafb7feffffffeb8f51f4
038dc17e6313cf831d4f02281c2a468bde0fafd37f1bf882729e7fd3000000006a473044022078
99531a52d59a6de200179928ca900254a36b8dff8bb75f5f5d71b1cdc26125022008b422690b84
61cb52c3cc30330b23d574351872b7c361e9aae3649071c1a7160121035d5c93d9ac96881f19ba
1f686f15f009ded7c62efe85a872e6a19b43c15a2937fefffffff567bf40595119d1bb8a3037c35
6efd56170b64cbcc160fb028fa10704b45d775000000006a47304402204c7c7818424c7f7911da
6cddc59655a70af1cb5eaf17c69dadbfc74ffa0b662f02207599e08bc8023693ad4e9527dc42c3
4210f7a7d1d1ddfc8492b654a11e7620a0012102158b46fbdff65d0172b7989aec8850aa0dae49
abfb84c81ae6e5b251a58ace5cfeffffffd63a5e6c16e620f86f375925b21cabaf736c779f88fd
04dcad51d26690f7f345010000006a47304402200633ea0d3314bea0d95b3cd8dadb2ef79ea833
1ffe1e61f762c0f6daea0fabde022029f23b3e9c30f080446150b23852028751635dcee2be669c
2a1686a4b5edf304012103ffd6f4a67e94aba353a00882e563ff2722eb4cff0ad6006e86ee20df
e7520d55fefffffff0251430f00000000001976a914ab0c0b2e98b1ab6dbf67d4750b0a56244948
a87988ac005a62020000000001976a9143c82d7df364eb6c75be8c80df2b3eda8db57397088ac46
430600

Coding Transactions

We've parsed the transaction; now we want to do the opposite, which is serializing the transaction. Let's start with TxOut:

```
class TxOut:
...
    def serialize(self):  ❶
        '''Returns the byte serialization of the transaction output'''
        result = int_to_little_endian(self.amount, 8)
        result += self.script_pubkey.serialize()
        return result
```

❶ We're going to serialize the TxOut object to a bunch of bytes.

We can then proceed to TxIn:

```
class TxIn:
...
    def serialize(self):
        '''Returns the byte serialization of the transaction input'''
        result = self.prev_tx[::-1]
        result += int_to_little_endian(self.prev_index, 4)
        result += self.script_sig.serialize()
        result += int_to_little_endian(self.sequence, 4)
        return result
```

Lastly, we can serialize Tx:

```
class Tx:
...
    def serialize(self):
        '''Returns the byte serialization of the transaction'''
```

```
    result = int_to_little_endian(self.version, 4)
    result += encode_varint(len(self.tx_ins))
    for tx_in in self.tx_ins:
        result += tx_in.serialize()
    result += encode_varint(len(self.tx_outs))
    for tx_out in self.tx_outs:
        result += tx_out.serialize()
    result += int_to_little_endian(self.locktime, 4)
    return result
```

We've used the `serialize` methods of both `TxIn` and `TxOut` to serialize `Tx`.

Note that the transaction fee is not specified anywhere! This is because the fee is an implied amount, as described in the next section.

Transaction Fee

One of the consensus rules of Bitcoin is that for any non-coinbase transactions (more on coinbase transactions in Chapter 9), the sum of the inputs has to be greater than or equal to the sum of the outputs. You may be wondering why the inputs and outputs can't just be forced to be equal. This is because if every transaction had zero cost, there wouldn't be any incentive for miners to include transactions in blocks (see Chapter 9). Fees are a way to incentivize miners to include transactions. Transactions not in blocks (so-called *mempool transactions*) are not part of the blockchain and are not final.

The transaction fee is simply the sum of the inputs minus the sum of the outputs. This difference is what the miner gets to keep. As inputs don't have an amount field, we have to look up the amount. This requires access to the blockchain, specifically the UTXO set. If you are not running a full node, this can be tricky, as you now need to trust some other entity to provide you with this information.

We are creating a new class to handle this, called `TxFetcher`:

```
class TxFetcher:
    cache = {}

    @classmethod
    def get_url(cls, testnet=False):
        if testnet:
            return 'http://testnet.programmingbitcoin.com'
        else:
            return 'http://mainnet.programmingbitcoin.com'

    @classmethod
    def fetch(cls, tx_id, testnet=False, fresh=False):
        if fresh or (tx_id not in cls.cache):
            url = '{}/tx/{}.hex'.format(cls.get_url(testnet), tx_id)
            response = requests.get(url)
            try:
```

```
            raw = bytes.fromhex(response.text.strip())
        except ValueError:
            raise ValueError('unexpected response: {}'.format(response.text))
        if raw[4] == 0:
            raw = raw[:4] + raw[6:]
            tx = Tx.parse(BytesIO(raw), testnet=testnet)
            tx.locktime = little_endian_to_int(raw[-4:])
        else:
            tx = Tx.parse(BytesIO(raw), testnet=testnet)
        if tx.id() != tx_id:   ❶
            raise ValueError('not the same id: {} vs {}'.format(tx.id(),
                             tx_id))
        cls.cache[tx_id] = tx
    cls.cache[tx_id].testnet = testnet
    return cls.cache[tx_id]
```

❶ We check that the ID is what we expect it to be.

You may be wondering why we don't get just the specific output for the transaction and instead get the entire transaction. This is because we don't want to be trusting a third party! By getting the entire transaction, we can verify the transaction ID (the hash256 of its contents) and be sure that we are indeed getting the transaction we asked for. This is impossible unless we receive the entire transaction.

Why We Minimize Trusting Third Parties

As Nick Szabo eloquently wrote in his seminal essay "Trusted Third Parties are Security Holes" (*https://nakamotoinstitute.org/ trusted-third-parties/*), trusting third parties to provide correct data is *not* a good security practice. The third party may be behaving well now, but you never know when it may get hacked, have an employee go rogue, or start implementing policies that are against your interests. Part of what makes Bitcoin secure is *not* trusting, but verifying the data that we're given.

We can now create the appropriate method in TxIn to fetch the previous transaction and methods to get the previous transaction output's amount and ScriptPubKey (the latter to be used in Chapter 6):

```
class TxIn:
...
    def fetch_tx(self, testnet=False):
        return TxFetcher.fetch(self.prev_tx.hex(), testnet=testnet)

    def value(self, testnet=False):
        '''Get the output value by looking up the tx hash.
        Returns the amount in satoshi.
        '''
        tx = self.fetch_tx(testnet=testnet)
```

```
        return tx.tx_outs[self.prev_index].amount

    def script_pubkey(self, testnet=False):
        '''Get the ScriptPubKey by looking up the tx hash.
        Returns a Script object.
        '''
        tx = self.fetch_tx(testnet=testnet)
        return tx.tx_outs[self.prev_index].script_pubkey
```

Calculating the Fee

Now that we have the `value` method in `TxIn` that lets us access how many bitcoins are in each transaction input, we can calculate the fee for a transaction.

Exercise 6

Write the `fee` method for the `Tx` class.

Conclusion

We've covered exactly how to parse and serialize transactions and defined what the fields mean. There are two fields that require more explanation, both related to Bitcoin's smart contract language, Script. To that topic we go in Chapter 6.

CHAPTER 6

Script

The ability to lock and unlock coins is the mechanism by which we transfer bitcoin. *Locking* is giving some bitcoins to some entity. *Unlocking* is spending some bitcoins that you have received.

In this chapter we examine this locking/unlocking mechanism, which is often called a *smart contract*. Elliptic curve cryptography (Chapter 3) is used by Script to validate that a transaction was properly authorized (Chapter 5). Script essentially allows people to prove that they have the right to spend certain UTXOs. We're getting a little ahead of ourselves, though, so let's start with how Script works and go from there.

Mechanics of Script

If you are confused about what a smart contract is, don't worry. "Smart contract" is a fancy way of saying "programmable," and the "smart contract language" is simply a programming language. In Bitcoin, Script is the smart contract language, or the programming language used to express the conditions under which bitcoins are spendable.

Bitcoin has the digital equivalent of a contract in Script. Script is a stack-based language similar to Forth. It's intentionally limited in the sense that it avoids certain features. Specifically, Script avoids any mechanism for loops and is therefore not Turing complete.

Why Bitcoin Isn't Turing Complete

Turing completeness in a programming language essentially means that the program has the ability to loop. Loops are a useful construct in programming, so you may be wondering at this point why Script doesn't have the ability to loop.

There are a lot of reasons for this, but let's start with program execution. Anyone can create a Script program that every full node on the network executes. If Script were Turing complete, it would be possible for the loop to go on executing forever. This would cause validating nodes to enter and never leave that loop. This would be an easy way to attack the network through what would be called a denial-of-service (DoS) attack. A single Script program with an infinite loop could take down Bitcoin! This would be a large systematic vulnerability, and protecting against this vulnerability is one of the major reasons why Turing completeness is avoided. Ethereum, which has Turing completeness in its smart contract language, Solidity, handles this problem by forcing contracts to pay for program execution with something called "gas." An infinite loop will exhaust whatever gas is in the contract because, by definition, it will run an infinite number of times.

Another reason to avoid Turing completeness is because smart contracts with Turing completeness are very difficult to analyze. A Turing-complete smart contract's execution conditions are very difficult to enumerate, and thus it's easy to create unintended behavior, causing bugs. Bugs in a smart contract mean that the coins are vulnerable to being unintentionally spent, which means the contract participants could lose money. Such bugs are not just theoretical: this was the major problem in the DAO (Decentralized Autonomous Organization), a Turing-complete smart contract that ended with the Ethereum Classic hard fork.

Transactions assign bitcoins to a *locking* script. The locking script is what's specified in the ScriptPubKey field (see Chapter 5). You can think of this as a lockbox where some money is deposited that only a particular key can open. The money inside, of course, can only be accessed by the owner who has the key.

The unlocking of the lockbox is done in the ScriptSig field (see Chapter 5); this proves ownership of the locked box, which authorizes spending of the funds.

How Script Works

Script is a programming language, and like most programming languages, it processes one command at a time. The commands operate on a stack of elements. There are two possible types of commands: elements and operations.

Elements are data. Technically, processing an element pushes that element onto the stack. Elements are byte strings of length 1 to 520. A typical element might be a DER signature or a SEC pubkey (Figure 6-1).

Figure 6-1. Elements

Operations do something to the data (Figure 6-2). They consume zero or more elements from the processing stack and push zero or more elements back to the stack.

Figure 6-2. Operations

A typical operation is OP_DUP (Figure 6-3), which will duplicate the top element (consuming 0) and push the new element to the stack (pushing 1).

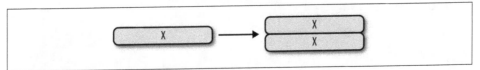

Figure 6-3. OP_DUP duplicates the top element

After all the commands are evaluated, the top element of the stack must be nonzero for the script to resolve as valid. Having no elements in the stack or the top element being 0 would resolve as invalid. Resolving as invalid means that the transaction that includes the unlocking script is not accepted on the network.

Example Operations

There are many other operations besides OP_DUP. OP_HASH160 (Figure 6-4) does a sha256 followed by a ripemd160 (aka a hash160) to the top element of the stack (consuming 1) and pushes a new element to the stack (pushing 1). Note in the diagram that y = hash160(x).

Figure 6-4. OP_HASH160 does a sha256 followed by ripemd160 to the top element

Another very important operation is OP_CHECKSIG (Figure 6-5). OP_CHECKSIG con-sumes two elements from the stack, the first being the pubkey and the second being a signature, and examines whether the signature is good for the given pubkey. If so, OP_CHECKSIG pushes a 1 to the stack; otherwise, it pushes a 0 to the stack.

Figure 6-5. OP_CHECKSIG checks if the signature for the pubkey is valid or not

Coding Opcodes

We can now code OP_DUP, given a stack. OP_DUP simply duplicates the top element of the stack:

```
def op_dup(stack):
    if len(stack) < 1:  ❶
        return False
    stack.append(stack[-1])  ❷
    return True
...
OP_CODE_FUNCTIONS = {
...
    118: op_dup,  ❸
...
}
```

❶ We have to have at least one element to duplicate; otherwise, we can't execute this opcode.

❷ This is how we duplicate the top element of the stack.

❸ 118 = 0x76, which is the code for OP_DUP.

Note that we return a Boolean with this opcode, as a way to tell whether the operation was successful. A failed operation automatically fails script evaluation.

Here's another one, for OP_HASH256. This opcode will consume the top element, per-form a hash256 operation on it, and push the result onto the stack:

```
def op_hash256(stack):
    if len(stack) < 1:
        return False
    element = stack.pop()
    stack.append(hash256(element))
    return True
...
OP_CODE_FUNCTIONS = {
...
    170: op_hash256,
...
}
```

Exercise 1

Write the op_hash160 function.

Parsing the Script Fields

Both the ScriptPubKey and ScriptSig are parsed the same way. If the byte is between
0x01 and 0x4b (whose value we call *n*), we read the next *n* bytes as an element. Otherwise, the byte represents an operation, which we have to look up. Here are some operations and their byte codes:

- 0x00 - OP_0
- 0x51 - OP_1
- 0x60 - OP_16
- 0x76 - OP_DUP
- 0x93 - OP_ADD
- 0xa9 - OP_HASH160
- 0xac - OP_CHECKSIG

Elements Longer Than 75 Bytes

You might be wondering what would happen if you had an element with a length greater than 0x4b (75 in decimal). There are three specific opcodes for handling such elements: OP_PUSHDATA1, OP_PUSHDATA2, and OP_PUSHDATA4. OP_PUSHDATA1 means that the next byte contains how many bytes we need to read for the element. OP_PUSHDATA2 means that the next 2 bytes contain how many bytes we need to read for the element. OP_PUSHDATA4 means that the next 4 bytes contain how many bytes we need to read for the element.

Practically speaking, this means if we have an element that's between 76 and 255 bytes inclusive, we use OP_PUSHDATA1 *<1-byte length of the element> <element>*. For anything between 256 bytes and 520 bytes inclusive, we use OP_PUSHDATA2 *<2-byte length of the element in little-endian> <element>*. Anything larger than 520 bytes is not allowed on the network, so OP_PUSHDATA4 is unnecessary, though OP_PUSHDATA4 *<4-byte length of the element in little-endian, but value less than or equal to 520> <element>* is still legal.

It is possible to encode a number below 76 using OP_PUSHDATA1 or a number below 256 using OP_PUSHDATA2 or even any number below 521 using OP_PUSHDATA4. However, these are considered nonstandard transactions, meaning most Bitcoin nodes (particularly those running Bitcoin Core software) will not relay them.

There are many more opcodes, which are coded in *op.py*, and the full list can be found at *https://en.bitcoin.it/wiki/Script*.

Coding a Script Parser and Serializer

Now that we know how Script works, we can write a script parser:

```
class Script:

    def __init__(self, cmds=None):
        if cmds is None:
            self.cmds = []
        else:
            self.cmds = cmds        ❶
    ...
    @classmethod
    def parse(cls, s):
        length = read_varint(s)     ❷
        cmds = []
        count = 0
        while count < length:       ❸
```

```
    current = s.read(1)  ❹
    count += 1
    current_byte = current[0]  ❺
    if current_byte >= 1 and current_byte <= 75:  ❻
        n = current_byte
        cmds.append(s.read(n))
        count += n
    elif current_byte == 76:  ❼
        data_length = little_endian_to_int(s.read(1))
        cmds.append(s.read(data_length))
        count += data_length + 1
    elif current_byte == 77:  ❽
        data_length = little_endian_to_int(s.read(2))
        cmds.append(s.read(data_length))
        count += data_length + 2
    else:  ❾
        op_code = current_byte
        cmds.append(op_code)
if count != length:  ❿
    raise SyntaxError('parsing script failed')
return cls(cmds)
```

❶ Each command is either an opcode to be executed or an element to be pushed onto the stack.

❷ Script serialization always starts with the length of the entire script.

❸ We parse until the right amount of bytes are consumed.

❹ The byte determines if we have an opcode or element.

❺ This converts the byte into an integer in Python.

❻ For a number between 1 and 75 inclusive, we know the next n bytes are an element.

❼ 76 is OP_PUSHDATA1, so the next byte tells us how many bytes to read.

❽ 77 is OP_PUSHDATA2, so the next two bytes tell us how many bytes to read.

❾ We have an opcode that we store.

❿ The script should have consumed exactly the length of bytes we expected; otherwise, we raise an error.

We can similarly write a script serializer:

```
class Script:
...
    def raw_serialize(self):
        result = b''
        for cmd in self.cmds:
            if type(cmd) == int:    ❶
                result += int_to_little_endian(cmd, 1)
            else:
                length = len(cmd)
                if length < 75:    ❷
                    result += int_to_little_endian(length, 1)
                elif length > 75 and length < 0x100:    ❸
                    result += int_to_little_endian(76, 1)
                    result += int_to_little_endian(length, 1)
                elif length >= 0x100 and length <= 520:    ❹
                    result += int_to_little_endian(77, 1)
                    result += int_to_little_endian(length, 2)
                else:    ❺
                    raise ValueError('too long an cmd')
                result += cmd
        return result

    def serialize(self):
        result = self.raw_serialize()
        total = len(result)
        return encode_varint(total) + result    ❻
```

❶ If the command is an integer, we know that's an opcode.

❷ If the length is between 1 and 75 inclusive, we encode the length as a single byte.

❸ For any element with length from 76 to 255, we put OP_PUSHDATA1 first, then encode the length as a single byte, followed by the element.

❹ For an element with a length from 256 to 520, we put OP_PUSHDATA2 first, then encode the length as two bytes in little endian, followed by the element.

❺ Any element longer than 520 bytes cannot be serialized.

❻ Script serialization starts with the length of the entire script.

Note that both the parser and the serializer were used in Chapter 5, for parsing/serializing the ScriptSig and ScriptPubKey fields.

Combining the Script Fields

The `Script` object represents the command set that requires evaluation. To evaluate a script, we need to combine the ScriptPubKey and ScriptSig fields. The lockbox (ScriptPubKey) and the unlocking mechanism (ScriptSig) are in *different* transactions. Specifically, the lockbox is where the bitcoins are received, and the unlocking script is where the bitcoins are spent. The input in the spending transaction *points to the receiving transaction*. Essentially, we have a situation like Figure 6-6.

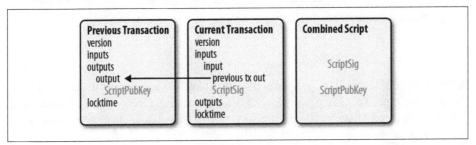

Figure 6-6. Combining the ScriptPubKey and ScriptSig

Since the ScriptSig unlocks a ScriptPubKey, we need a mechanism by which the two scripts combine. To evaluate the two together, we take the commands from the ScriptSig and ScriptPubKey and combine them as in Figure 6-6. The commands from the ScriptSig go on top of all the commands from the ScriptPubKey. Instructions are processed one at a time until no commands are left to be processed (or the script fails).

Coding the Combined Instruction Set

The evaluation of a script requires that we take the ScriptSig and ScriptPubKey, combine them into a single command set, and execute the commands. To do this, we require a way to combine the scripts:

```
class Script:
...
    def __add__(self, other):
        return Script(self.cmds + other.cmds)    ❶
```

❶ We are combining the command set to create a new, combined `Script` object.

We will use this ability to combine scripts for evaluation later in this chapter.

Standard Scripts

There are many types of standard scripts in Bitcoin, including the following:

p2pk

> Pay-to-pubkey

p2pkh

> Pay-to-pubkey-hash

p2sh

> Pay-to-script-hash

p2wpkh

> Pay-to-witness-pubkey-hash

p2wsh

> Pay-to-witness-script-hash

Addresses are known script templates like these. Wallets know how to interpret various address types (p2pkh, p2sh, p2wpkh) and create the appropriate ScriptPubKeys. All of the examples here have a particular type of address format (Base58, Bech32) so wallets can pay to them.

To show exactly how all this works, we'll start with one of the original scripts, pay-to-pubkey.

p2pk

Pay-to-pubkey (p2pk) was used largely during the early days of Bitcoin. Most coins thought to belong to Satoshi are in p2pk UTXOs—that is, transaction outputs whose ScriptPubKeys have the p2pk form. There are some limitations that we'll discuss in "Problems with p2pk" on page 118, but first, let's look at how p2pk works.

Back in Chapter 3, we learned about both ECDSA signing and verification. To verify an ECDSA signature, we need the message, z, the public key, P, and the signature, r and s. In p2pk, bitcoins are sent to a public key, and the owner of the private key can unlock or spend the bitcoins by creating a signature. The ScriptPubKey of a transaction puts the assigned bitcoins under the control of the private key owner.

Specifying where the bitcoins go is the job of the ScriptPubKey—this is the lockbox that receives the bitcoins. The p2pk ScriptPubKey looks like Figure 6-7.

```
410411db93e1dcdb8a016b49840f8c53bc1eb68a382e97b1482ecad7b148a6909a5cb2e0eaddfb84c
cf9744464f82e160bfa9b8b64f9d4c03f999b8643f656b412a3ac

        - 41 - length of pubkey
        - 0411...a3 - <pubkey>
        - ac - OP_CHECKSIG
```

Figure 6-7. Pay-to-pubkey (p2pk) ScriptPubKey

Note the OP_CHECKSIG, as that will be very important. The ScriptSig is the part that unlocks the received bitcoins. The pubkey can be compressed or uncompressed, though early on in Bitcoin's history when p2pk was more prominent, the uncompressed format was the only one being used (see Chapter 4).

For p2pk, the ScriptSig required to unlock the corresponding ScriptPubKey is the signature followed by a single sighash byte, as shown in Figure 6-8.

```
47304402204e45e16932b8af514961a1d3a1a25fdf3f4f7732e9d624c6c61548ab5fb8cd410220181
522ec8eca07de4860a4acdd12909d831cc56cbbac4622082221a8768d1d0901


        - 47 - length of signature
        - 3044...01 - <signature>
```

Figure 6-8. Pay-to-pubkey (p2pk) ScriptSig

The ScriptPubKey and ScriptSig combine to make a command set that looks like Figure 6-9.

Figure 6-9. p2pk combined

The two columns in Figure 6-10 are Script commands and the elements stack. At the end of the processing, the top element of the stack must be nonzero to be considered a valid ScriptSig. The Script commands are processed one at a time. In Figure 6-10, we start with the commands as combined in Figure 6-9.

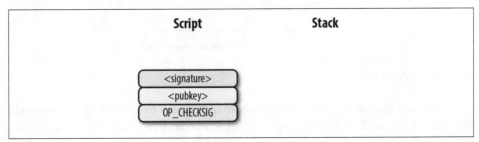

Figure 6-10. p2pk start

The first command is the signature, which is an element. This is data that is pushed to the stack (Figure 6-11).

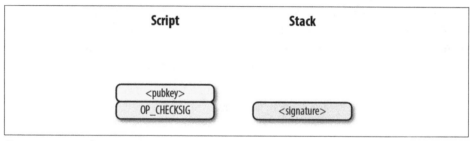

Figure 6-11. p2pk step 1

The second command is the pubkey, which is also an element. Again, this is data that is pushed to the stack (Figure 6-12).

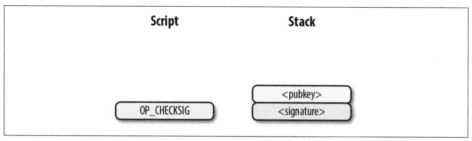

Figure 6-12. p2pk step 2

OP_CHECKSIG consumes two stack commands (pubkey and signature) and determines if they are valid for this transaction. OP_CHECKSIG will push a 1 to the stack if the signature is valid, and a 0 if not. Assuming that the signature is valid for this public key, we have the situation shown in Figure 6-13.

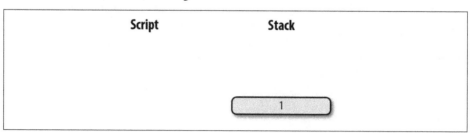

Figure 6-13. p2pk step 3

We're finished processing all the Script commands, and we've ended up with a single element on the stack. Since the top element is nonzero (1 is definitely not 0), this script is valid.

If this transaction instead had an invalid signature, the result from OP_CHECKSIG would be 0, ending our script processing (as shown in Figure 6-14).

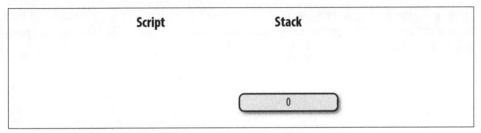

Figure 6-14. p2pk end

If the top element is 0, the combined script is invalid and a transaction with this ScriptSig in the input is invalid.

The combined script will validate if the signature is valid, but fail if the signature is invalid. The ScriptSig will only unlock the ScriptPubKey if the signature is valid for that public key. In other words, only someone with knowledge of the private key can produce a valid ScriptSig.

Incidentally, we can see where ScriptPubKey got its name. The public key in uncompressed SEC format is the main command in the ScriptPubKey for p2pk (the other command being OP_CHECKSIG). Similarly, ScriptSig is named as such because the ScriptSig for p2pk has the DER signature.

Coding Script Evaluation

We'll now code a way to evaluate scripts. This requires us to go through each command and evaluate whether the script is valid. What we want to be able to do is this:

```
>>> from script import Script
>>> z = 0x7c076ff316692a3d7eb3c3bb0f8b1488cf72e1afcd929e29307032997a838a3d
>>> sec = bytes.fromhex('04887387e452b8eacc4acfde10d9aaf7f6d9a0f975aabb10d006e\
4da568744d06c61de6d95231cd89026e286df3b6ae4a894a3378e393e93a0f45b666329a0ae34')
>>> sig = bytes.fromhex('3045022000eff69ef2b1bd93a66ed5219add4fb51e11a840f4048\
76325a1e8ffe0529a2c022100c7207fee197d27c618aea621406f6bf5ef6fca38681d82b2f06fd\
dbdce6feab601')
>>> script_pubkey = Script([sec, 0xac])  ❶
>>> script_sig = Script([sig])
>>> combined_script = script_sig + script_pubkey  ❷
>>> print(combined_script.evaluate(z))  ❸
True
```

❶ The p2pk ScriptPubkey is the SEC format pubkey followed by OP_CHECKSIG, which is 0xac or 172.

❷ We can do this because of the __add__ method we just created.

❸ We want to evaluate the commands and see if the script validates.

Here is the method that we'll use for the *combined* command set (combination of the ScriptPubKey of the previous transaction and the ScriptSig of the current transaction):

```
from op import OP_CODE_FUNCTIONS, OP_CODE_NAMES
...
class Script:
...
    def evaluate(self, z):
        cmds = self.cmds[:]  ❶
        stack = []
        altstack = []
        while len(cmds) > 0:  ❷
            cmd = cmds.pop(0)
            if type(cmd) == int:
                operation = OP_CODE_FUNCTIONS[cmd]  ❸
                if cmd in (99, 100):  ❹
                    if not operation(stack, cmds):
                        LOGGER.info('bad op: {}'.format(OP_CODE_NAMES[cmd]))
                        return False
                elif cmd in (107, 108):  ❺
                    if not operation(stack, altstack):
                        LOGGER.info('bad op: {}'.format(OP_CODE_NAMES[cmd]))
                        return False
                elif cmd in (172, 173, 174, 175):  ❻
                    if not operation(stack, z):
                        LOGGER.info('bad op: {}'.format(OP_CODE_NAMES[cmd]))
                        return False
                else:
                    if not operation(stack):
                        LOGGER.info('bad op: {}'.format(OP_CODE_NAMES[cmd]))
                        return False
            else:
                stack.append(cmd)  ❼
        if len(stack) == 0:
            return False  ❽
        if stack.pop() == b'':
            return False  ❾
        return True  ❿
```

❶ As the commands list will change, we make a copy.

❷ We execute until the commands list is empty.

❸ The function that executes the opcode is in the OP_CODE_FUNCTIONS array (e.g., OP_DUP, OP_CHECKSIG, etc.).

❹ 99 and 100 are OP_IF and OP_NOTIF, respectively. They require manipulation of the cmds array based on the top element of the stack.

⑤ 107 and 108 are OP_TOALTSTACK and OP_FROMALTSTACK, respectively. They move stack elements to/from an "alternate" stack, which we call altstack.

⑥ 172, 173, 174, and 175 are OP_CHECKSIG, OP_CHECKSIGVERIFY, OP_CHECKMULTI SIG, and OP_CHECKMULTISIGVERIFY, which all require the signature hash, z, from Chapter 3 for signature validation.

⑦ If the command is not an opcode, it's an element, so we push that element to the stack.

⑧ If the stack is empty at the end of processing all the commands, we fail the script by returning False.

⑨ If the stack's top element is an empty byte string (which is how the stack stores a 0), then we also fail the script by returning False.

⑩ Any other result means that the script has validated.

Making Script Evaluation Safe

The code shown here is a little bit of a cheat, as the combined script is not exactly executed this way. The ScriptSig is evaluated separately from the ScriptPubKey so as to not allow operations from the ScriptSig to affect the ScriptPubKey commands.

Specifically, the stack after all the ScriptSig commands are evaluated is stored, and then the ScriptPubkey commands are evaluated on their own with the stack from the first execution.

Stack Elements Under the Hood

It may be confusing that the stack elements are sometimes numbers like 0 or 1 and other times byte strings like a DER signature or SEC pubkey. Under the hood, they're all bytes, but some are interpreted as numbers for certain opcodes. For example, 1 is stored on the stack as the 01 byte, 2 is stored as the 02 byte, 999 as the e703 byte, and so on. Any byte string is interpreted as a little-endian number for arithmetic opcodes. The integer 0 is *not* stored as the 00 byte, but as the empty byte string.

The code in *op.py* can clarify what's going on:

```
def encode_num(num):
    if num == 0:
        return b''
    abs_num = abs(num)
    negative = num < 0
    result = bytearray()
```

```
        while abs_num:
            result.append(abs_num & 0xff)
            abs_num >>= 8
        if result[-1] & 0x80:
            if negative:
                result.append(0x80)
            else:
                result.append(0)
        elif negative:
            result[-1] |= 0x80
        return bytes(result)


    def decode_num(element):
        if element == b'':
            return 0
        big_endian = element[::-1]
        if big_endian[0] & 0x80:
            negative = True
            result = big_endian[0] & 0x7f
        else:
            negative = False
            result = big_endian[0]
        for c in big_endian[1:]:
            result <<= 8
            result += c
        if negative:
            return -result
        else:
            return result


    def op_0(stack):
        stack.append(encode_num(0))
        return True
```

Numbers being pushed to the stack are encoded into bytes and decoded from bytes when the numerical value is needed.

Exercise 2

Write the op_checksig function in *op.py*.

Problems with p2pk

Pay-to-pubkey is intuitive in the sense that there is a public key that anyone can send bitcoins to and a signature that can only be produced by the owner of the private key. This works well, but there are some problems.

First, the public keys are long. We know from Chapter 4 that secp256k1 public points are 33 bytes in compressed SEC and 65 bytes in uncompressed SEC format. Unfortunately, humans can't interpret 33 or 65 raw bytes easily. Most character encodings don't render certain byte ranges, as they are control characters, newlines, or similar. The SEC format is typically encoded instead in hexadecimal, doubling the length (hex encodes 4 bits per character instead of 8). This makes the compressed and uncompressed SEC formats 66 and 130 characters, respectively, which is bigger than most identifiers (your username on a website, for instance, is usually less than 20 characters). To compound this, early Bitcoin transactions didn't use the compressed versions, so the hexadecimal addresses were 130 characters each! This is not fun or easy for people to transcribe, much less communicate by voice.

That said, the original use cases for p2pk were for IP-to-IP payments and mining outputs. For IP-to-IP payments, IP addresses were queried for their public keys; communicating the public keys was done machine-to-machine, which meant that human communication wasn't necessarily a problem. Use for mining outputs also doesn't require human communication. Incidentally, this IP-to-IP payment system was phased out because it's not secure and prone to man-in-the-middle attacks.

Why Did Satoshi Use the Uncompressed SEC Format?

It seems the uncompressed SEC format doesn't make sense for Bitcoin given that block space is at a premium. So why did Satoshi use it? Satoshi was using the OpenSSL library to do the SEC format conversions, and the OpenSSL library at the time Satoshi wrote Bitcoin (circa 2008) did not document the compressed format very well. It's speculated this is why Satoshi used the uncompressed SEC format.

When Pieter Wuille discovered that the compressed SEC format existed in OpenSSL, more people started using the compressed SEC format in Bitcoin.

Second, the length of the public keys causes a subtler problem: because they have to be kept around and indexed to see if the outputs are spendable, the UTXO set becomes bigger. This requires more resources on the part of full nodes.

Third, because we're storing the public keys in the ScriptPubKey field, they're known to everyone. That means should ECDSA someday be broken, these outputs could be stolen. For example, quantum computing has the potential to reduce the calculation times significantly for RSA and ECDSA, so having something else in addition to protect these outputs would be more secure. However, this is not a very big threat since ECDSA is used in a lot of applications besides Bitcoin and breaking it would affect all of those things, too.

Solving the Problems with p2pkh

Pay-to-pubkey-hash (p2pkh) is an alternative script format that has two key advantages over p2pk:

1. The addresses are shorter.
2. It's additionally protected by sha256 and ripemd160.

The addresses are shorter because it uses the sha256 and ripemd160 hashing algorithms. We do both in succession and call that hash160. The result of hash160 is 160 bits or 20 bytes, which are encoded into an address.

The result is what you may have seen on the Bitcoin network and coded in Chapter 4:

    1PMycacnJaSqwwJqjawXBErnLsZ7RkXUAs

This address encodes within 20 bytes that look like this in hexadecimal:

    f54a5851e9372b87810a8e60cdd2e7cfd80b6e31

These 20 bytes are the result of doing a hash160 operation on this (compressed) SEC public key:

    0250863ad64a87ae8a2fe83c1af1a8403cb53f53e486d8511dad8a04887e5b2352

Given that p2pkh is shorter and more secure, p2pk use declined significantly after 2010, though it's still fully supported today.

p2pkh

Pay-to-pubkey-hash was used during the early days of Bitcoin, though not as much as p2pk.

The p2pkh ScriptPubKey, or locking script, looks like Figure 6-15.

```
76a914bc3b654dca7e56b04dca18f2566cdaf02e8d9ada88ac

            - 76 - OP_DUP
            - a9 - OP_HASH160
            - 14 - Length of <hash>
            - bc3b...da - <hash>
            - 88 - OP_EQUALVERIFY
            - ac - OP_CHECKSIG
```

Figure 6-15. Pay-to-pubkey-hash (p2pkh) ScriptPubKey

Like p2pk, OP_CHECKSIG is here and OP_HASH160 makes an appearance. Unlike p2pk, the SEC pubkey is not here, but a 20-byte hash is. There is also a new opcode here: OP_EQUALVERIFY.

The p2pkh ScriptSig, or unlocking script, looks like Figure 6-16.

```
483045022100ed81ff192e75a3fd2304004dcadb746fa5e24c5031ccfcf2
1320b0277457c98f02207a986d955c6e0cb35d446a89d3f56100f4d7f678
01c31967743a9c8e10615bed01210349fc4e631e3624a545de3f89f5d868
4c7b8138bd94bdd531d2e213bf016b278a

        - 48 - Length of <signature>
        - 30...01 - <signature>
        - 21 - Length of <pubkey>
        - 0349...8a - <pubkey>
```

Figure 6-16. Pay-to-pubkey-hash (p2pkh) ScriptSig

Like p2pk, the ScriptSig has the DER signature. Unlike p2pk, the ScriptSig also has the SEC pubkey. The main difference between p2pk and p2pkh ScriptSigs is that the SEC pubkey has moved from the ScriptPubKey to the ScriptSig.

The ScriptPubKey and ScriptSig combine to form a list of commands that looks like Figure 6-17.

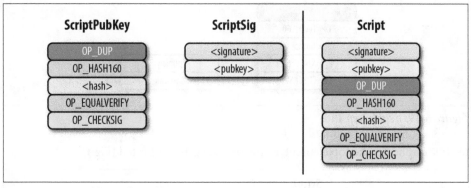

Figure 6-17. p2pkh combined

At this point, the script is processed one command at a time. We start with the commands as combined in Figure 6-18.

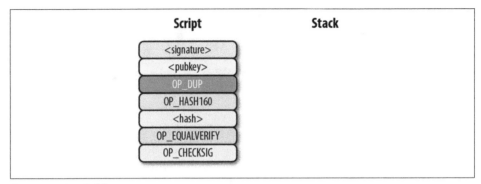

Figure 6-18. p2pkh start

The first two commands are elements, so they are pushed to the stack (Figure 6-19).

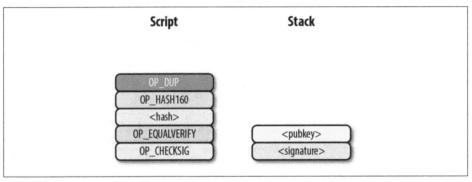

Figure 6-19. p2pkh step 1

OP_DUP duplicates the top element, so the pubkey gets duplicated (Figure 6-20).

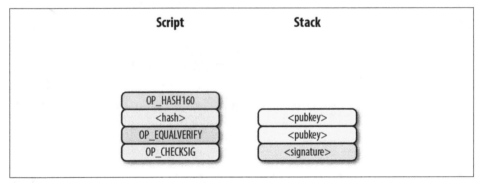

Figure 6-20. p2pkh step 2

OP_HASH160 takes the top element and performs the hash160 operation on it (sha256 followed by ripemd160), creating a 20-byte hash (Figure 6-21).

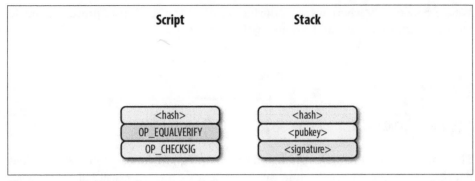

Figure 6-21. p2pkh step 3

The 20-byte hash is an element and is pushed to the stack (Figure 6-22).

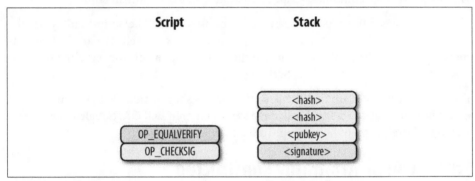

Figure 6-22. p2pkh step 4

We are now at `OP_EQUALVERIFY`. This opcode consumes the top two elements and checks if they're equal. If they are equal, the script continues execution. If they are not equal, the script stops immediately and fails. We assume here that they're equal, leading to Figure 6-23.

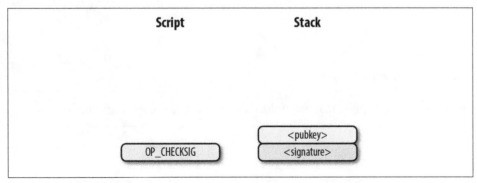

Figure 6-23. p2pkh step 5

We are now exactly where we were during the OP_CHECKSIG part of processing p2pk. Once again, we assume that the signature is valid (Figure 6-24).

Figure 6-24. p2pkh end

There are two ways this script can fail. If the ScriptSig provides a public key that does not hash160 to the 20-byte hash in the ScriptPubKey, the script will fail at OP_EQUAL VERIFY (Figure 6-22). The other failure condition is if the ScriptSig has a public key that hash160s to the 20-byte hash in the ScriptPubKey, but has an invalid signature. That would end the combined script evaluation with a 0, ending in failure.

This is why we call this type of script pay-to-pubkey-*hash*. The ScriptPubKey has the 20-byte *hash160* of the public key and not the public key itself. We are locking bitcoins to a *hash* of the public key, and the spender is responsible for revealing the public key as part of constructing the ScriptSig.

The major advantages are that the ScriptPubKey is shorter (just 25 bytes) and a thief would not only have to solve the discrete log problem in ECDSA, but also figure out a way to find preimages of both ripemd160 and sha256.

Scripts Can Be Arbitrarily Constructed

Note that a script can be any arbitrary program. Script is a smart contract language and can lock bitcoins in many different ways. Figure 6-25 is an example ScriptPubKey.

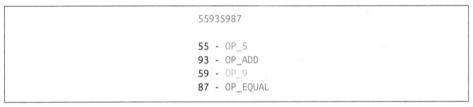

Figure 6-25. Example ScriptPubKey

Figure 6-26 is a ScriptSig that will unlock the the ScriptPubKey from Figure 6-25.

```
                              54

                        54 - OP_4
```

Figure 6-26. Example ScriptSig

The combined script is shown in Figure 6-27.

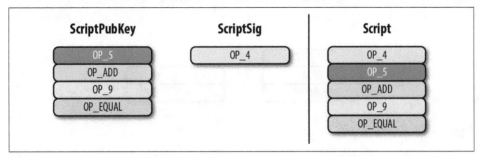

Figure 6-27. Example combined

Script evaluation will start as shown in Figure 6-28.

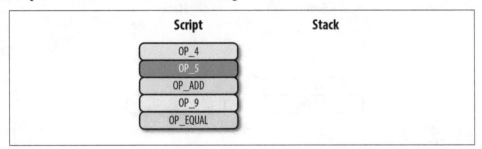

Figure 6-28. Example start

OP_4 will push a 4 to the stack (Figure 6-29).

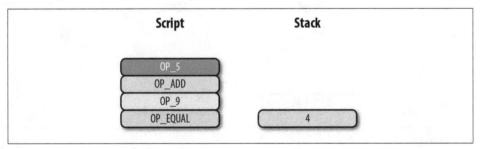

Figure 6-29. Example step 1

OP_5 will likewise push a 5 to the stack (Figure 6-30).

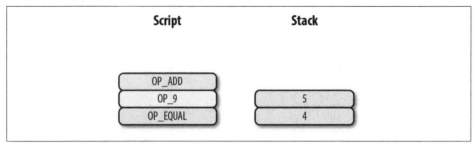

Figure 6-30. Example step 2

OP_ADD will consume the top two elements of the stack, add them together, and push the sum to the stack (Figure 6-31).

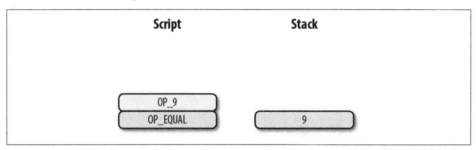

Figure 6-31. Example step 3

OP_9 will push a 9 to the stack (Figure 6-32).

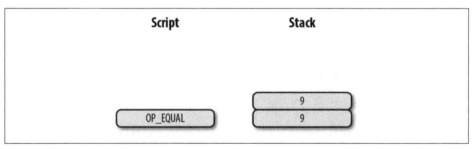

Figure 6-32. Example step 4

OP_EQUAL will consume two elements and push a 1 if they're equal and a 0 if not (Figure 6-33).

Figure 6-33. Example end

Note that the ScriptSig here isn't particularly hard to figure out and contains no signature. As a result, the ScriptPubKey is vulnerable to being taken by anyone who can solve it. Think of this ScriptPubKey as a lockbox with a very flimsy lock that anyone can break into. It is for this reason that most transactions have a signature requirement in the ScriptSig.

Once a UTXO has been spent, included in a block, and secured by proof-of-work, the coins are locked to a different ScriptPubKey and no longer as easily spendable. Someone attempting to spend already spent coins would have to provide proof-of-work, which is expensive (see Chapter 9).

Exercise 3

Create a ScriptSig that can unlock this ScriptPubKey:

```
767695935687
```

Note that OP_MUL multiplies the top two elements of the stack.

- 56 = OP_6
- 76 = OP_DUP
- 87 = OP_EQUAL
- 93 = OP_ADD
- 95 = OP_MUL

Utility of Scripts

The previous exercise was a bit of a cheat, as OP_MUL is no longer allowed on the Bitcoin network. Version 0.3.5 of Bitcoin disabled a lot of different opcodes (anything that had even a little bit of potential to create vulnerabilities on the network).

This is just as well, since most of the functionality in Script is actually not used much. From a software maintenance standpoint, this is not a great situation as the code has to be maintained despite its lack of usage. Simplifying and getting rid of certain capabilities can be seen as a way to make Bitcoin more secure.

This is in stark contrast to other projects, which try to expand their smart contract languages, often increasing the attack surface along with new features.

Exercise 4

Figure out what this script is doing:

```
6e879169a77ca787
```

- 69 = OP_VERIFY

- 6e = OP_2DUP

- 7c = OP_SWAP

- 87 = OP_EQUAL

- 91 = OP_NOT

- a7 = OP_SHA1

Use the `Script.parse` method and look up what various opcodes do at *https://en.bitcoin.it/wiki/Script*.

SHA-1 Piñata

In 2013, Peter Todd created a script very similar to the one in Exercise 4 and put some bitcoins into it to create an economic incentive for people to find hash collisions. The donations reached 2.49153717 BTC, and when Google actually found a hash collision for SHA-1 in February 2017 (*https://security.googleblog.com/2017/02/announcing-first-sha1-collision.html*), this script was promptly redeemed. The transaction output was 2.48 BTC, which was 2,848.88 USD at the time.

Peter created more piñatas for sha256, hash256, and hash160, which add economic incentives to find collisions for these hashing functions.

Conclusion

We've covered Script and how it works. We can now proceed to the creation and validation of transactions.

CHAPTER 7

Transaction Creation and Validation

One of the trickiest things to code in Bitcoin is validating transactions. Another one is creating transactions. In this chapter, we'll cover the exact steps to do both. Toward the end of the chapter, we'll be creating a testnet transaction and broadcasting it.

Validating Transactions

Every node, when receiving transactions, makes sure that each transaction adheres to the network rules. This process is called *transaction validation*. Here are the main things that a node checks:

1. The inputs of the transaction are previously unspent.
2. The sum of the inputs is greater than or equal to the sum of the outputs.
3. The ScriptSig successfully unlocks the previous ScriptPubKey.

#1 prevents double-spending. Any input that's been spent (that is, included in the blockchain) cannot be spent again.

#2 makes sure no new bitcoins are created (except in a special type of transaction called a coinbase transaction; more on that in Chapter 9).

#3 makes sure that the combined script is valid. In the vast majority of transactions, this means checking that the one or more signatures in the ScriptSig are valid.

Let's look at how each condition is checked.

Checking the Spentness of Inputs

To prevent double-spending, a node checks that each input exists and has not been spent. This can be checked by any full node by looking at the UTXO set (see Chapter 5). We cannot determine from the transaction itself whether it's double-spending, much like we cannot look at a personal check and determine whether it's overdrafting. The only way to know is to have access to the UTXO set, which requires calculation from the entire set of transactions.

In Bitcoin, we can determine whether an input is being double-spent by keeping track of the UTXOs. If an input is in the UTXO set, that transaction input both exists and is *not* double-spending. If the transaction passes the rest of the validity tests, then we remove all the inputs of the transaction from the UTXO set. Light clients that do not have access to the blockchain have to trust other nodes for a lot of the information, including whether an input has already been spent.

A full node can check the spentness of an input pretty easily, but a light client has to get this information from someone else.

Checking the Sum of the Inputs Versus the Sum of the Outputs

Nodes also make sure that the sum of the inputs is greater than or equal to the sum of the outputs. This ensures that the transaction does not create new coins. The one exception is a coinbase transaction, which we'll study more in Chapter 9. Since inputs don't have an amount field, this must be looked up on the blockchain. Once again, full nodes have access to the amounts associated with the unspent output, but light clients have to depend on full nodes to supply this information.

We covered how to calculate fees in Chapter 5. Checking that the sum of the inputs is greater than or equal to the sum of the outputs is the same as checking that the fee is not negative (that is, creating money). Recall the last exercise in Chapter 5. The method fee looks like this:

```
class Tx:
    ...
    def fee(self):
        '''Returns the fee of this transaction in satoshi'''
        input_sum, output_sum = 0, 0
        for tx_in in self.tx_ins:
            input_sum += tx_in.value(self.testnet)
        for tx_out in self.tx_outs:
            output_sum += tx_out.amount
        return input_sum - output_sum
```

We can test to see if this transaction is trying to create money by using this method:

```
>>> from tx import Tx
>>> from io import BytesIO
>>> raw_tx = ('0100000001813f79011acb80925dfe69b3def355fe914bd1d96a3f5f71bf830\
3c6a989c7d1000000006b483045022100ed81ff192e75a3fd2304004dcadb746fa5e24c5031ccf\
cf21320b0277457c98f02207a986d955c6e0cb35d446a89d3f56100f4d7f67801c31967743a9c8\
e10615bed01210349fc4e631e3624a545de3f89f5d8684c7b8138bd94bdd531d2e213bf016b278\
afefffffff02a135ef010000000001976a914bc3b654dca7e56b04dca18f2566cdaf02e8d9ada88a\
c99c39800000000001976a9141c4bc762dd5423e332166702cb75f40df79fea1288ac19430600')
>>> stream = BytesIO(bytes.fromhex(raw_tx))
>>> transaction = Tx.parse(stream)
>>> print(transaction.fee() >= 0)  ❶
True
```

❶ This only works because we're using Python (see The Value Overflow Incident).

If the fee is negative, we know that the output_sum is greater than the input_sum, which is another way of saying that this transaction is trying to create bitcoins out of the ether.

The Value Overflow Incident

Back in 2010, there was a transaction that created 184 billion new bitcoins. This was due to the fact that in C++, the amount field is a *signed* integer and not an *unsigned* integer. That is, the value could be negative!

The clever transaction passed all the checks, including the one for not creating new bitcoins, but only because the output amounts overflowed past the maximum number. 2^{64} is ~1.84×10^{19} satoshis, which is 184 billion bitcoins. The fee was negative by enough that the C++ code was tricked into believing that the fee was actually positive by 0.1 BTC!

The vulnerability is detailed in CVE-2010-5139 and was patched via a soft fork in Bitcoin Core 0.3.11. The transaction and the extra bitcoins it created were invalidated retroactively by a block reorganization, which is another way of saying that the block including the value overflow transaction and all the blocks built on top of it were replaced.

Checking the Signature

Perhaps the trickiest part of validating a transaction is the process of checking its signatures. A transaction typically has at least one signature per input. If there are multisig outputs being spent, there may be more than one. As we learned in Chapter 3, the ECDSA signature algorithm requires the public key P, the signature hash z, and the signature (r,s). Once these are known, the process of verifying the signature is pretty simple, as we already coded in Chapter 3:

```
>>> from ecc import S256Point, Signature
>>> sec = bytes.fromhex('0349fc4e631e3624a545de3f89f5d8684c7b8138bd94bdd531d2e\
213bf016b278a')
>>> der = bytes.fromhex('3045022100ed81ff192e75a3fd2304004dcadb746fa5e24c5031c\
cfcf21320b0277457c98f02207a986d955c6e0cb35d446a89d3f56100f4d7f67801c31967743a9\
c8e10615bed')
>>> z = 0x27e0c5994dec7824e56dec6b2fcb342eb7cdb0d0957c2fce9882f715e85d81a6
>>> point = S256Point.parse(sec)
>>> signature = Signature.parse(der)
>>> print(point.verify(z, signature))
True
```

SEC public keys and DER signatures are in the stack when a command like OP_CHECK
SIG is executed, making getting the public key and signature pretty straightforward
(see Chapter 6). The hard part is getting the signature hash. A naive way to do this
would be to hash the transaction serialization as shown in Figure 7-1. Unfortunately,
we can't do that, since the signature is part of the ScriptSig and a signature can't sign
itself.

```
0100000001813f79011acb80925dfe69b3def355fe914bd1d96a3f5f71bf8303c6a989c7d10000000
06b483045022100ed81ff192e75a3fd2304004dcadb746fa5e24c5031ccfcf21320b0277457c98f02
207a986d955c6e0cb35d446a89d3f56100f4d7f67801c31967743a9c8e10615bed01210349fc4e631
e3624a545de3f89f5d8684c7b8138bd94bdd531d2e213bf016b278afeffffff02a135ef0100000000
1976a914bc3b654dca7e56b04dca18f2566cdaf02e8d9ada88ac99c39800000000001976a9141c4bc
762dd5423e332166702cb75f40df79fea1288ac19430600
```

Figure 7-1. A signature is in the yellow highlighted part, or the ScriptSig

Instead, we modify the transaction before signing it. That is, we compute a different
signature hash *for each input*. The procedure is as follows.

Step 1: Empty all the ScriptSigs

The first step is to empty all the ScriptSigs when checking the signature (Figure 7-2).
The same procedure is used for creating the signature, except the ScriptSigs are usually already empty.

```
0100000001813f79011acb80925dfe69b3def355fe914bd1d96a3f5f71bf8303c6a989c7d10000000
000feffffff02a135ef01000000001976a914bc3b654dca7e56b04dca18f2566cdaf02e8d9ada88ac
99c39800000000001976a9141c4bc762dd5423e332166702cb75f40df79fea1288ac19430600
```

Figure 7-2. Empty each input's ScriptSig (in yellow highlighted field, now 00)

Note that this example has only one input, so only that input's ScriptSig is emptied,
but it's possible to have more than one input. In that case, each of those would be
emptied.

Step 2: Replace the ScriptSig of the input being signed with the previous ScriptPubKey

Each input points to a previous transaction output, which has a ScriptPubKey. Recall the diagram from Chapter 6, shown again in Figure 7-3.

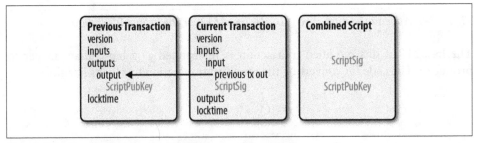

Figure 7-3. Combining the ScriptPubKey and ScriptSig

We take the ScriptPubKey that the input is pointing to and put that in place of the empty ScriptSig (Figure 7-4). This may require a lookup on the blockchain, but in practice the signer already knows the ScriptPubKey, as the input is one where the signer has the private key.

```
0100000001813f79011acb80925dfe69b3def355fe914bd1d96a3f5f71bf8303c6a989c7d10000000
01976a914a802fc56c704ce87c42d7c92eb75e7896bdc41ae88acfeffffff02a135ef010000000019
76a914bc3b654dca7e56b04dca18f2566cdaf02e8d9ada88ac99c39800000000001976a9141c4bc76
2dd5423e332166702cb75f40df79fea1288ac19430600
```

Figure 7-4. Replace the ScriptSig (yellow highlighted field) for one of the inputs with the previous ScriptPubKey

Step 3: Append the hash type

Last, we add a 4-byte hash type to the end. This is to specify what the signature is authorizing. The signature can authorize this input to go with all the other inputs and outputs (SIGHASH_ALL), go with a specific output (SIGHASH_SINGLE), or go with any output whatsoever (SIGHASH_NONE). The latter two have some theoretical use cases, but in practice, almost every transaction is signed with SIGHASH_ALL. There's also a rarely used hash type called SIGHASH_ANYONECANPAY that can be combined with any of the previous three, which we won't get into here. For SIGHASH_ALL, the final transaction must have the exact outputs that were signed or the input signature is invalid.

The integer corresponding to SIGHASH_ALL is 1 and this has to be encoded in little-endian over 4 bytes, which makes the modified transaction look like Figure 7-5.

```
0100000001813f79011acb80925dfe69b3def355fe914bd1d96a3f5f71bf8303c6a989c7d10000000
01976a914a802fc56c704ce87c42d7c92eb75e7896bdc41ae88acfefffff02a135ef0100000000019
76a914bc3b654dca7e56b04dca18f2566cdaf02e8d9ada88ac99c39800000000001976a9141c4bc76
2dd5423e332166702cb75f40df79fea1288ac1943060001000000
```

Figure 7-5. Append the hash type (SIGHASH_ALL), or the brown 01000000

The hash256 of this modified transaction is interpreted as a big-endian integer to produce *z*. The code for converting the modified transaction to *z* looks like this:

```
>>> from helper import hash256
>>> modified_tx = bytes.fromhex('0100000001813f79011acb80925dfe69b3def355fe914\
bd1d96a3f5f71bf8303c6a989c7d1000000001976a914a802fc56c704ce87c42d7c92eb75e7896\
bdc41ae88acfefffff02a135ef010000000001976a914bc3b654dca7e56b04dca18f2566cdaf02\
e8d9ada88ac99c398000000000001976a9141c4bc762dd5423e332166702cb75f40df79fea1288a\
c1943060001000000')
>>> h256 = hash256(modified_tx)
>>> z = int.from_bytes(h256, 'big')
>>> print(hex(z))
0x27e0c5994dec7824e56dec6b2fcb342eb7cdb0d0957c2fce9882f715e85d81a6
```

Now that we have our *z*, we can take the public key in SEC format and the signature in DER format from the ScriptSig to verify the signature:

```
>>> from ecc import S256Point, Signature
>>> sec = bytes.fromhex('0349fc4e631e3624a545de3f89f5d8684c7b8138bd94bdd531d2e\
213bf016b278a')
>>> der = bytes.fromhex('3045022100ed81ff192e75a3fd2304004dcadb746fa5e24c5031c\
cfcf21320b0277457c98f02207a986d955c6e0cb35d446a89d3f56100f4d7f67801c31967743a9\
c8e10615bed')
>>> z = 0x27e0c5994dec7824e56dec6b2fcb342eb7cdb0d0957c2fce9882f715e85d81a6
>>> point = S256Point.parse(sec)
>>> signature = Signature.parse(der)
>>> point.verify(z, signature)
True
```

We can code this transaction validation process into a method for Tx. Thankfully, the Script engine can already handle signature verification (see Chapter 6), so our task here is to glue everything together. We need *z*, or the signature hash, to pass into the **evaluate** method and we need to combine the ScriptSig and ScriptPubKey.

Quadratic Hashing

The signature hashing algorithm is inefficient and wasteful. The *quadratic hashing problem* states that time required to calculate the signature hashes increases quadratically with the number of inputs in a transaction. Specifically, not only will the number of hash256 operations for calculating z increase on a per-input basis, but in addition, the length of the transaction will increase, slowing down each hash256 operation because the entire signature hash will need to be calculated anew for each input.

This was particularly obvious with the biggest transaction mined to date:

> bb41a757f405890fb0f5856228e23b715702d714d59bf2b1feb70d8b2 b4e3e08

This transaction had 5,569 inputs and 1 output and took many miners over a minute to validate, as the signature hashes for the transaction were expensive to calculate.

Segwit (Chapter 13) fixes this with a different way of calculating the signature hash, which is specified in BIP0143.

Exercise 1

Write the sig_hash method for the Tx class.

Exercise 2

Write the verify_input method for the Tx class. You will want to use the TxIn.script_pubkey, Tx.sig_hash, and Script.evaluate methods.

Verifying the Entire Transaction

Now that we can verify an input, the task of verifying the entire transaction is straightforward:

```
class Tx:
...
    def verify(self):
        '''Verify this transaction'''
        if self.fee() < 0:  ❶
            return False
        for i in range(len(self.tx_ins)):
            if not self.verify_input(i):  ❷
                return False
        return True
```

❶ We make sure that we are not creating money.

❷ We make sure that each input has a correct ScriptSig.

Note that a full node would verify more things, like checking for double-spends and checking some other consensus rules not discussed in this chapter (max sigops, size of ScriptSig, etc.), but this is good enough for our library.

Creating Transactions

The code to verify transactions will help quite a bit with creating transactions. We can create transactions that fit the verification process. Transactions we create will require the sum of the inputs to be greater than or equal to the sum of the outputs. Similarly, transactions we create will require a ScriptSig that, when combined with the Script-PubKey, will be valid.

To create a transaction, we need at least one output we've received. That is, we need an output from the UTXO set whose ScriptPubKey we can unlock. The vast majority of the time, we need one or more private keys corresponding to the public keys that are hashed in the ScriptPubKey.

The rest of this chapter will be concerned with creating a transaction whose inputs are locked by p2pkh ScriptPubKeys.

Constructing the Transaction

The construction of a transaction requires answering some basic questions:

1. Where do we want the bitcoins to go?

2. What UTXOs can we spend?

3. How quickly do we want this transaction to get into the blockchain?

We'll be using testnet for this example, though this can easily be applied to mainnet.

The first question is about how much we want to pay whom. We can pay one or more addresses. In this example, we will pay 0.1 testnet bitcoins (tBTC) to mnrVtF8DWjMu839VW3rBfgYaAfKk8983Xf.

The second question is about what's in our wallet. What do we have available to spend? In this example, we have an output denoted by a transaction ID and output index:

    0d6fe5213c0b3291f208cba8bfb59b7476dffacc4e5cb66f6eb20a080843a299:13

When we view this output on a testnet block explorer (Figure 7-6), we can see that our output is worth 0.44 tBTC.

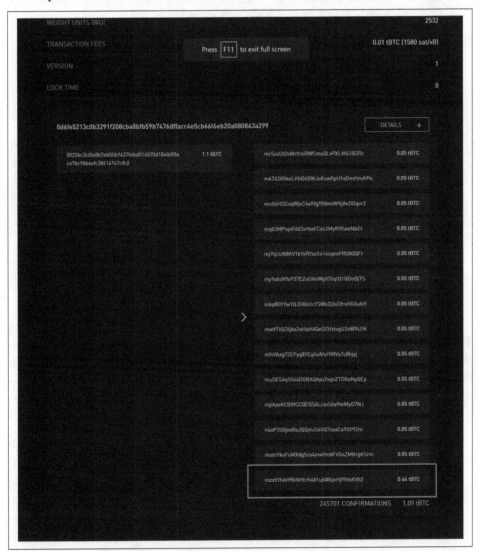

Figure 7-6. UTXO that we're spending

Since this is more than 0.1 tBTC, we'll want to send the rest back to ourselves. Though it's generally bad privacy and security practice to reuse addresses, we'll send the bitcoins back to mzx5YhAH9kNHtcN481u6WkjeHjYtVeKVh2 to make the transaction construction easier.

Why Reusing Addresses Is a Bad Idea

Back in Chapter 6, we went through how p2pk was inferior to p2pkh, in part because it was only protected by ECDSA. p2pkh, on the other hand, is also protected by sha256 and ripemd160. However, because the blockchain is public, once we spend from a ScriptPubKey corresponding to our address, we reveal our public key as part of the ScriptSig. Once we've revealed that public key, sha256 and ripemd160 no longer protect us, as the attacker knows the public key and doesn't have to guess it.

As of this writing, we are still protected by the discrete log problem, which is unlikely to be broken any time soon. It's important from a security perspective, however, to understand what we're protected by.

The other reason to not reuse addresses is for privacy. Having a single address for all our transactions means that people can link our transactions together. If, for example, we bought something private (say, medication to treat some disease we don't want others to know about) and spent another output with the same ScriptPubKey for a donation to some charity, the charity and the medication vendor could identify that we had done business with the other.

Privacy leaks tend to become security holes over time.

The third question is really about fees. If we want to get the transaction in the blockchain faster, we'll have to pay more fees; if we don't mind waiting, we can pay less. In our case, we'll use 0.01 tBTC as our fee.

Fee Estimation

Fee estimation is done on a per-byte basis. If your transaction is 600 bytes, it will have double the fees as a transaction that's 300 bytes. This is because block space is limited and larger transactions take up more space. This calculation has changed a bit since Segwit (see Chapter 13), but the general principle still applies. We want to pay enough on a per-byte basis so that miners are motivated to include our transaction as soon as possible.

When blocks aren't full, almost any amount above the default relay limit (1 satoshi/byte) is enough to get a transaction included. When blocks are full, this is not an easy thing to estimate. There are multiple ways to estimate fees, including:

- Looking at various fee levels and estimating the probability of inclusion based on past blocks and the mempools at the time
- Looking at the current mempool and adding a fee that roughly corresponds to enough economic incentivization
- Going with some fixed fee

Many wallets use different strategies, and this is an active area of research.

Making the Transaction

We have a plan for a new transaction with one input and two outputs. But first, let's look at some other tools we'll need.

We need a way to take an address and get the 20-byte hash out of it. This is the opposite of encoding an address, so we call the function decode_base58:

```
def decode_base58(s):
    num = 0
    for c in s:  ❶
        num *= 58
        num += BASE58_ALPHABET.index(c)
    combined = num.to_bytes(25, byteorder='big')  ❷
    checksum = combined[-4:]
    if hash256(combined[:-4])[:4] != checksum:
        raise ValueError('bad address: {} {}'.format(checksum,
            hash256(combined[:-4])[:4]))
    return combined[1:-4]  ❸
```

❶ We get what number is encoded in this Base58 address.

❷ Once we have the number, we convert it to big-endian bytes.

❸ The first byte is the network prefix and the last 4 are the checksum. The middle 20 are the actual 20-byte hash (aka hash160).

We also need a way to convert the 20-byte hash to a ScriptPubKey. We call this function p2pkh_script since we're converting the hash160 to a p2pkh:

```python
def p2pkh_script(h160):
    '''Takes a hash160 and returns the p2pkh ScriptPubKey'''
    return Script([0x76, 0xa9, h160, 0x88, 0xac])
```

Note that 0x76 is OP_DUP, 0xa9 is OP_HASH160, h160 is a 20-byte element, 0x88 is OP_EQUALVERIFY, and 0xac is OP_CHECKSIG. This is the p2pkh ScriptPubKey command set from Chapter 6.

Given these tools, we can proceed to transaction creation:

```python
>>> from helper import decode_base58, SIGHASH_ALL
>>> from script import p2pkh_script, Script
>>> from tx import TxIn, TxOut, Tx
>>> prev_tx = bytes.fromhex('0d6fe5213c0b3291f208cba8bfb59b7476dffacc4e5cb66f6\
eb20a080843a299')
>>> prev_index = 13
>>> tx_in = TxIn(prev_tx, prev_index)
>>> tx_outs = []
>>> change_amount = int(0.33*100000000)          ❶
>>> change_h160 = decode_base58('mzx5YhAH9kNHtcN481u6WkjeHjYtVeKVh2')
>>> change_script = p2pkh_script(change_h160)
>>> change_output = TxOut(amount=change_amount, script_pubkey=change_script)
>>> target_amount = int(0.1*100000000)           ❶
>>> target_h160 = decode_base58('mnrVtF8DWjMu839VW3rBfgYaAfKk8983Xf')
>>> target_script = p2pkh_script(target_h160)
>>> target_output = TxOut(amount=target_amount, script_pubkey=target_script)
>>> tx_obj = Tx(1, [tx_in], [change_output, target_output], 0, True)  ❷
>>> print(tx_obj)
tx: cd30a8da777d28ef0e61efe68a9f7c559c1d3e5bcd7b265c850ccb4068598d11
version: 1
tx_ins:
0d6fe5213c0b3291f208cba8bfb59b7476dffacc4e5cb66f6eb20a080843a299:13
tx_outs:
33000000:OP_DUP OP_HASH160 d52ad7ca9b3d096a38e752c2018e6fbc40cdf26f OP_EQUALVE\
RIFY OP_CHECKSIG
10000000:OP_DUP OP_HASH160 507b27411ccf7f16f10297de6cef3f291623eddf OP_EQUALVE\
RIFY OP_CHECKSIG
locktime: 0
```

❶ The amount must be in satoshis; given there are 100,000,000 satoshis per BTC, we have to multiply and cast to an integer.

❷ We have to designate which network to look up using the testnet=True argument.

We have created the actual transaction, but every ScriptSig in this transaction is currently empty. Filling it is where we turn next.

Signing the Transaction

Signing the transaction could be tricky, but we know how to get the signature hash, z, from earlier in this chapter. If we have the private key whose public key hash160s to the 20-byte hash in the ScriptPubKey, we can sign z and produce the DER signature:

```
>>> from ecc import PrivateKey
>>> from helper import SIGHASH_ALL
>>> z = transaction.sig_hash(0)  ❶
>>> private_key = PrivateKey(secret=8675309)
>>> der = private_key.sign(z).der()
>>> sig = der + SIGHASH_ALL.to_bytes(1, 'big')  ❷
>>> sec = private_key.point.sec()
>>> script_sig = Script([sig, sec])  ❸
>>> transaction.tx_ins[0].script_sig = script_sig  ❹
>>> print(transaction.serialize().hex())
0100000001813f79011acb80925dfe69b3def355fe914bd1d96a3f5f71bf8303c6a989c7d10000\
00006a47304402207db2402a3311a3b845b038885e3dd889c08126a8570f26a844e3e4049c482a\
11022010178cdca4129eacbeab7c44648bf5ac1f9cac217cd609d216ec2ebc8d242c0a01210393\
5581e52c354cd2f484fe8ed83af7a3097005b2f9c60bff71d35bd795f54b67fefffffff02a135ef\
01000000001976a914bc3b654dca7e56b04dca18f2566cdaf02e8d9ada88ac99c3980000000000\
1976a9141c4bc762dd5423e332166702cb75f40df79fea1288ac19430600
```

❶ We only need to sign the first input—there's only one. Multiple inputs would require us to sign each input with the right private key.

❷ The signature is actually a combination of the DER signature and the hash type, which is SIGHASH_ALL in our case.

❸ The ScriptSig of a p2pkh has exactly two elements, as we saw in Chapter 6: the signature and SEC format public key.

❹ We only have one input that we need to sign, but if there were more, this process of creating the ScriptSig would need to be done for each input.

Exercise 3

Write the sign_input method for the Tx class.

Creating Your Own Transactions on testnet

To create your own transaction, get some coins for yourself. To do that you'll need an address. If you completed the last exercise in Chapter 4, you should have your own testnet address and private key. If you don't remember, here's how:

```
>>> from ecc import PrivateKey
>>> from helper import hash256, little_endian_to_int
>>> secret = little_endian_to_int(hash256(b'Jimmy Song secret'))  ❶
>>> private_key = PrivateKey(secret)
>>> print(private_key.point.address(testnet=True))
mn81594PzKZa9K3Jyy1ushpuEzrnTnxhVg
```

❶ Please use a phrase other than `Jimmy Song secret`.

Once you have an address, you can get some coins from one of the testnet faucets that provide free testnet coins for testing purposes. You can Google "testnet bitcoin faucet" to find one, or use one from the list on the wiki (*https://en.bitcoin.it/wiki/Test net#Faucets*). My website, *https://faucet.programmingbitcoin.com*, is also updated to point to a testnet faucet that works. Enter your new testnet address into any of these faucets to get some testnet coins.

After receiving some coins, spend them using this library. This is a big accomplishment for a budding Bitcoin developer, so please take some time to complete these exercises.

Exercise 4

Create a testnet transaction that sends 60% of a single UTXO to mwJn1YPMq7y5F8J3LkC5Hxg9PHyZ5K4cFv. The remaining amount minus fees should go back to your own change address. This should be a one-input, two-output transaction.

You can broadcast the transaction at *https://blockstream.info/testnet/tx/push*.

Exercise 5

Advanced: Get some more testnet coins from a testnet faucet and create a two-input, one-output transaction. One input should be from the faucet, the other should be from the previous exercise; the output can be your own address.

You can broadcast the transaction at *https://blockstream.info/testnet/tx/push*.

Conclusion

We've successfully validated existing transactions on the blockchain, and you've also created your own transactions on testnet! This is a major achievement, and you should be proud.

The code we have so far will do p2pkh and p2pk. In the next chapter, we turn to a more advanced smart contract, p2sh.

CHAPTER 8

Pay-to-Script Hash

Up to this point in the book, we've been doing single-key transactions, or transactions with only a single private key per input. What if we wanted something a little more complicated? A company that has $100 million in bitcoin might not want the funds locked to a single private key: if that single key were lost or stolen, all funds would then be lost. What can we do to reduce the risk of this single point of failure?

The solution is *multisig*, or multiple signatures. This was built into Bitcoin from the beginning, but was clunky at first and so wasn't used. As we'll discover later in this chapter, Satoshi probably didn't test multisig, as it has an off-by-one error (see OP_CHECKMULTISIG Off-by-One Bug). The bug has had to stay in the protocol because fixing it would require a hard fork.

Multiple Private Keys to a Single Aggregated Public Key

It is possible to "split" a single private key into multiple private keys and use an interactive method to aggregate signatures without ever reconstructing the private key, but this is not a common practice. Schnorr signatures will make aggregating signatures easier and perhaps more common in the future.

Bare Multisig

Bare multisig was the first attempt at creating transaction outputs that require signatures from multiple parties. The idea is to change from a single point of failure to something a little more resilient to hacks. To understand bare multisig, one must first understand the OP_CHECKMULTISIG opcode. As discussed in Chapter 6, Script has a lot of different opcodes. OP_CHECKMULTISIG is one of them, at 0xae. The opcode consumes a lot of elements from the stack and returns whether or not the required number of signatures are valid for a transaction input.

The transaction output is called "bare" multisig because it's a long ScriptPubKey. Figure 8-1 shows what a ScriptPubKey for a 1-of-2 multisig looks like.

```
5141 04fcf07bb1222f7925f2b7cc15183a40443c578e62ea17100aa3b44b
a66905c95d4980aec4cd2f6eb426d1b1ec45d76724f26901099416b9265b
76ba67c8b0b73d21 0202be80a0ca69c0e000b97d507f45b98c49f58fec66
50b64ff70e6ffccc3e6d00 52ae

     - 51 - OP_1
     - 41 - Length of <pubkey1>
     - 04fc...3d - <pubkey1>
     - 21 - Length of <pubkey2>
     - 0202...00 - <pubkey2>
     - 52 - OP_2
     - ae - OP_CHECKMULTISIG
```

Figure 8-1. Bare multisig ScriptPubKey

Among bare multisig ScriptPubKeys, this one is on the small end, and we can already see that it's long. The ScriptPubKey for p2pkh is only 25 bytes, whereas this bare multisig is 101 bytes (though obviously, compressed SEC format would reduce it some), and this is a 1-of-2! Figure 8-2 shows what the ScriptSig looks like.

```
0048 3045022100e222a0a6816475d85ad28fbeb66e97c931081076dc9655
da3afc6c1d81b43f9802204681f9ea9d52a31c9c47cf78b71410ecae6188
d7c31495f5f1adfe0df5864a7401

     - 00 - OP_0
     - 48 - Length of <signature1>
     - 3045...01 - <signature1>
```

Figure 8-2. Bare multisig ScriptSig

We only need 1 signature for this 1-of-2 multisig, so this is relatively short; something like a 5-of-7 would require 5 DER signatures and would be a lot longer (360 bytes or so). Figure 8-3 shows how the ScriptSig and ScriptPubKey combine.

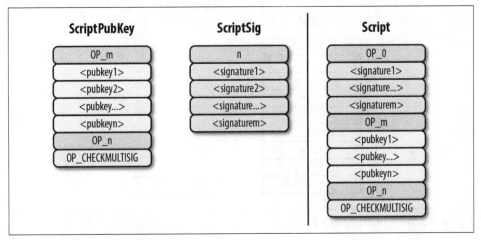

Figure 8-3. Bare multisig combined script

I've generalized here to show what an *m*-of-*n* bare multisig would look like (*m* and *n* can be anything from 1 to 20 inclusive, though the numerical opcodes only go up to OP_16; values of 17 to 20 would require 0112 to push a number like 18 to the stack). The starting state looks like Figure 8-4.

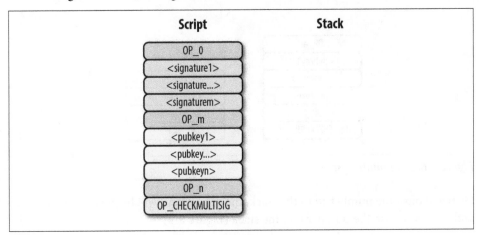

Figure 8-4. Bare multisig start

OP_0 will push the number 0 to the stack (Figure 8-5).

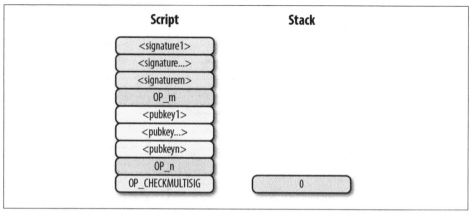

Figure 8-5. Bare multisig step 1

The signatures are elements, so they'll be pushed directly to the stack (Figure 8-6).

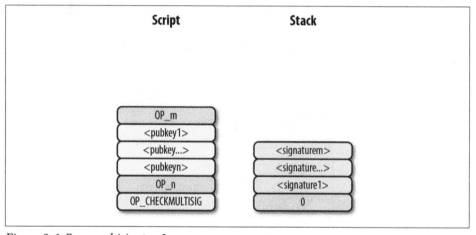

Figure 8-6. Bare multisig step 2

OP_m will push the number *m* to the stack, the public keys will be pushed to the stack, and OP_n will push the number *n* to the stack (Figure 8-7).

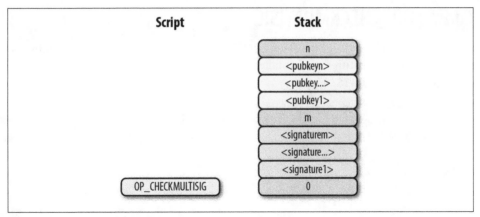

Figure 8-7. Bare multisig step 3

At this point, OP_CHECKMULTISIG will consume $m + n + 3$ elements (see OP_CHECK-MULTISIG Off-by-One Bug) and push a 1 to the stack if m of the signatures are valid for m distinct public keys from the list of n public keys; otherwise, it pushes a 0. Assuming that the signatures are valid, the stack has a single 1, which validates the combined script (Figure 8-8).

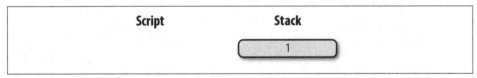

Figure 8-8. Bare multisig end

OP_CHECKMULTISIG Off-by-One Bug

The stack elements consumed by OP_CHECKMULTISIG are supposed to be m, m different signatures, n and n different pubkeys. The number of elements consumed should be 2 (m and n themselves) + m (signatures) + n (pubkeys). Unfortunately, the opcode consumes one more element than the $m + n + 2$ elements that it's supposed to. OP_CHECKMULTISIG consumes $m + n + 3$ elements, so an extra element is added (OP_0 in our example) so as to not cause a failure.

The opcode does nothing with that extra element, and that extra element can be anything. As a way to combat malleability, however, most nodes on the Bitcoin network will not relay the transaction unless the extra element is OP_0. Note that if we had $m + n + 2$ elements, OP_CHECKMULTISIG would fail as there are not enough elements to be consumed and the combined script would fail, causing the transaction to be invalid.

Coding OP_CHECKMULTISIG

In an *m*-of-*n* bare multisig, the stack contains *n* as the top element, then *n* pubkeys, then *m*, then *m* signatures, and finally a filler item due to the off-by-one bug. The code for OP_CHECKMULTISIG in *op.py* is mostly written here:

```
def op_checkmultisig(stack, z):
    if len(stack) < 1:
        return False
    n = decode_num(stack.pop())
    if len(stack) < n + 1:
        return False
    sec_pubkeys = []
    for _ in range(n):
        sec_pubkeys.append(stack.pop())
    m = decode_num(stack.pop())
    if len(stack) < m + 1:
        return False
    der_signatures = []
    for _ in range(m):
        der_signatures.append(stack.pop()[:-1])  ❶
    stack.pop()  ❷
    try:
        raise NotImplementedError  ❸
    except (ValueError, SyntaxError):
        return False
    return True
```

❶ Each DER signature is assumed to be signed with SIGHASH_ALL.

❷ We take care of the off-by-one error by consuming the only remaining element of the stack and not doing anything with the element.

❸ This is the part that you will need to code for the next exercise.

Exercise 1

Write the op_checkmultisig function of *op.py*.

Problems with Bare Multisig

Bare multisig is a bit ugly, but it is functional. It avoids the single point of failure by requiring *m* of *n* signatures to unlock a UTXO. There is plenty of utility in making outputs multisig, especially if you're a business. However, bare multisig suffers from a few problems:

1. A bare multisig ScriptPubKey has many different public keys, and that makes the ScriptPubKey long. Unlike p2pkh or even p2pk ScriptPubKeys, these are not easily communicated using voice or even text messages.

2. Because the output is so long—5 to 20 times larger than a normal p2pkh output —it requires more resources for node software. Nodes keep track of the UTXO set, and a big ScriptPubKey is more expensive to keep track of. A large output is more expensive to keep in fast-access storage (like RAM).

3. Because the ScriptPubKey can be so big, bare multisig can and has been abused. The entire PDF of Satoshi's original whitepaper is encoded in this transaction in block 230009:

   ```
   54e48e5f5c656b26c3bca14a8c95aa583d07ebe84dde3b7dd4a78f4e4186e713
   ```

   The creator of this transaction split up the whitepaper PDF into 64-byte chunks, which were then made into invalid uncompressed public keys. The whitepaper was encoded into 947 1-of-3 bare multisig outputs. These outputs are not spendable but have to be indexed in the UTXO sets of full nodes. This is a tax every full node has to pay and is in that sense abusive.

To mitigate these problems, pay-to-script-hash (p2sh) was born.

Pay-to-Script-Hash (p2sh)

Pay-to-script-hash (p2sh) is a general solution to the long address/ScriptPubKey problem. More complicated ScriptPubKeys than bare multisig can easily be made, and they have the same problems as bare multisig.

The solution that p2sh implements is to take the hash of some Script commands and then reveal the preimage Script commands later. Pay-to-script-hash was introduced in 2011 to a lot of controversy. There were multiple proposals, but as we'll see, p2sh is kludgy but works.

In p2sh, a special rule gets executed only when the pattern shown in Figure 8-9 is encountered.

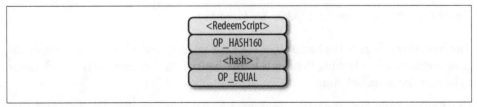

Figure 8-9. Pay-to-script-hash pattern (p2sh) that executes the special rule

If this exact command set ends with a 1 on the stack, then the RedeemScript (the top item in Figure 8-9) is parsed and then added to the Script command set. This special pattern was introduced in BIP0016, and Bitcoin software that implements BIP0016 (anything post 2011) checks for the pattern. The RedeemScript does not add new Script commands for processing unless this *exact* sequence is encountered and ends with a 1.

If this sounds hacky, it is. But before we get to that, let's look a little more closely at exactly how this plays out.

Let's say we have a 2-of-2 multisig ScriptPubKey (Figure 8-10).

```
5221022626e955ea6ea6d98850c994f9107b036b1334f18ca8830bfff129
5d21cfdb702103b287eaf122eea69030a0e9feed096bed8045c8b98bec45
3e1ffac7fbdbd4bb7152ae

          - 52 - OP_2
          - 21 - Length of <pubkey1>
          - 02...db70 - <pubkey1>
          - 21 - Length of <pubkey2>
          - 03...bb71 - <pubkey2>
          - 52 - OP_2
          - ae - OP_CHECKMULTISIG
```

Figure 8-10. Pay-to-script-hash (p2sh) RedeemScript

This is a ScriptPubKey for a bare multisig. What we need to do to convert this to p2sh is to take a hash of this script and keep the script handy for when we want to redeem it. We call this the RedeemScript, because the script is only revealed during redemption. We put the hash of the RedeemScript as the ScriptPubKey (Figure 8-11).

```
a91474d691da1574e6b3c192ecfb52cc8984ee7b6c5687

          - a9 - OPHASH160
          - 14 - Length of <hash>
          - 74d6...56 - <hash>
          - 87 - OP_EQUAL
```

Figure 8-11. Pay-to-script-hash (p2sh) ScriptPubKey

The hash digest here is the hash160 of the RedeemScript, or what was previously the ScriptPubKey. We're locking the funds to the *hash* of the RedeemScript, which needs to be revealed at unlock time.

Creating the ScriptSig for a p2sh script involves not only revealing the RedeemScript, but also unlocking the RedeemScript. At this point, you might be wondering where the RedeemScript is stored. It's not on the blockchain until actual redemption, so it must be stored by the creator of the p2sh address. If the RedeemScript is lost and cannot be reconstructed, the funds are lost, so it's very important to keep track of it!

Importance of Keeping the RedeemScript

If you are receiving to a p2sh address, be sure to store and back up the RedeemScript! Better yet, make it easy to reconstruct!

The ScriptSig for the 2-of-2 multisig looks like Figure 8-12.

```
00483045022100dc92655fe37036f47756db8102e0d7d5e28b3beb83a8fef4f5dc0559bddfb94e022
05a36d4e4e6c7fcd16658c50783e00c341609977aed3ad00937bf4ee942a8993701483045022100da
6bee3c93766232079a01639d07fa8695987497 29ae323eab8eef53577d611b02207bef15429dcadce
2121ea07f233115c6f09034c0be68db99980b9a6c5e75402201475221022626e955ea6ea6d98850c9
94f9107b036b1334f18ca8830bfff1295d21cfdb702103b287eaf122eea69030a0e9feed096bed804
5c8b98bec453e1ffac7fbdbd4bb7152ae

    - 00 - OP_0
    - 48 - Length of <signature1>
    - 3045...3701 - <signature1>
    - 48 - Length of <signature2>
    - 3045...2201 - <signature2>
    - 47 - Length of <RedeemScript>
    - 5221...ae - <RedeemScript>
```

Figure 8-12. Pay-to-script-hash (p2sh) ScriptSig

This produces the combined script in Figure 8-13.

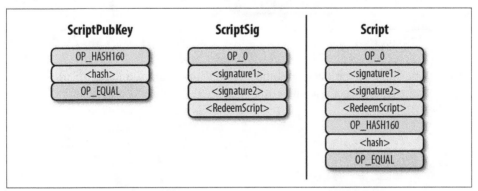

Figure 8-13. p2sh combined script

As before, `OP_0` is there because of the `OP_CHECKMULTISIG` bug. The key to understanding p2sh is the execution of the exact sequence shown in Figure 8-14.

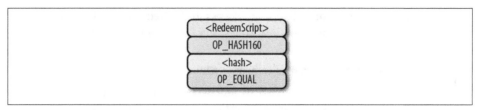

Figure 8-14. p2sh pattern that executes the special rule

Upon execution of this sequence, if the stack is left with a 1, the RedeemScript is inserted into the Script command set. In other words, if we reveal a RedeemScript whose hash160 is the same as the hash160 in the ScriptPubKey, that RedeemScript acts like the ScriptPubKey instead. We hash the script that locks the funds and put that into the blockchain instead of the script itself. This is why we call this ScriptPub-Key pay-to-script-*hash*.

Let's go through exactly how this works. We start with the Script commands (Figure 8-15).

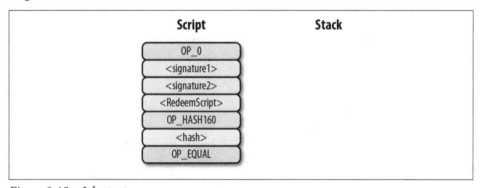

Figure 8-15. p2sh start

OP_0 will push a 0 to the stack, and the two signatures and the RedeemScript will be pushed to the stack directly, leading to Figure 8-16.

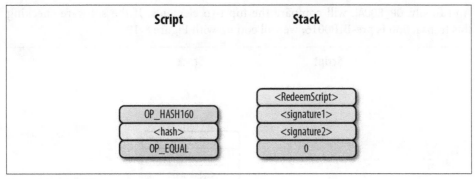

Figure 8-16. p2sh step 1

OP_HASH160 will hash the RedeemScript, which will make the stack look like Figure 8-17.

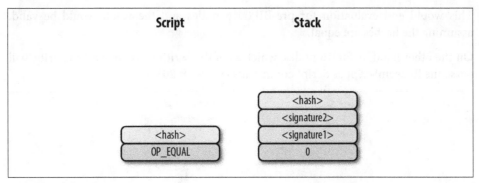

Figure 8-17. p2sh step 2

The 20-byte hash will be pushed to the stack (Figure 8-18).

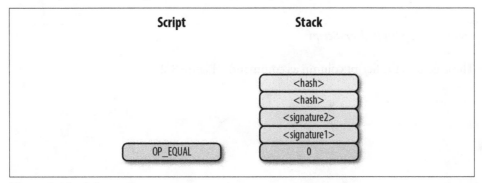

Figure 8-18. p2sh step 3

And finally, OP_EQUAL will compare the top two elements. If the software checking this transaction is pre-BIP0016, we will end up with Figure 8-19.

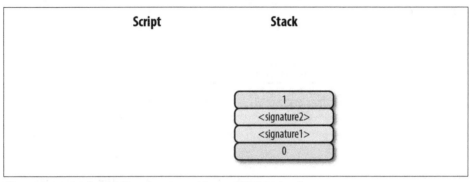

Figure 8-19. p2sh end if evaluating with pre-BIP0016 software

This would end evaluation for pre-BIP0016 nodes and the result would be valid, assuming the hashes are equal.

On the other hand, BIP0016 nodes, which as of this writing are the vast majority, will parse the RedeemScript as Script commands (Figure 8-20).

```
5221022626e955ea6ea6d98850c994f9107b036b1334f18ca8830bfff129
5d21cfdb702103b287eaf122eea69030a0e9feed096bed8045c8b98bec45
3e1ffac7fbdbd4bb7152ae

 - 52 - OP_2
 - 21 - Length of <pubkey1>
 - 02...db70 - <pubkey1>
 - 21 - Length of <pubkey2>
 - 03...bb71 - <pubkey2>
 - 52 - OP_2
 - ae - OP_CHECKMULTISIG
```

Figure 8-20. p2sh RedeemScript

These go into the Script column as commands (Figure 8-21).

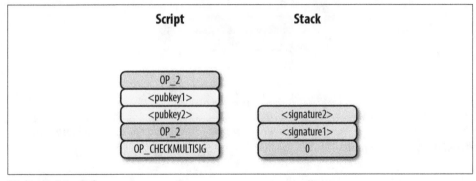

Figure 8-21. p2sh step 4

OP_2 pushes a 2 to the stack, the pubkeys are also pushed, and a final OP_2 pushes another 2 to the stack (Figure 8-22).

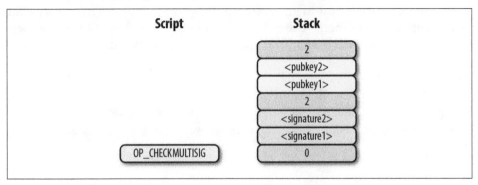

Figure 8-22. p2sh step 5

OP_CHECKMULTISIG consumes $m + n + 3$ elements, which is the entire stack, and we end the same way we did for bare multisig (Figure 8-23).

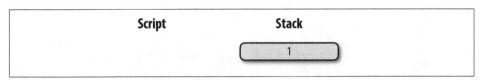

Figure 8-23. p2sh end for post-BIP0016 software

The RedeemScript substitution is a bit hacky, and there's special-cased code in Bitcoin software to handle this. Why wasn't something a lot less hacky and more intuitive chosen? BIP0012 was a competing proposal at the time that used OP_EVAL and was considered more elegant. A ScriptPubKey like Figure 8-24 would have worked with BIP0012.

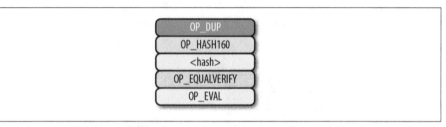

Figure 8-24. OP_EVAL would have been a command that adds additional commands based on the top element

`OP_EVAL` would have consumed the top element of the stack and interpreted that as Script commands to be put into the Script column.

Unfortunately, this more elegant solution comes with an unwanted side effect, namely Turing completeness. Turing completeness is undesirable as it makes the security of a smart contract much harder to guarantee (see Chapter 6). Thus, the more hacky but more secure option of special-casing was chosen in BIP0016. BIP0016 (or p2sh) was implemented in 2011 and continues to be a part of the network today.

Coding p2sh

The special pattern of RedeemScript, `OP_HASH160`, hash160, and `OP_EQUAL` needs handling. The `evaluate` method in *script.py* is where we handle the special case:

```python
class Script:
...
    def evaluate(self, z):
...
        while len(commands) > 0:
            command = commands.pop(0)
            if type(command) == int:
...
            else:
                stack.append(cmd)
                if len(cmds) == 3 and cmds[0] == 0xa9 \
                    and type(cmds[1]) == bytes and len(cmds[1]) == 20 \
                    and cmds[2] == 0x87:           ❶
                    cmds.pop()                     ❷
                    h160 = cmds.pop()
                    cmds.pop()
                    if not op_hash160(stack):      ❸
                        return False
                    stack.append(h160)
                    if not op_equal(stack):
                        return False
                    if not op_verify(stack):       ❹
                        LOGGER.info('bad p2sh h160')
                        return False
```

```
redeem_script = encode_varint(len(cmd)) + cmd  ❺
stream = BytesIO(redeem_script)
cmds.extend(Script.parse(stream).cmds)  ❻
```

❶ 0xa9 is OP_HASH160, 0x87 is OP_EQUAL. We're checking that the next three commands conform to the BIP0016 special pattern.

❷ We know that this is OP_HASH160, so we just pop it off. Similarly, we know the next command is the 20-byte hash value and the third command is OP_EQUAL, which is what we tested for in the if statement above it.

❸ We run the OP_HASH160, 20-byte hash push to the stack, and OP_EQUAL as normal.

❹ There should be a 1 remaining, which is what op_verify checks for (OP_VERIFY consumes one element and does not put anything back).

❺ Because we want to parse the RedeemScript, we need to prepend the length.

❻ We extend the command set with the parsed commands from the RedeemScript.

More Complicated Scripts

The nice thing about p2sh is that the RedeemScript can be as long as the largest single element from OP_PUSHDATA2, which is 520 bytes. Multisig is just one possibility. You can have scripts that define more complicated logic, like "2 of 3 of these keys or 5 of 7 of these other keys." The main feature of p2sh is that it's flexible and at the same time reduces the UTXO set size by pushing the burden of storing part of the script back to the user.

In Chapter 13, p2sh is also used to make Segwit backward compatible.

Addresses

To compute p2sh addresses, we use a process similar to how we compute p2pkh addresses. The hash160 is prepended with a prefix byte and appended with a checksum.

Mainnet p2sh uses the 0x05 byte, which causes addresses to start with a 3 in Base58, while testnet p2sh uses the 0xc4 byte to cause addresses to start with a 2. We can calculate the address using the encode_base58_checksum function from *helper.py*:

```
>>> from helper import encode_base58_checksum
>>> h160 = bytes.fromhex('74d691da1574e6b3c192ecfb52cc8984ee7b6c56')
>>> print(encode_base58_checksum(b'\x05' + h160))
3CLoMMyuoDQTPRD3XYZtCvgvkadrAdvdXh
```

Exercise 2

Write the `h160_to_p2pkh_address` function that converts a 20-byte hash160 into a p2pkh address.

Exercise 3

Write the `h160_to_p2sh_address` function that converts a 20-byte hash160 into a p2sh address.

p2sh Signature Verification

As with p2pkh, one of the tricky aspects of p2sh is verifying the signatures. p2sh signature verification is different from the p2pkh process covered in Chapter 7.

Unlike with p2pkh, where there's only one signature and one public key, we have some number of pubkeys (in SEC format in the RedeemScript) and some equal or smaller number of signatures (in DER format in the ScriptSig). Thankfully, the signatures have to be in the same order as the pubkeys or the signatures are not considered valid.

Once we have a particular signature and public key, we only need the signature hash, or z, to figure out whether the signature is valid (Figure 8-25).

```
0100000001868278ed6ddfb6c1ed3ad5f8181eb0c7a385aa0836f01d5e4789e6bd304d87221a00000
0db00483045022100dc92655fe37036f47756db8102e0d7d5e28b3beb83a8fef4f5dc0559bddfb94e
02205a36d4e4e6c7fcd16658c50783e00c341609977aed3ad00937bf4ee942a899370148304502210
0da6bee3c93766232079a01639d07fa869598749729ae323eab8eef53577d611b02207bef15429dca
dce2121ea07f233115c6f09034c0be68db99980b9a6c5e75402201475221022626e955ea6ea6d9885
0c994f9107b036b1334f18ca8830bfff1295d21cfdb702103b287eaf122eea69030a0e9feed096bed
8045c8b98bec453e1ffac7fbdbd4bb7152aeffffffff04d3b11400000000001976a914904a49878c0
adfc3aa05de7afad2cc15f483a56a88ac7f400900000000001976a914418327e3f3dda4cf5b908932
5a4b95abdfa0334088ac722c0c00000000001976a914ba35042cfe9fc66fd35ac2224eebdafd1028a
d2788acdc4ace020000000017a91474d691da1574e6b3c192ecfb52cc8984ee7b6c56870000000000
```

Figure 8-25. Validation of p2sh inputs

As with p2pkh, finding the signature hash is the most difficult part of the p2sh signature validation process. We'll now proceed to cover this in detail.

Step 1: Empty all the ScriptSigs

The first step is to empty all the ScriptSigs when checking the signature (Figure 8-26). The same procedure is used for creating the signature.

```
0100000001868278ed6ddfb6c1ed3ad5f8181eb0c7a385aa0836f01d5e4789e6bd304d87221a00000
000ffffffff04d3b11400000000001976a914904a49878c0adfc3aa05de7afad2cc15f483a56a88ac
7f400900000000001976a914418327e3f3dda4cf5b9089325a4b95abdfa0334088ac722c0c0000000
0001976a914ba35042cfe9fc66fd35ac2224eebdafd1028ad2788acdc4ace020000000017a91474d6
91da1574e6b3c192ecfb52cc8984ee7b6c568700000000
```

Figure 8-26. Empty each input's ScriptSig

Step 2: Replace the ScriptSig of the p2sh input being signed with the RedeemScript

Each p2sh input has a RedeemScript. We take the RedeemScript and put that in place of the empty ScriptSig (Figure 8-27). This is different from p2pkh in that it's not the ScriptPubKey.

```
0100000001868278ed6ddfb6c1ed3ad5f8181eb0c7a385aa0836f01d5e4789e6bd304d87221a00000
0475221022626e955ea6ea6d98850c994f9107b036b1334f18ca8830bfff1295d21cfdb702103b287
eaf122eea69030a0e9feed096bed8045c8b98bec453e1ffac7fbdbd4bb7152aeffffffff04d3b1140
0000000001976a914904a49878c0adfc3aa05de7afad2cc15f483a56a88ac7f400900000000001976
a914418327e3f3dda4cf5b9089325a4b95abdfa0334088ac722c0c00000000001976a914ba35042cf
e9fc66fd35ac2224eebdafd1028ad2788acdc4ace020000000017a91474d691da1574e6b3c192ecfb
52cc8984ee7b6c568700000000
```

Figure 8-27. Replace the ScriptSig of the input we're checking with the RedeemScript

Step 3: Append the hash type

Last, we add a 4-byte hash type to the end. This is the same as in p2pkh. The integer corresponding to SIGHASH_ALL is 1 and this has to be encoded in little-endian over 4 bytes, which makes the transaction look like Figure 8-28.

```
0100000001868278ed6ddfb6c1ed3ad5f8181eb0c7a385aa0836f01d5e4789e6bd304d87221a00000
0475221022626e955ea6ea6d98850c994f9107b036b1334f18ca8830bfff1295d21cfdb702103b287
eaf122eea69030a0e9feed096bed8045c8b98bec453e1ffac7fbdbd4bb7152aeffffffff04d3b1140
0000000001976a914904a49878c0adfc3aa05de7afad2cc15f483a56a88ac7f400900000000001976
a914418327e3f3dda4cf5b9089325a4b95abdfa0334088ac722c0c00000000001976a914ba35042cf
e9fc66fd35ac2224eebdafd1028ad2788acdc4ace020000000017a91474d691da1574e6b3c192ecfb
52cc8984ee7b6c56870000000001000000
```

Figure 8-28. Append the hash type (SIGHASH_ALL), 01000000

The hash256 of this interpreted as a big-endian integer is our *z*. The code for getting our signature hash looks like this:

```
>>> from helper import hash256
>>> modified_tx = bytes.fromhex('0100000001868278ed6ddfb6c1ed3ad5f8181eb0c7a38\
5aa0836f01d5e4789e6bd304d87221a000000475221022626e955ea6ea6d98850c994f9107b036\
b1334f18ca8830bfff1295d21cfdb702103b287eaf122eea69030a0e9feed096bed8045c8b98be\
c453e1ffac7fbdbd4bb7152aeffffffff04d3b11400000000001976a914904a49878c0adfc3aa0\
5de7afad2cc15f483a56a88ac7f400900000000001976a914418327e3f3dda4cf5b9089325a4b9\
5abdfa0334088ac722c0c00000000001976a914ba35042cfe9fc66fd35ac2224eebdafd1028ad2\
```

```
788acdc4ace020000000017a91474d691da1574e6b3c192ecfb52cc8984ee7b6c5687000000000\
1000000')
>>> s256 = hash256(modified_tx)
>>> z = int.from_bytes(s256, 'big')
>>> print(hex(z))
0xe71bfa115715d6fd33796948126f40a8cdd39f187e4afb03896795189fe1423c
```

Now that we have our *z*, we can grab the SEC public key and DER signature from the ScriptSig and RedeemScript (Figure 8-29).

```
0100000001868278ed6ddfb6c1ed3ad5f8181eb0c7a385aa0836f01d5e4789e6bd304d87221a00000
0db00483045022100dc92655fe37036f47756db8102e0d7d5e28b3beb83a8fef4f5dc0559bddfb94e
02205a36d4e4e6c7fcd16658c50783e00c341609977aed3ad00937bf4ee942a899370148304502210
0da6bee3c93766232079a01639d07fa869598749729ae323eab8eef53577d611b02207bef15429dca
dce2121ea07f233115c6f09034c0be68db99980b9a6c5e754022014752210022626e955ea6ea6d9885
0c994f9107b036b1334f18ca8830bfff1295d21cfdb702103b287eaf122eea69030a0e9feed096bed
8045c8b98bec453e1ffac7fbdbd4bb7152aeffffffff04d3b11400000000001976a914904a49878c0
adfc3aa05de7afad2cc15f483a56a88ac7f400900000000001976a914418327e3f3dda4cf5b908932
5a4b95abdfa0334088ac722c0c00000000001976a914ba35042cfe9fc66fd35ac2224eebdafd1028a
d2788acdc4ace020000000017a91474d691da1574e6b3c192ecfb52cc8984ee7b6c56870000000000
```

Figure 8-29. DER signature and SEC pubkey within the p2sh ScriptSig and Redeem-Script

We can now validate the signature:

```
>>> from ecc import S256Point, Signature
>>> from helper import hash256
>>> modified_tx = bytes.fromhex('0100000001868278ed6ddfb6c1ed3ad5f8181eb0c7a38\
5aa0836f01d5e4789e6bd304d87221a000000475221022626e955ea6ea6d98850c994f9107b036\
b1334f18ca8830bfff1295d21cfdb702103b287eaf122eea69030a0e9feed096bed8045c8b98be\
c453e1ffac7fbdbd4bb7152aeffffffff04d3b11400000000001976a914904a49878c0adfc3aa0\
5de7afad2cc15f483a56a88ac7f400900000000001976a914418327e3f3dda4cf5b9089325a4b9\
5abdfa0334088ac722c0c00000000001976a914ba35042cfe9fc66fd35ac2224eebdafd1028ad2\
788acdc4ace020000000017a91474d691da1574e6b3c192ecfb52cc8984ee7b6c5687000000000\
1000000')
>>> h256 = hash256(modified_tx)
>>> z = int.from_bytes(h256, 'big')   ❶
>>> sec = bytes.fromhex('022626e955ea6ea6d98850c994f9107b036b1334f18ca8830bfff\
1295d21cfdb70')
>>> der = bytes.fromhex('3045022100dc92655fe37036f47756db8102e0d7d5e28b3beb83a\
8fef4f5dc0559bddfb94e02205a36d4e4e6c7fcd16658c50783e00c341609977aed3ad00937bf4\
ee942a89937')
>>> point = S256Point.parse(sec)
>>> sig = Signature.parse(der)
>>> print(point.verify(z, sig))
True
```

❶ z is from the code on page 185.

We've verified one of the two signatures that are required to unlock this p2sh multisig.

Exercise 4

Validate the second signature from the preceding transaction.

Exercise 5

Modify the `sig_hash` and `verify_input` methods to be able to verify p2sh transactions.

Conclusion

In this chapter we learned how p2sh ScriptPubKeys are created and how they're redeemed. We've covered transactions for the last four chapters; we now turn to how they are grouped in blocks.

CHAPTER 9

Blocks

Transactions transfer bitcoins from one party to another and are unlocked, or authorized, by signatures. This ensures that the sender authorized the transaction, but what if the sender sends the same coins to multiple people? The owner of a lockbox may try to spend the same output twice. This is called the *double-spending problem*. Much like being given a check that has the possibility of bouncing, the receiver needs to be assured that the transaction is valid.

This is where a major innovation of Bitcoin comes in, with *blocks*. Think of blocks as a way to order transactions. If we order transactions, a double-spend can be prevented by making any later, conflicting transaction invalid. This is the equivalent to accepting the earlier transaction as the valid one.

Implementing this rule would be easy (earliest transaction is valid, subsequent transactions that conflict are invalid) if we could order transactions one at a time. Unfortunately, that would require nodes on the network to agree on which transaction is supposed to be next and would cause a lot of transmission overhead in coming to consensus. We could also order large batches of transactions, maybe once per day, but that wouldn't be very practical as transactions would settle only once per day and not have finality before then.

Bitcoin finds a middle ground between these extremes by settling every 10 minutes in batches of transactions. These batches of transactions are what we call blocks. In this chapter we'll review how to parse blocks and how to check the proof-of-work. We'll start with a special transaction called the coinbase transaction, which is the first transaction of every block.

Coinbase Transactions

Coinbase transactions have nothing to do with the US company of the same name. Coinbase is the required first transaction of every block and is the only transaction allowed to bring bitcoins into existence. The coinbase transaction's outputs are kept by whomever the mining entity designates and usually include all the transaction fees of the other transactions in the block as well as something called the *block reward*.

The coinbase transaction is what makes it worthwhile for a miner to mine. Figure 9-1 shows what a coinbase transaction looks like.

```
010000000100000000000000000000000000000000000000000000000000000000000000000000ffffffff
f5e03d71b07254d696e656420627920416e74506f6f6c20626a31312f4542312f4144362f43205914
293101fabe6d6d678e2c8c34afc36896e7d9402824ed38e856676ee94bfdb0c6c4bcd8b2e5666a040
0000000000000c7270000a5e00e00ffffffffff01faf20b58000000001976a914338c84849423992471
bffb1a54a8d9b1d69dc28a88ac00000000

         - 01000000 - version
         - 01 - # of inputs
         - 000...00 - previous tx hash
         - ffffffff - previous tx index
         - 5e0...00 - ScriptSig
         - ffffffff - sequence
         - 01 - # of outputs
         - faf20b58...00 - output amount
         - 1976...ac - p2pkh ScriptPubKey
         - 00000000 - locktime
```

Figure 9-1. Coinbase transaction

The transaction structure is no different from that of other transactions on the Bitcoin network, with a few exceptions:

1. Coinbase transactions must have exactly one input.

2. The one input must have a previous transaction of 32 bytes of 00.

3. The one input must have a previous index of ffffffff.

These three conditions determine whether a transaction is a coinbase transaction or not.

Exercise 1

Write the is_coinbase method of the Tx class.

ScriptSig

The coinbase transaction has no previous output that it's spending, so the input is not unlocking anything. So what's in the ScriptSig?

The ScriptSig of the coinbase transaction is set by whoever mined the transaction. The main restriction is that the ScriptSig has to be at least 2 bytes and no longer than 100 bytes. Other than those restrictions and BIP0034 (described in the next section), the ScriptSig can be anything the miner wants as long as the evaluation of the Script-Sig by itself, with no corresponding ScriptPubKey, is valid. Here is the ScriptSig for the genesis block's coinbase transaction:

```
4d04ffff001d0104455468652054696d65732030332f4a616e2f32303039204368616e63656c6c
6f72206f6e206272696e6b206f66207365636f6e64206261696c6f757420666f722062616e6b73
```

This ScriptSig was composed by Satoshi and contains a message that we can read:

```
>>> from io import BytesIO
>>> from script import Script
>>> stream = BytesIO(bytes.fromhex('4d04ffff001d0104455468652054696d6573203033\
2f4a616e2f32303039204368616e63656c6c6f72206f6e206272696e6b206f66207365636f6e64\
206261696c6f757420666f722062616e6b73'))
>>> s = Script.parse(stream)
>>> print(s.cmds[2])
b'The Times 03/Jan/2009 Chancellor on brink of second bailout for banks'
```

This was the headline from the *Times* of London on January 3, 2009. This proves that the genesis block was created some time *at or after* that date, and not *before*. Other coinbase transactions' ScriptSigs contain similarly arbitrary data.

BIP0034

BIP0034 regulates the first element of the ScriptSig of coinbase transactions. This was due to a network problem where miners were using the *same* coinbase transaction for different blocks.

The coinbase transaction being the same byte-wise means that the transaction IDs are also the same, since the hash256 of the transaction is deterministic. To prevent transaction ID duplication, Gavin Andresen authored BIP0034, which is a soft-fork rule that adds the height of the block being mined into the first element of the coinbase ScriptSig.

The height is interpreted as a little-endian integer and must equal the height of the block (that is, the number of blocks since the genesis block). Thus, a coinbase transaction cannot be byte-wise the same across different blocks, since the block height will differ. Here's how we can parse the height from the coinbase transaction in Figure 9-1:

```
>>> from io import BytesIO
>>> from script import Script
>>> from helper import little_endian_to_int
>>> stream = BytesIO(bytes.fromhex('5e03d71b07254d696e656420627920416e74506f6f\
6c20626a31312f4542312f4144362f43205914293101fabe6d6d678e2c8c34afc36896e7d94028\
24ed38e856676ee94bfdb0c6c4bcd8b2e5666a0400000000000000c7270000a5e00e00'))
>>> script_sig = Script.parse(stream)
>>> print(little_endian_to_int(script_sig.cmds[0]))
465879
```

A coinbase transaction reveals the block it was in! Coinbase transactions in different blocks are required to have different ScriptSigs and thus different transaction IDs. This rule continues to be needed as it would otherwise allow the duplicate coinbase transaction IDs across multiple blocks.

Exercise 2

Write the `coinbase_height` method for the `Tx` class.

Block Headers

Blocks are batches of transactions, and the block header is metadata about the transactions included in a block. The block header as shown in Figure 9-2 consists of:

- Version
- Previous block
- Merkle root
- Timestamp
- Bits
- Nonce

```
020000208ec39428b17323fa0ddec8e887b4a7c53b8c0a0
a220cfd00000000000000000000005b0750fce0a889502d4050
8d39576821155e9c9e3f5c3157f961db38fd8b25be1e77a
759e93c0118a4ffd71d

     - 02000020 - version, 4 bytes, LE
     - 8ec3...00 - previous block, 32 bytes, LE
     - 5b07...be - merkle root, 32 bytes, LE
     - 1e77a759 - timestamp, 4 bytes, LE
     - e93c0118 - bits, 4 bytes
     - a4ffd71d - nonce, 4 bytes
```

Figure 9-2. Parsed block

The block header is the metadata for the block. Unlike in transactions, each field in a block header is of a fixed length, as listed in Figure 9-2; a block header takes up exactly 80 bytes. As of this writing there are roughly 550,000 blocks, or ~45 MB in block headers. The entire blockchain, on the other hand, is roughly 200 GB, so the headers are roughly .023% of the size. The fact that headers are so much smaller is an important feature, as we'll see when we look at simplified payment verification in Chapter 11.

Like the transaction ID, the block ID is the hex representation of the hash256 of the header interpreted in little-endian. The block ID is interesting:

```
>>> from helper import hash256
>>> block_hash = hash256(bytes.fromhex('020000208ec39428b17323fa0ddec8e887b4a7\
c53b8c0a0a220cfd0000000000000000005b0750fce0a889502d40508d39576821155e9c9e3f5c\
3157f961db38fd8b25be1e77a759e93c0118a4ffd71d'))[::-1]
>>> block_id = block_hash.hex()
>>> print(block_id)
0000000000000000007e9e4c586439b0cdbe13b1370bdd9435d76a644d047523
```

This ID is what gets put into prev_block for a block building on top of this one. For now, notice that the ID starts with a lot of zeros. We'll come back to this in "Proof-of-Work" on page 170, after we take a closer look at the fields in the block header.

We can start coding a Block class based on what we already know:

```
class Block:

    def __init__(self, version, prev_block, merkle_root, timestamp, bits, nonce):
        self.version = version
        self.prev_block = prev_block
        self.merkle_root = merkle_root
        self.timestamp = timestamp
        self.bits = bits
        self.nonce = nonce
```

Exercise 3

Write the parse method for Block.

Exercise 4

Write the serialize method for Block.

Exercise 5

Write the hash method for Block.

Version

Version in normal software refers to a particular set of features. For a block, this is similar, in the sense that the version field reflects the capabilities of the software that produced the block. In the past this was used as a way to indicate a single feature that was ready to be deployed by the block's miner. Version 2 meant that the software was ready for BIP0034, which introduced the coinbase transaction block height feature mentioned earlier in this chapter. Version 3 meant that the software was ready for BIP0066, which enforced strict DER encoding. Version 4 meant that the software was ready for BIP0065, which specified OP_CHECKLOCKTIMEVERIFY.

Unfortunately, the incremental increase in version number meant that only one feature was signaled on the network at a time. To alleviate this, the developers came up with BIP0009, which allows up to 29 different features to be signaled at the same time.

The way BIP0009 works is by fixing the first 3 bits of the 4-byte (32-bit) header to be 001 to indicate that the miner is using BIP0009. The first 3 bits have to be 001, as that forces older clients to interpret the version field as a number greater than or equal to 4, which was the last version number that was used pre-BIP0009.

This means that in hexadecimal, the first character will always be 2 or 3. The other 29 bits can be assigned to different soft-fork features for which miners can signal readiness. For example, bit 0 (the rightmost bit) can be flipped to 1 to signal readiness for one soft fork, bit 1 (the second bit from the right) can be flipped to 1 to signal readiness for another, bit 2 (the third bit from the right) can be flipped to 1 to signal readiness for another, and so on.

BIP0009 requires that 95% of blocks signal readiness in a given 2,016-block epoch (the period for a difficulty adjustment; more on that later in this chapter) before the soft fork feature gets activated on the network. Soft forks that used BIP0009 as of this writing have been BIP0068/BIP0112/BIP0113 (OP_CHECKSEQUENCEVERIFY and related changes) and BIP0141 (Segwit). These BIPs used bits 0 and 1 for signaling, respectively. BIP0091 used something like BIP0009 but with an 80% threshold and a smaller block period, so it wasn't strictly using BIP0009. Bit 4 was used to signal BIP0091.

Checking for these features is relatively straightforward:

```
>>> from io import BytesIO
>>> from block import Block
>>> b = Block.parse(BytesIO(bytes.fromhex('020000208ec39428b17323fa0ddec8e887b\
4a7c53b8c0a0a220cfd000000000000000000005b0750fce0a889502d40508d39576821155e9c9e3\
f5c3157f961db38fd8b25be1e77a759e93c0118a4ffd71d')))
>>> print('BIP9: {}'.format(b.version >> 29 == 0b001))    ❶
BIP9: True
>>> print('BIP91: {}'.format(b.version >> 4 & 1 == 1))    ❷
BIP91: False
```

```
>>> print('BIP141: {}'.format(b.version >> 1 & 1 == 1))   ❸
BIP141: True
```

❶ The >> operator is the right bit-shift operator, which throws away the rightmost 29 bits, leaving just the top 3 bits. The 0b001 is a way of writing a number in binary in Python.

❷ The & operator is the "bitwise and" operator. In our case, we right-shift by 4 bits first and then check that the rightmost bit is 1.

❸ We shift 1 to the right because BIP0141 was assigned to bit 1.

Exercise 6

Write the bip9 method for the Block class.

Exercise 7

Write the bip91 method for the Block class.

Exercise 8

Write the bip141 method for the Block class.

Previous Block

All blocks have to point to a previous block. This is why the data structure is called a *blockchain*. Blocks link back all the way to the very first block, or the *genesis block*. The previous block field ends in a bunch of 00 bytes, which we will discuss more later in this chapter.

Merkle Root

The Merkle root encodes all the ordered transactions in a 32-byte hash. We will discuss how this is important for simplified payment verification (SPV) clients and how they can use the Merkle root along with data from the server to get a proof of inclusion in Chapter 11.

Timestamp

The timestamp is a Unix-style timestamp taking up 4 bytes. Unix timestamps are the number of seconds since January 1, 1970. This timestamp is used in two places: for validating timestamp-based locktimes on transactions included in the block and for calculating a new bits/target/difficulty every 2,016 blocks. The locktimes were at one point used directly for transactions within a block, but BIP0113 changed the behavior to not use the current block's timestamp directly, but the median time past (MTP) of the past 11 blocks.

Will Bitcoin Overflow on the Timestamp?

Bitcoin's timestamp field in the block header is 4 bytes, or 32 bits. This means that once the Unix timestamp exceeds $2^{32} - 1$, there is no room to go further. 2^{32} seconds is roughly 136 years, which means that this field will have no more room in 2106 (136 years after 1970).

Many people mistakenly believe that we only have until 68 years after 1970, or 2038, but that's only when the field is a signed integer (2^{31} seconds is 68 years), so we get the benefit of that extra bit, giving us until 2106.

In 2106, the block header will need some sort of fork as the timestamp in the block header will no longer continuously increase.

Bits

Bits is a field that encodes the proof-of-work necessary in this block. This will be discussed more in the next section.

Nonce

Nonce stands for "number used only once," or *n-once*. This number is what is changed by miners when looking for proof-of-work.

Proof-of-Work

Proof-of-work is what secures Bitcoin and, at a deep level, allows the decentralized mining of Bitcoin. Finding a proof-of-work gives a miner the right to put the attached block into the blockchain. As proof-of-work is very rare, this is not an easy task. But because proof-of-work is objective and easy to verify, anyone can be a miner if they so choose.

Proof-of-work is called "mining" for a very good reason. Like with physical mining, there is something that miners are searching for. A typical gold mining operation processes 45 tons of dirt and rock before accumulating 1 oz of gold. This is because gold is very rare. However, once gold is found, it's very easy to verify that the gold is real. There are chemical tests, touchstones, and many other ways to tell relatively cheaply whether the thing found is gold.

Similarly, proof-of-work is a number that provides a very rare result. To find a proof-of-work, the miners on the Bitcoin network have to churn through the numerical equivalent of dirt and rock. Like with gold, verifying proof-of-work is much cheaper than actually finding it.

So what is proof-of-work? Let's look at the hash256 of the block header we saw before to find out:

```
020000208ec39428b17323fa0ddec8e887b4a7c53b8c0a0a220cfd000000000000000000
5b0750fce0a889502d40508d39576821155e9c9e3f5c3157f961db38fd8b25be1e77a759
e93c0118a4ffd71d

>>> from helper import hash256
>>> block_id = hash256(bytes.fromhex('020000208ec39428b17323fa0ddec8e887b4a7c5\
3b8c0a0a220cfd000000000000000000005b0750fce0a889502d40508d39576821155e9c9e3f5c31\
57f961db38fd8b25be1e77a759e93c0118a4ffd71d'))[::-1]
>>> print('{}'.format(block_id.hex()).zfill(64))    ❶
0000000000000000007e9e4c586439b0cdbe13b1370bdd9435d76a644d047523
```

❶   We are purposefully printing this number as 64 hexadecimal digits to show how small it is in 256-bit terms.

sha256 is known to generate uniformly distributed values. Given this, we can treat two rounds of sha256, or hash256, as a random number. The probability of any random 256-bit number being this small is tiny. The probability of the first bit in a 256-bit number being 0 is 0.5, the first two bits being 00, 0.25, the first three bits being 000, 0.125, and so on. Note that each 0 in the hexadecimal just shown represents four 0- bits. In this case, we have the first 73 bits being 0, which has a probability of 0.5^{73}, or about 1 in 10^{22}. This is a really tiny probability. On average, 10^{22} (or 10 trillion trillion) random 256-bit numbers have to be generated before finding one this small. In other words, we need to calculate 10^{22} in hashes on average to find one this small. Getting back to the analogy, the process of finding proof-of-work requires us to process around 10^{22} numerical bits of dirt and rock to find our numerical gold nugget.

How a Miner Generates New Hashes

Where does the miner get new numerical dirt to process to see if it satisfies proof-of-work? This is where the nonce field comes in. The miners can change the nonce field at will to change the hash of the block header.

Unfortunately, the 4 bytes or 32 bits of the nonce field (or 2^{32} possible nonces that a miner can try) is insufficient for the required proof-of-work. Modern ASIC equipment can calculate way more than 2^{32} different hashes per second. The AntMiner S9, for example, calculates 12 terahashes per second (Th/s). That is approximately 2^{43} hashes per second, which means that the entire nonce space can be consumed in just 0.0003 seconds.

What miners can do when the nonce field is exhausted is change the coinbase transaction, which then changes the Merkle root, giving miners a fresh nonce space each time. The other option is to roll the version field or use overt ASICBOOST. The mechanics of how the Merkle root changes whenever any transaction in the block changes will be discussed in Chapter 11.

The Target

Proof-of-work is the requirement that the hash of every block header in Bitcoin must be below a certain target. The *target* is a 256-bit number that is computed directly from the bits field (in our example, e93c0118). The target is very small compared to an average 256-bit number.

The bits field is actually two different numbers. The first is the exponent, which is the last byte. The second is the coefficient, which is the other three bytes in little-endian. The formula for calculating the target from these two numbers is:

$$\text{target} = \text{coefficient} \times 256^{\text{exponent}-3}$$

This is how we calculate the target given the bits field in Python:

```
>>> from helper import little_endian_to_int
>>> bits = bytes.fromhex('e93c0118')
>>> exponent = bits[-1]
>>> coefficient = little_endian_to_int(bits[:-1])
>>> target = coefficient * 256**(exponent - 3)
>>> print('{:x}'.format(target).zfill(64))   ❶
0000000000000000013ce9000000000000000000000000000000000000000000
```

❶ We are purposefully printing this number as 64 hexadecimal digits to show how small the number is in 256-bit terms.

A valid proof-of-work is a hash of the block header that, when interpreted as a little-endian integer, is below the target number. Proof-of-work hashes are exceedingly rare, and the process of mining is the process of finding one of these hashes. To find a single proof-of-work with the preceding target, the network as a whole must calculate 3.8×10^{21} hashes, which, when this block was found, could be done roughly every 10 minutes. To give this number some context, the best GPU mining card in the world would need to run for 50,000 years on average to find a single proof-of-work below this target.

We can check that this block header's hash satisfies the proof-of-work as follows:

```
>>> from helper import little_endian_to_int
>>> proof = little_endian_to_int(hash256(bytes.fromhex('020000208ec39428b17323\
fa0ddec8e887b4a7c53b8c0a0a220cfd0000000000000000005b0750fce0a889502d40508d3957\
6821155e9c9e3f5c3157f961db38fd8b25be1e77a759e93c0118a4ffd71d')))
>>> print(proof < target)   ❶
True
```

❶ target is calculated above.

We can see that the proof-of-work is lower by lining up the numbers in 64 hex characters:

```
TG: 000000000000000013ce9000000000000000000000000000000000000000000000
```

```
ID: 0000000000000000007e9e4c586439b0cdbe13b1370bdd9435d76a644d047523
```

Exercise 9

Write the bits_to_target function in *helper.py*.

Difficulty

Targets are hard for human beings to comprehend. The target is the number that the hash must be below, but as humans, it's not easy to see the difference between a 180-bit number and a 190-bit number. The first is a thousand times smaller, but from looking at targets, such large numbers are not easy to contextualize.

To make different targets easier to compare, the concept of *difficulty* was born. The trick is that difficulty is inversely proportional to the target, to make comparisons easier. The specific formula is:

$$\text{difficulty} = \text{0xffff} \times 256^{\text{0x1d}-3} / \text{target}$$

The code looks like this:

```
>>> from helper import little_endian_to_int
>>> bits = bytes.fromhex('e93c0118')
>>> exponent = bits[-1]
>>> coefficient = little_endian_to_int(bits[:-1])
>>> target = coefficient*256**(exponent-3)
>>> difficulty = 0xffff * 256**(0x1d-3) / target
>>> print(difficulty)
888171856257.3206
```

The difficulty of Bitcoin at the genesis block was 1. This gives us context for how difficult mainnet currently is. The difficulty can be thought of as how much more difficult mining is now than it was at the start. The mining difficulty in the preceding code is roughly 888 billion times harder than when Bitcoin started.

Difficulty is often shown in block explorers and Bitcoin price charting services, as it's a much more intuitive way to understand the effort required to create a new block.

Exercise 10

Write the difficulty method for Block.

Checking That the Proof-of-Work Is Sufficient

We already learned that proof-of-work can be calculated by computing the hash256 of the block header and interpreting this as a little-endian integer. If this number is lower than the target, we have a valid proof-of-work. If not, the block is not valid as it doesn't have proof-of-work.

Exercise 11

Write the check_pow method for Block.

Difficulty Adjustment

In Bitcoin, each group of 2,016 blocks is called a *difficulty adjustment period*. At the end of every difficulty adjustment period, the target is adjusted according to this formula:

time_differential = (block timestamp of last block in difficulty adjustment period) – (block timestamp of first block in difficulty adjustment period)

new_target = *previous_target* * *time_differential* / (2 weeks)

The *time_differential* is calculated so that if it's greater than 8 weeks, 8 weeks is used, and if it's less than 3.5 days, 3.5 days is used. This way, the new target cannot change more than four times in either direction. That is, the target will be reduced or increased by four times at the most.

If each block took on average 10 minutes to create, 2,016 blocks should take 20,160 minutes. There are 1,440 minutes per day, which means that 2,016 blocks will take 20,160 / 1,440 = 14 days to create. The effect of the difficulty adjustment is that block times are regressed toward the mean of 10 minutes per block. This means that long-term, blocks will always go toward 10-minute blocks even if a lot of hashing power has entered or left the network.

The new bits calculation should be using the timestamp field of the last block of each of the current and previous difficulty adjustment periods. Satoshi unfortunately had another off-by-one error here, as the timestamp differential calculation looks at the first and last blocks of the 2,016-block difficulty adjustment period instead. The time differential is therefore the difference of blocks that are 2,015 blocks apart instead of 2,016 blocks apart.

We can code this formula like so:

```
>>> from block import Block
>>> from helper import TWO_WEEKS  ❶
>>> last_block = Block.parse(BytesIO(bytes.fromhex('00000020fdf740b0e49cf75bb3\
d5168fb3586f7613dcc5cd89675b0100000000000000002e37b144c0baced07eb7e7b64da916cd\
```

```
3121f2427005551aeb0ec6a6402ac7d7f0e4235954d801187f5da9f5')))
>>> first_block = Block.parse(BytesIO(bytes.fromhex('000000201ecd89664fd205a37\
566e694269ed76e425803003628ab010000000000000000bfcade29d080d9aae8fd461254b0418\
05ae442749f2a40100440fc0e3d5868e55019345954d80118a1721b2e')))
>>> time_differential = last_block.timestamp - first_block.timestamp
>>> if time_differential > TWO_WEEKS * 4:   ❷
...     time_differential = TWO_WEEKS * 4
>>> if time_differential < TWO_WEEKS // 4:   ❸
...     time_differential = TWO_WEEKS // 4
>>> new_target = last_block.target() * time_differential // TWO_WEEKS
>>> print('{:x}'.format(new_target).zfill(64))
0000000000000000007615000000000000000000000000000000000000000000
```

❶ Note that `TWO_WEEKS = 60*60*24*14` is the number of seconds in 2 weeks: 60 seconds × 60 minutes × 24 hours × 14 days.

❷ This makes sure that if it took more than 8 weeks to find the last 2,015 blocks, we don't decrease the difficulty too much.

❸ This makes sure that if it took less than 3.5 days to find the last 2,015 blocks, we don't increase the difficulty too much.

Note that we only need the headers to calculate what the next block's target should be. Once we have the target, we can convert the target to bits. The inverse operation looks like this:

```
def target_to_bits(target):
    '''Turns a target integer back into bits'''
    raw_bytes = target.to_bytes(32, 'big')
    raw_bytes = raw_bytes.lstrip(b'\x00')    ❶
    if raw_bytes[0] > 0x7f:   ❷
        exponent = len(raw_bytes) + 1
        coefficient = b'\x00' + raw_bytes[:2]
    else:
        exponent = len(raw_bytes)    ❸
        coefficient = raw_bytes[:3]   ❹
    new_bits = coefficient[::-1] + bytes([exponent])   ❺
    return new_bits
```

❶ Get rid of all the leading zeros.

❷ The bits format is a way to express really large numbers succinctly and can be used with both negative and positive numbers. If the first bit in the coefficient is a 1, the bits field is interpreted as a negative number. Since the target is always positive for us, we shift everything over by 1 byte if the first bit is 1.

❸ The exponent is how long the number is in base 256.

❹ The coefficient is the first three digits of the base 256 number.

❺ The coefficient is in little-endian and the exponent goes last in the bits format.

If the block doesn't have the correct bits calculated using the difficulty adjustment formula, then we can safely reject that block.

Exercise 12

Calculate the new bits given the first and last blocks of this 2,016-block difficulty adjustment period:

- Block 471744:

  ```
  000000203471101bbda3fe307664b3283a9ef0e97d9a38a7eacd88000000000000000000
  10c8aba8479bbaa5e0848152fd3c2289ca50e1c3e58c9a4faaafbdf5803c5448ddb84559
  7e8b0118e43a81d3
  ```

- Block 473759:

  ```
  02000020f1472d9db4b563c35f97c428ac903f23b7fc055d1cfc260000000000000000000
  b3f449fcbe1bc4cfbcb8283a0d2c037f961a3fdf2b8bedc144973735eea707e126425859
  7e8b0118e5f00474
  ```

Exercise 13

Write the `calculate_new_bits` function in *helper.py*.

Conclusion

We've learned how to calculate proof-of-work, how to calculate the new bits for a block after a difficulty adjustment period, and how to parse coinbase transactions. We'll now move on to networking in Chapter 10 on our way to the block header field we haven't covered, the Merkle root, in Chapter 11.

CHAPTER 10

Networking

The peer-to-peer network that Bitcoin runs on is what gives it a lot of its robustness. More than 65,000 nodes are running on the network as of this writing and are communicating constantly.

The Bitcoin network is a broadcast network, or gossip network. Every node is announcing different transactions, blocks, and peers that it knows about. The protocol is rich and has a lot of features that have been added to it over the years.

One thing to note about the networking protocol is that it is not consensus-critical. The same data can be sent from one node to another using some other protocol and the blockchain itself will not be affected.

With that in mind, we'll work in this chapter toward requesting, receiving, and validating block headers using the network protocol.

Network Messages

All network messages look like Figure 10-1.

The first 4 bytes are always the same and are referred to as the *network magic*. Magic bytes are common in network programming as the communication is asynchronous and can be intermittent. Magic bytes give the receiver of the message a place to start should the communication get interrupted (say, by your phone dropping signal). They are also useful for identifying the network. You would not want a Bitcoin node to connect to a Litecoin node, for example. Thus, a Litecoin node has a different magic. Bitcoin testnet also has a different magic, 0b110907, as opposed to the Bitcoin mainnet magic, f9beb4d9.

```
f9beb4d976657273696f6e000000000000650000005f1a69d27211010001000000000000000bc8f5e540
000000001000000000000000000000000000000000000000ffffc61b6409208d010000000000000000000000
00000000000000000ffffcb0071c0208d128035cbc97953f80f2f5361746f7368693a302e392e332fcf0
5050001

                - f9beb4d9 - network magic (always 0xf9beb4d9 for mainnet)
                - 76657273696f6e0000000000 - command, 12 bytes, human-readable
                - 65000000 - payload length, 4 bytes, little-endian
                - 5f1a69d2 - payload checksum, first 4 bytes of hash256 of the
                            payload
                - 7211...01 - payload
```

Figure 10-1. A network message—the envelope that contains the actual payload

The next 12 bytes are the command field, or a description of what the payload actually carries. There are many different commands; an exhaustive list can be seen in the documentation (*https://en.bitcoin.it/wiki/Protocol_documentation*). The command field is meant to be human-readable and this particular message is the byte string "version" in ASCII with 0-byte padding.

The next 4 bytes are the length of the payload in little-endian. As we saw in Chapters 5 and 9, the length of the payload is necessary since the payload is variable. 2^{32} is about 4 billion, so payloads can be as big as 4 GB, though the reference client rejects any payloads over 32 MB. In the message in Figure 10-1, our payload is 101 bytes.

The next 4 bytes are the checksum field. The checksum algorithm is something of an odd choice, as it's the first 4 bytes of the hash256 of the payload. It's an odd choice because networking protocol checksums are normally designed to have error-correcting capability and hash256 has none. That said, hash256 is common in the rest of the Bitcoin protocol, which is probably the reason it's used here.

The code to handle network messages requires us to create a new class:

```python
NETWORK_MAGIC = b'\xf9\xbe\xb4\xd9'
TESTNET_NETWORK_MAGIC = b'\x0b\x11\x09\x07'


class NetworkEnvelope:

    def __init__(self, command, payload, testnet=False):
        self.command = command
        self.payload = payload
        if testnet:
            self.magic = TESTNET_NETWORK_MAGIC
        else:
            self.magic = NETWORK_MAGIC

    def __repr__(self):
        return '{}: {}'.format(
            self.command.decode('ascii'),
```

```
                    self.payload.hex(),
                )
```

Exercise 1

Write the `parse` method for `NetworkEnvelope`.

Exercise 2

Determine what this network message is:

```
f9beb4d976657261636b0000000000000000000005df6e0e2
```

Exercise 3

Write the `serialize` method for `NetworkEnvelope`.

Parsing the Payload

Each command has a separate payload specification. Figure 10-2 is the parsed payload for `version`.

```
7f11010000000000000000000ad17835b000000000000000000000000000000000000000000000000000000000ffff0
00000000208d000000000000000000000000000000000000000000ffff00000000208df6a8d7a440ec27a11b
2f70726f6772616d6d696e67626c6f636b636861696e3a302e312f0000000001

7f110100 - Protocol version, 4 bytes, little-endian, 70015
0000000000000000 - Network services of sender, 8 bytes, little-endian
ad17835b00000000 - Timestamp, 8 bytes, little-endian
0000000000000000 - Network services of receiver, 8 bytes, little-endian
00000000000000000000ffff00000000 - Network address of receiver, 16 bytes, IPv4
        0.0.0.0
208d - Network port of receiver, 2 bytes, 8333
0000000000000000 - Network services of sender, 8 bytes, little-endian
00000000000000000000ffff00000000 - Network address of sender, 16 bytes, IPv4
        0.0.0.0
208d - Network port of sender, 2 bytes, 8333
f6a8d7a440ec27a1 - Nonce, 8 bytes, used for communicating responses
1b2f70726f6772616d6d696e67626c6f636b636861696e3a302e312f - User agent
        /programmingblockchain:0.1/
00000000 - Height, 0
01 - Optional flag for relay, based on BIP37
```

Figure 10-2. Parsed version

The fields are meant to give enough information for two nodes to be able to
communicate.

The first field is the network protocol version, which specifies what messages may be communicated. The service field gives information about what capabilities are available to connecting nodes. The timestamp field is 8 bytes (as opposed to 4 bytes in the block header) and is the Unix timestamp in little-endian.

IP addresses can be IPv6, IPv4, or OnionCat (a mapping of TOR's .onion addresses to IPv6). If IPv4, the first 12 bytes are 00000000000000000000ffff and the last 4 bytes are the IP. The port is 2 bytes in big-endian. The default on mainnet is 8333, which maps to 208d in big-endian hex.

A nonce is a number used by a node to detect a connection to itself. The user agent identifies the software being run. The height or latest block field helps the other node know which block a node is synced up to.

Relay is used for Bloom filters, which we'll get to in Chapter 12.

Setting some reasonable defaults, our VersionMessage class looks like this:

```
class VersionMessage:
    command = b'version'

    def __init__(self, version=70015, services=0, timestamp=None,
                 receiver_services=0,
                 receiver_ip=b'\x00\x00\x00\x00', receiver_port=8333,
                 sender_services=0,
                 sender_ip=b'\x00\x00\x00\x00', sender_port=8333,
                 nonce=None, user_agent=b'/programmingbitcoin:0.1/',
                 latest_block=0, relay=False):
        self.version = version
        self.services = services
        if timestamp is None:
            self.timestamp = int(time.time())
        else:
            self.timestamp = timestamp
        self.receiver_services = receiver_services
        self.receiver_ip = receiver_ip
        self.receiver_port = receiver_port
        self.sender_services = sender_services
        self.sender_ip = sender_ip
        self.sender_port = sender_port
        if nonce is None:
            self.nonce = int_to_little_endian(randint(0, 2**64), 8)
        else:
            self.nonce = nonce
        self.user_agent = user_agent
        self.latest_block = latest_block
        self.relay = relay
```

At this point, we need a way to serialize this message.

Exercise 4

Write the `serialize` method for `VersionMessage`.

Network Handshake

The network handshake is how nodes establish communication:

- A wants to connect to B and sends a version message.
- B receives the version message, responds with a verack message, and sends its own version message.
- A receives the version and verack messages and sends back a verack message.
- B receives the verack message and continues communication.

Once the handshake is finished, A and B can communicate however they want. Note that there is no authentication here, and it's up to the nodes to verify all data that they receive. If a node sends a bad transaction or block, it can expect to get banned or disconnected.

Connecting to the Network

Network communication is tricky due to its asynchronous nature. To experiment, we can establish a connection to a node on the network synchronously:

```
>>> import socket
>>> from network import NetworkEnvelope, VersionMessage
>>> host = 'testnet.programmingbitcoin.com'  ❶
>>> port = 18333
>>> socket = socket.socket(socket.AF_INET, socket.SOCK_STREAM)
>>> socket.connect((host, port))
>>> stream = socket.makefile('rb', None)  ❷
>>> version = VersionMessage()  ❸
>>> envelope = NetworkEnvelope(version.command, version.serialize())
>>> socket.sendall(envelope.serialize())  ❹
>>> while True:
...     new_message = NetworkEnvelope.parse(stream)  ❺
...     print(new_message)
```

❶ This is a server I've set up for testnet. The testnet port is 18333 by default.

❷ We create a stream to be able to read from the socket. A stream made this way can be passed to all the parse methods.

❸ The first step of the handshake is to send a version message.

❹ We now send the message in the right envelope.

❺ This line will read any messages coming in through our connected socket.

Connecting in this way, we can't send until we've received and can't respond intelligently to more than one message at a time. A more robust implementation would use an asynchronous library (like asyncio in Python 3) to send and receive without being blocked.

We also need a verack message class, which we'll create here:

```python
class VerAckMessage:
    command = b'verack'

    def __init__(self):
        pass

    @classmethod
    def parse(cls, s):
        return cls()

    def serialize(self):
        return b''
```

A VerAckMessage is a minimal network message.

Let's now automate this by creating a class that will handle the communication for us:

```python
class SimpleNode:

    def __init__(self, host, port=None, testnet=False, logging=False):
        if port is None:
            if testnet:
                port = 18333
            else:
                port = 8333
        self.testnet = testnet
        self.logging = logging
        self.socket = socket.socket(socket.AF_INET, socket.SOCK_STREAM)
        self.socket.connect((host, port))
        self.stream = self.socket.makefile('rb', None)

    def send(self, message):  ❶
        '''Send a message to the connected node'''
        envelope = NetworkEnvelope(
            message.command, message.serialize(), testnet=self.testnet)
        if self.logging:
            print('sending: {}'.format(envelope))
        self.socket.sendall(envelope.serialize())

    def read(self):  ❷
        '''Read a message from the socket'''
```

```
        envelope = NetworkEnvelope.parse(self.stream, testnet=self.testnet)
        if self.logging:
            print('receiving: {}'.format(envelope))
        return envelope

    def wait_for(self, *message_classes):  ❸
        '''Wait for one of the messages in the list'''
        command = None
        command_to_class = {m.command: m for m in message_classes}
        while command not in command_to_class.keys():
            envelope = self.read()
            command = envelope.command
            if command == VersionMessage.command:
                self.send(VerAckMessage())
            elif command == PingMessage.command:
                self.send(PongMessage(envelope.payload))
        return command_to_class[command].parse(envelope.stream())
```

❶ The send method sends a message over the socket. The command property and serialize methods are expected to exist in the message object.

❷ The read method reads a new message from the socket.

❸ The wait_for method lets us wait for any one of several commands (specifically, message classes). Along with the synchronous nature of this class, a method like this makes for easier programming. A commercial-strength node would definitely not use something like this.

Now that we have a node, we can handshake with another node:

```
>>> from network import SimpleNode, VersionMessage
>>> node = SimpleNode('testnet.programmingbitcoin.com', testnet=True)
>>> version = VersionMessage()  ❶
>>> node.send(version)  ❷
>>> verack_received = False
>>> version_received = False
>>> while not verack_received and not version_received:  ❸
...     message = node.wait_for(VersionMessage, VerAckMessage)  ❹
...     if message.command == VerAckMessage.command:
...         verack_received = True
...     else:
...         version_received = True
...         node.send(VerAckMessage())
```

❶ Most nodes don't care about the fields in version like IP address. We can connect with the defaults and everything will be just fine.

❷ We start the handshake by sending the version message.

❸ We only finish when we've received both verack and version.

❹ We expect to receive a verack for our version and the other node's version. We don't know in which order they will arrive, though.

Exercise 5

Write the `handshake` method for `SimpleNode`.

Getting Block Headers

Now that we have code to connect to a node, what can we do? When any node first connects to the network, the data that's most crucial to get and verify is the block headers. For full nodes, downloading the block headers allows them to asynchronously ask for full blocks from multiple nodes, parallelizing the download of the blocks. For light clients, downloading headers allows them to verify the proof-of-work in each block. As we'll see in Chapter 11, light clients will be able to get proofs of inclusion through the network, but that requires the light clients to have the block headers.

Nodes can give us the block headers without taking up much bandwidth. The command to get the block headers is called `getheaders`, and it looks like Figure 10-3.

```
7f11010001a35bd0ca2f4a88c4eda6d213e2378a5758dfcd6af43712000000000000000000000000000000
000000000000000000000000000000000000000000000000000000000000

        - 7f110100 - Protocol version, 4 bytes, little-endian, 70015
        - 01 - Number of hashes, varint
        - a35b...00 - Starting block, little-endian
        - 0000...00 - Ending block, little-endian
```

Figure 10-3. Parsed getheaders

As with version, we start with the protocol version, then the number of block header groups in this list (this number can be more than 1 if there's a chain split), then the starting block header, and finally the ending block header. If we specify the ending block to be 000...000, we're indicating that we want as many as the other node will give us. The maximum number of headers that we can get back is 2,000, or almost a single difficulty adjustment period (2,016 blocks).

Here's what the class looks like:

```
class GetHeadersMessage:
    command = b'getheaders'

    def __init__(self, version=70015, num_hashes=1,
```

```
            start_block=None, end_block=None):
        self.version = version
        self.num_hashes = num_hashes    ❶
        if start_block is None:    ❷
            raise RuntimeError('a start block is required')
        self.start_block = start_block
        if end_block is None:
            self.end_block = b'\x00' * 32    ❸
        else:
            self.end_block = end_block
```

❶ For the purposes of this chapter, we're going to assume that the number of block header groups is 1. A more robust implementation would handle more than a single block group, but we can download the block headers using a single group.

❷ A starting block is needed, otherwise we can't create a proper message.

❸ The ending block we assume to be null, or as many as the server will send to us if not defined.

Exercise 6

Write the `serialize` method for `GetHeadersMessage`.

Headers Response

We can now create a node, handshake, and then ask for some headers:

```
>>> from io import BytesIO
>>> from block import Block, GENESIS_BLOCK
>>> from network import SimpleNode, GetHeadersMessage
>>> node = SimpleNode('mainnet.programmingbitcoin.com', testnet=False)
>>> node.handshake()
>>> genesis = Block.parse(BytesIO(GENESIS_BLOCK))
>>> getheaders = GetHeadersMessage(start_block=genesis.hash())
>>> node.send(getheaders)
```

Now we need a way to receive the headers from the other node. The other node will send back the `headers` command. This is a list of block headers (Figure 10-4), which we already learned how to parse in Chapter 9. The `HeadersMessage` class can take advantage of this when parsing.

```
0200000020df3b053dc46f162a9b00c7f0d5124e2676d47bbe7c5d0793a50000000000000000ef445fef
2ed495c275892206ca533e7411907971013ab83e3b47bd0d692d14d4dc7c835b67d8001ac157e6700
00000002030eb2540c41025690160a1014c577061596e32e426b712c7ca000000000000000768b89f07
044e6130ead292a3f51951adbd2202df447d98789339937fd006bd44880835b67d8001ade09204600
```
- 02 - Number of block headers
- 00...67 - Block header
- 00 - Number of transactions (always 0)

Figure 10-4. Parsed headers

The headers message starts with the number of headers as a varint, which is a number from 1 to 2,000 inclusive. Each block header, we know, is 80 bytes. Then we have the number of transactions. The number of transactions in the headers message is always 0. This may be a bit confusing at first, since we only asked for the headers and not the transactions. The reason nodes bother sending the number of transactions at all is because the headers message is meant to be compatible with the format for the block message, which is the block header, the number of transactions, and then the transactions themselves. By specifying that the number of transactions is 0, we can use the same parsing engine as when parsing a full block:

```python
class HeadersMessage:
    command = b'headers'

    def __init__(self, blocks):
        self.blocks = blocks

    @classmethod
    def parse(cls, stream):
        num_headers = read_varint(stream)
        blocks = []
        for _ in range(num_headers):
            blocks.append(Block.parse(stream))      ❶
            num_txs = read_varint(stream)           ❷
            if num_txs != 0:                         ❸
                raise RuntimeError('number of txs not 0')
        return cls(blocks)
```

❶ Each block gets parsed with the `Block` class's `parse` method, using the same stream that we have.

❷ The number of transactions is always 0 and is a remnant of block parsing.

❸ If we didn't get 0, something is wrong.

Given the network connection that we've set up, we can download the headers, check their proof-of-work, and validate the block header difficulty adjustments as follows:

```
>>> from io import BytesIO
>>> from network import SimpleNode, GetHeadersMessage, HeadersMessage
>>> from block import Block, GENESIS_BLOCK, LOWEST_BITS
>>> from helper import calculate_new_bits
>>> previous = Block.parse(BytesIO(GENESIS_BLOCK))
>>> first_epoch_timestamp = previous.timestamp
>>> expected_bits = LOWEST_BITS
>>> count = 1
>>> node = SimpleNode('mainnet.programmingbitcoin.com', testnet=False)
>>> node.handshake()
>>> for _ in range(19):
...     getheaders = GetHeadersMessage(start_block=previous.hash())
...     node.send(getheaders)
...     headers = node.wait_for(HeadersMessage)
...     for header in headers.blocks:
...         if not header.check_pow():                                      ❶
...             raise RuntimeError('bad PoW at block {}'.format(count))
...         if header.prev_block != previous.hash():                        ❷
...             raise RuntimeError('discontinuous block at {}'.format(count))
...         if count % 2016 == 0:
...             time_diff = previous.timestamp - first_epoch_timestamp
...             expected_bits = calculate_new_bits(previous.bits, time_diff)  ❹
...             print(expected_bits.hex())
...             first_epoch_timestamp = header.timestamp                    ❺
...         if header.bits != expected_bits:                                ❸
...             raise RuntimeError('bad bits at block {}'.format(count))
...         previous = header
...         count += 1
ffff001d
ffff001d
ffff001d
ffff001d
ffff001d
ffff001d
ffff001d
ffff001d
ffff001d
ffff001d
ffff001d
ffff001d
ffff001d
ffff001d
ffff001d
6ad8001d
28c4001d
71be001d
```

❶ Check that the proof-of-work is valid.

❷ Check that the current block is after the previous one.

❸ Check that the bits/target/difficulty is what we expect based on the previous epoch calculation.

❹ At the end of the epoch, calculate the next bits/target/difficulty.

❺ Store the first block of the epoch to calculate bits at the end of the epoch.

Note that this won't work on testnet as the difficulty adjustment algorithm is different. To make sure blocks can be found consistently for testing, if a block hasn't been found on testnet in 20 minutes, the difficulty drops to 1, making it very easy to find a block. This is set up this way to allow testers to be able to keep building blocks on the network without expensive mining equipment. A $30 USB ASIC can typically find a few blocks per minute at the minimum difficulty.

Conclusion

We've managed to connect to a node on the network, handshake, download the block headers, and verify that they meet the consensus rules. In the next chapter, we focus on getting information about transactions that we're interested in from another node in a private yet provable way.

CHAPTER 11

Simplified Payment Verification

The one block header field that we didn't investigate much in Chapter 9 was the Merkle root. To understand what makes the Merkle root useful, we first have to learn about Merkle trees and what properties they have. In this chapter, we're going to learn exactly what a Merkle root is. This will be motivated by something called a *proof of inclusion*.

Motivation

For a device that doesn't have much disk space, bandwidth, or computing power, it's expensive to store, receive, and validate the entire blockchain. As of this writing, the entire Bitcoin blockchain is around 200 GB, which is more than many phones can store; it can be very difficult to download efficiently and will certainly tax the CPU. If the entire blockchain cannot be put on the phone, what else can we do? Is it possible to create a Bitcoin wallet on a phone without having all the data?

For any wallet, there are two scenarios that we're concerned with:

1. Paying someone
2. Getting paid by someone

If you are paying someone with your Bitcoin wallet, it is up to the person receiving your bitcoins to verify that they've been paid. Once they've verified that the transaction has been included in a block sufficiently deep, the other side of the trade, or the good or service, will be given to you. Once you've sent the transaction to the other party, there really isn't anything for you to do other than wait until you receive whatever it is you're exchanging the bitcoins for.

When getting paid bitcoins, however, we have a dilemma. If we are connected and have the full blockchain, we can easily see when the transaction is in a sufficiently deep block, at which point we give the other party our goods or services. But if we don't have the full blockchain, as with a phone, what can we do?

The answer lies in the Merkle root field from the block header that we saw in Chapter 9. As we saw in the last chapter, we can download the block headers and verify that they meet the Bitcoin consensus rules. In this chapter we're going to work toward getting proof that a particular transaction is in a block that we know about. Since the block header is secured by proof-of-work, a transaction with a proof of inclusion in that block means, at a minimum, there was a good deal of energy spent to produce that block. This means that the cost to deceive you would be at least the cost of the proof-of-work for the block. The rest of this chapter goes into what the proof of inclusion is and how to verify it.

Merkle Tree

A Merkle tree is a computer science structure designed for efficient proofs of inclusion. The prerequisites are an ordered list of items and a cryptographic hash function. In our case, the items in the ordered list are transactions in a block and the hash function is hash256. To construct the Merkle tree, we follow this algorithm:

1. Hash all the items of the ordered list with the provided hash function.
2. If there is exactly 1 hash, we are done.
3. Otherwise, if there is an odd number of hashes, we duplicate the last hash in the list and add it to the end so that we have an even number of hashes.
4. We pair the hashes in order and hash the concatenation to get the parent level, which should have half the number of hashes.
5. Go to #2.

The idea is to come to a single hash that "represents" the entire ordered list. Visually, a Merkle tree looks like Figure 11-1.

The bottom row is what we call the *leaves* of the tree. All other nodes besides the leaves are called *internal nodes*. The leaves get combined to produce a *parent level* (H_{AB} and H_{CD}), and when we calculate the parent level of that, we get the Merkle root.

We'll go through each part of this process in the following sections.

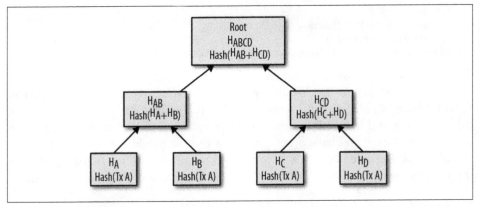

Figure 11-1. Merkle tree

Be Careful with Merkle Trees!

There was a vulnerability in Bitcoin 0.4–0.6 related to the Merkle root, which is detailed in CVE-2012-2459. There was a denial-of-service vector due to the duplication of the last item in Merkle trees, which caused some nodes to invalidate blocks even if they were valid.

Merkle Parent

Given two hashes, we produce another hash that represents both of them. As they are ordered, we will call the two hashes the *left* hash and the *right* hash. The hash of the left and right hashes is what we call the *parent* hash. To clarify, here's the formula for the parent hash:

- H = Hashing function
- P = Parent hash
- L = Left hash
- R = Right hash

$P=H(L||R)$

Note that the $||$ symbol denotes concatenation.

Here's how we can code this process in Python:

```
>>> from helper import hash256
>>> hash0 = bytes.fromhex('c117ea8ec828342f4dfb0ad6bd140e03a50720ece40169ee38b\
dc15d9eb64cf5')
>>> hash1 = bytes.fromhex('c131474164b412e3406696da1ee20ab0fc9bf41c8f05fa8ceea\
```

```
7a08d672d7cc5')
>>> parent = hash256(hash0 + hash1)
>>> print(parent.hex())
8b30c5ba100f6f2e5ad1e2a742e5020491240f8eb514fe97c713c31718ad7ecd
```

The reason why we hash the concatenation to get the parent is because we can provide a proof of inclusion. Specifically, we can show that *L* is represented in the parent, *P*, by revealing *R*. That is, if we want proof *L* is represented in *P*, the producer of *P* can show us *R* and let us know that *L* is the left child of *P*. We can then combine *L* and *R* to produce *P* and have proof that *L* was used to produce *P*. If *L* is not represented in *P*, being able to provide *R* would be the equivalent to providing a hash preimage, which we know is very difficult. This is what we mean by a proof of inclusion.

Exercise 1

Write the merkle_parent function.

Merkle Parent Level

Given an ordered list of more than two hashes, we can calculate the parents of each pair, or what we call the *Merkle parent level*. If we have an even number of hashes, this is straightforward, as we can simply pair them up in order. If we have an odd number of hashes, then we need to do something, as we have a lone hash at the end. We can solve this by duplicating the last item.

That is, for a list like [A, B, C] we can add C again to get [A, B, C, C]. Now we can calculate the Merkle parent of A and B and calculate the Merkle parent of C and C to get:

$$[H(A||B), H(C||C)]$$

Since the Merkle parent always consists of two hashes, the Merkle parent level always has exactly half the number of hashes, rounded up. Here is how we calculate a Merkle parent level:

```
>>> from helper import merkle_parent
>>> hex_hashes = [
...     'c117ea8ec828342f4dfb0ad6bd140e03a50720ece40169ee38bdc15d9eb64cf5',
...     'c131474164b412e3406696da1ee20ab0fc9bf41c8f05fa8ceea7a08d672d7cc5',
...     'f391da6ecfeed1814efae39e7fcb3838ae0b02c02ae7d0a5848a66947c0727b0',
...     '3d238a92a94532b946c90e19c49351c763696cff3db400485b813aecb8a13181',
...     '10092f2633be5f3ce349bf9ddbde36caa3dd10dfa0ec8106bce23acbff637dae',
... ]
>>> hashes = [bytes.fromhex(x) for x in hex_hashes]
>>> if len(hashes) % 2 == 1:
...     hashes.append(hashes[-1])  ❶
>>> parent_level = []
>>> for i in range(0, len(hashes), 2):  ❷
```

```
...         parent = merkle_parent(hashes[i], hashes[i+1])
...         parent_level.append(parent)
>>> for item in parent_level:
...     print(item.hex())
8b30c5ba100f6f2e5ad1e2a742e5020491240f8eb514fe97c713c31718ad7ecd
7f4e6f9e224e20fda0ae4c44114237f97cd35aca38d83081c9bfd41feb907800
3ecf6115380c77e8aae56660f5634982ee897351ba906a6837d15ebc3a225df0
```

❶ We add the last hash on the list, hashes[-1], to the end of hashes to make the length of hashes even.

❷ This is how we skip by two in Python. i will be 0 the first time through the loop, 2 the second, 4 the third, and so on.

This code results in a new list of hashes that correspond to the Merkle parent level.

Exercise 2

Write the merkle_parent_level function.

Merkle Root

To get the Merkle root we calculate successive Merkle parent levels until we get a single hash. If, for example, we have items A through G (7 items), we calculate the Merkle parent level first as follows:

$$[H(A||B), H(C||D), H(E||F), H(G||G)]$$

Then we calculate the Merkle parent level again:

$$[H(H(A||B)||H(C||D)), H(H(E||F)||H(G||G))]$$

We are left with just two items, so we calculate the Merkle parent level one more time:

$$H(H(H(A||B)||H(C||D))||H(H(E||F)||H(G||G)))$$

Since we are left with exactly one hash, we are done. Each level will halve the number of hashes, so doing this process over and over will eventually result in a final single item called the Merkle root:

```
>>> from helper import merkle_parent_level
>>> hex_hashes = [
...     'c117ea8ec828342f4dfb0ad6bd140e03a50720ece40169ee38bdc15d9eb64cf5',
...     'c131474164b412e3406696da1ee20ab0fc9bf41c8f05fa8ceea7a08d672d7cc5',
...     'f391da6ecfeed1814efae39e7fcb3838ae0b02c02ae7d0a5848a66947c0727b0',
...     '3d238a92a94532b946c90e19c49351c763696cff3db400485b813aecb8a13181',
...     '10092f2633be5f3ce349bf9ddbde36caa3dd10dfa0ec8106bce23acbff637dae',
...     '7d37b3d54fa6a64869084bfd2e831309118b9e833610e6228adacdbd1b4ba161',
```

```
...         '8118a77e542892fe15ae3fc771a4abfd2f5d5d5997544c3487ac36b5c85170fc',
...         'dff6879848c2c9b62fe652720b8df5272093acfaa45a43cdb3696fe2466a3877',
...         'b825c0745f46ac58f7d3759e6dc535a1fec7820377f24d4c2c6ad2cc55c0cb59',
...         '95513952a04bd8992721e9b7e2937f1c04ba31e0469fbe615a78197f68f52b7c',
...         '2e6d722e5e4dbdf2447ddecc9f7dabb8e299bae921c99ad5b0184cd9eb8e5908',
...         'b13a750047bc0bdceb2473e5fe488c2596d7a7124b4e716fdd29b046ef99bbf0',
... ]
>>> hashes = [bytes.fromhex(x) for x in hex_hashes]
>>> current_hashes = hashes
>>> while len(current_hashes) > 1:  ❶
...     current_hashes = merkle_parent_level(current_hashes)
>>> print(current_hashes[0].hex())  ❷
acbcab8bcc1af95d8d563b77d24c3d19b18f1486383d75a5085c4e86c86beed6
```

❶ We loop until there's one hash left.

❷ We've exited the loop so there should only be one item.

Exercise 3

Write the `merkle_root` function.

Merkle Root in Blocks

Calculating the Merkle root in blocks should be pretty straightforward, but due to endianness issues, it turns out to be tricky. Specifically, we use little-endian ordering for the leaves of the Merkle tree. After we calculate the Merkle root, we use little-endian ordering again.

In practice, this means reversing the leaves before we start and reversing the root at the end:

```
>>> from helper import merkle_root
>>> tx_hex_hashes = [
...         '42f6f52f17620653dcc909e58bb352e0bd4bd1381e2955d19c00959a22122b2e',
...         '94c3af34b9667bf787e1c6a0a009201589755d01d02fe2877cc69b929d2418d4',
...         '959428d7c48113cb9149d0566bde3d46e98cf028053c522b8fa8f735241aa953',
...         'a9f27b99d5d108dede755710d4a1ffa2c74af70b4ca71726fa57d68454e609a2',
...         '62af110031e29de1efcad103b3ad4bec7bdcf6cb9c9f4afdd586981795516577',
...         '766900590ece194667e9da2984018057512887110bf54fe0aa800157aec796ba',
...         'e8270fb475763bc8d855cfe45ed98060988c1bdcad2ffc8364f783c98999a208',
... ]
>>> tx_hashes = [bytes.fromhex(x) for x in tx_hex_hashes]
>>> hashes = [h[::-1] for h in tx_hashes]  ❶
>>> print(merkle_root(hashes)[::-1].hex())  ❷
654d6181e18e4ac4368383fdc5eead11bf138f9b7ac1e15334e4411b3c4797d9
```

❶ We reverse each hash before we begin using a Python list comprehension.

---

❷ We reverse the root at the end.

We want to calculate Merkle roots for a `Block`, so we add a `tx_hashes` parameter:

```
class Block:

    def __init__(self, version, prev_block, merkle_root,
                 timestamp, bits, nonce, tx_hashes=None):  ❶
        self.version = version
        self.prev_block = prev_block
        self.merkle_root = merkle_root
        self.timestamp = timestamp
        self.bits = bits
        self.nonce = nonce
        self.tx_hashes = tx_hashes
```

❶ We now allow the transaction hashes to be set as part of the initialization of the block. The transaction hashes have to be ordered.

As a full node, if we are given all of the transactions, we can calculate the Merkle root and check that the Merkle root is what we expect.

Exercise 4

Write the `validate_merkle_root` method for `Block`.

Using a Merkle Tree

Now that we know how a Merkle tree is constructed, we can create and verify proofs of inclusion. Light nodes can get proofs that transactions of interest were included in a block without having to know all the transactions of a block (Figure 11-2).

Say that a light client has two transactions that are of interest, which would be the hashes represented by the green boxes, H_K and H_N in Figure 11-2. A full node can construct a proof of inclusion by sending us all of the hashes marked by blue boxes: $H_{ABCDEFGH}$, H_{IJ}, H_L, H_M, and H_{OP}. The light client would then perform these calculations:

- $H_{KL} = merkle\_parent(H_K, H_L)$
- $H_{MN} = merkle\_parent(H_M, H_N)$
- $H_{IJKL} = merkle\_parent(H_{IJ}, H_{KL})$
- $H_{MNOP} = merkle\_parent(H_{MN}, H_{OP})$
- $H_{IJKLMNOP} = merkle\_parent(H_{IJKL}, H_{MNOP})$
- $H_{ABCDEFGHIJKLMNOP} = merkle\_parent(H_{ABCDEFGH}, H_{IJKLMNOP})$

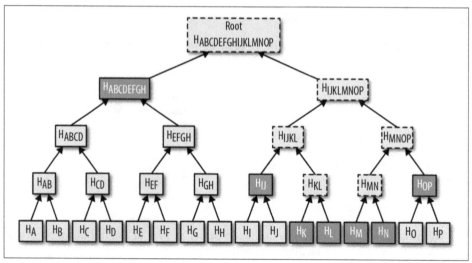

Figure 11-2. Merkle proof

You can see that in Figure 11-2, the dotted boxes correspond to the hashes that the light client calculates. In particular, the Merkle root is $H_{ABCDEFGHIJKLMNOP}$, which can then be checked against the block header whose proof-of-work has been validated.

How Secure Is an SPV Proof?

The full node can send a limited amount of information about the block and the light client can recalculate the Merkle root, which can then be verified against the Merkle root in the block header. This does not guarantee that the transaction is in the longest blockchain, but it does assure the light client that the full node would have had to spend a lot of hashing power or energy creating a valid proof-of-work. As long as the reward for creating such a proof-of-work is greater than the amounts in the transactions, the light client can at least know that the full node has no clear economic incentive to lie.

Since block headers can be requested from multiple nodes, light clients have a way to verify if one node is trying to show them block headers that are not the longest. It only takes a single honest node to invalidate a hundred dishonest ones, since proof-of-work is objective. Therefore, isolation of a light client (that is, control of who the light client is connected to) is required to deceive in this way. The security of SPV requires that there be lots of honest nodes on the network.

In other words, light client security is based on a robust network of nodes and the economic cost of producing proof-of-work. For small transactions relative to the block subsidy (currently 12.5 BTC), there's probably little to worry about. For large transactions (say, 100 BTC), the full nodes may have an economic incentive to deceive you. Transactions that large should generally be validated using a full node.

Merkle Block

When a full node sends a proof of inclusion, there are two pieces of information that need to be included. First, the light client needs the Merkle tree structure, and second, the light client needs to know which hash is at which position in the Merkle tree. Once both pieces of information are given, the light client can reconstruct the partial Merkle tree to reconstruct the Merkle root and validate the proof of inclusion. A full node communicates these two pieces of information to a light client using a Merkle block.

To understand what's in a Merkle block, we need to understand a bit about how a Merkle tree, or more generally, binary trees, can be traversed. In a binary tree, nodes can be traversed breadth-first or depth-first. Breadth-first traversal would go level by level like in Figure 11-3.

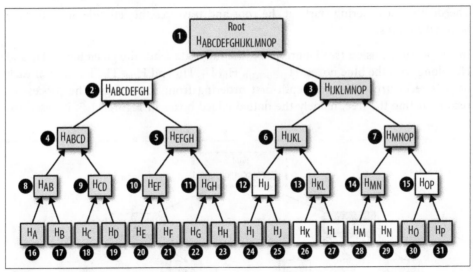

Figure 11-3. Breadth-first ordering

The breadth-first ordering starts at the root and goes from root to leaves, level by level, left to right.

Depth-first ordering is a bit different and looks like Figure 11-4.

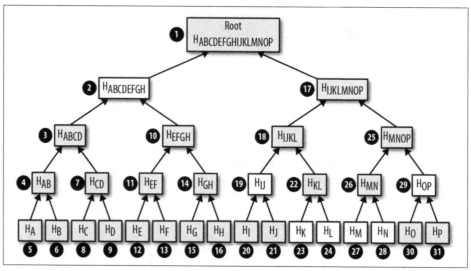

Figure 11-4. Depth-first ordering

The depth-first ordering starts at the root and traverses the left side at each node before the right side.

In a proof of inclusion (see Figure 11-5), the full node sends the green boxes, H_K and H_N, along with the blue boxes, $H_{ABCDEFGH}$, H_{IJ}, H_L, H_M and H_{OP}. The location of each hash is reconstructed using depth-first ordering from some flags. The process of reconstructing the tree, namely the dotted-edged boxes in Figure 11-5, is described next.

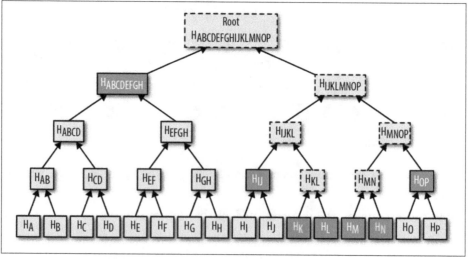

Figure 11-5. Merkle proof

Merkle Tree Structure

The first thing a light client does is create the general structure of the Merkle tree. Because Merkle trees are built from the leaves upward, the only thing a light client needs is the number of leaves that exist to know the structure. The tree from Figure 11-5 has 16 leaves. A light client can create the empty Merkle tree like so:

```
>>> import math
>>> total = 16
>>> max_depth = math.ceil(math.log(total, 2))  ❶
>>> merkle_tree = []  ❷
>>> for depth in range(max_depth + 1):  ❸
...     num_items = math.ceil(total / 2**(max_depth - depth))  ❹
...     level_hashes = [None] * num_items  ❺
...     merkle_tree.append(level_hashes)  ❻
>>> for level in merkle_tree:
...     print(level)
[None]
[None, None]
[None, None, None, None]
[None, None, None, None, None, None, None, None]
[None, None, None, None, None, None, None, None, None, None, None, None, None,\
 None, None, None]
```

❶ Since we halve at every level, $\log_2$ of the number of leaves is how many levels there are in the Merkle tree. Note we round up using `math.ceil` as we round up for halving at each level. We could also be clever and use `len(bin(total))-2`.

❷ The Merkle tree will hold the root level at index 0, the level below at index 1, and so on. In other words, the index is the "depth" from the top.

❸ There are levels 0 to `max_depth` in this Merkle tree.

❹ At any particular level, the number of nodes is the number of total leaves divided by 2 for every level above the leaf level.

❺ We don't know yet what any of the hashes are, so we set them to `None`.

❻ Note `merkle_tree` is a list of lists of hashes, or a two-dimensional array.

Exercise 5

Create an empty Merkle Tree with 27 items and print each level.

Coding a Merkle Tree

We can now create a `MerkleTree` class:

```
class MerkleTree:

    def __init__(self, total):
        self.total = total
        self.max_depth = math.ceil(math.log(self.total, 2))
        self.nodes = []
        for depth in range(self.max_depth + 1):
            num_items = math.ceil(self.total / 2**(self.max_depth - depth))
            level_hashes = [None] * num_items
            self.nodes.append(level_hashes)
        self.current_depth = 0  ❶
        self.current_index = 0

    def __repr__(self):  ❷
        result = []
        for depth, level in enumerate(self.nodes):
            items = []
            for index, h in enumerate(level):
                if h is None:
                    short = 'None'
                else:
                    short = '{}...'.format(h.hex()[:8])
                if depth == self.current_depth and index == self.current_index:
                    items.append('*{}*'.format(short[:-2]))
                else:
                    items.append('{}'.format(short))
            result.append(', '.join(items))
        return '\n'.join(result)
```

❶ We keep a pointer to a particular node in the tree, which will come in handy later.

❷ We print a representation of the tree.

Now that we have an empty tree, we can go about filling it to calculate the Merkle root. If we had every leaf hash, getting the Merkle root would look like this:

```
>>> from merkleblock import MerkleTree
>>> from helper import merkle_parent_level
>>> hex_hashes = [
...     "9745f7173ef14ee4155722d1cbf13304339fd00d900b759c6f9d58579b5765fb",
...     "5573c8ede34936c29cdfdfe743f7f5fdfbd4f54ba0705259e62f39917065cb9b",
...     "82a02ecbb6623b4274dfcab82b336dc017a27136e08521091e443e62582e8f05",
...     "507ccae5ed9b340363a0e6d765af148be9cb1c8766ccc922f83e4ae681658308",
...     "a7a4aec28e7162e1e9ef33dfa30f0bc0526e6cf4b11a576f6c5de58593898330",
...     "bb6267664bd833fd9fc82582853ab144fece26b7a8a5bf328f8a059445b59add",
...     "ea6d7ac1ee77fbacee58fc717b990c4fcccf1b19af43103c090f601677fd8836",
...     "457743861de496c429912558a106b810b0507975a49773228aa788df40730d41",
...     "7688029288efc9e9a0011c960a6ed9e5466581abf3e3a6c26ee317461add619a",
...     "b1ae7f15836cb2286cdd4e2c37bf9bb7da0a2846d06867a429f654b2e7f383c9",
...     "9b74f89fa3f93e71ff2c241f32945d877281a6a50a6bf94adac002980aafe5ab",
...     "b3a92b5b255019bdaf754875633c2de9fec2ab03e6b8ce669d07cb5b18804638",
...     "b5c0b915312b9bdaedd2b86aa2d0f8feffc73a2d37668fd9010179261e25e263",
```

```
...         "c9d52c5cb1e557b92c84c52e7c4bfbce859408bedffc8a5560fd6e35e10b8800",
...         "c555bc5fc3bc096df0a0c9532f07640bfb76bfe4fc1ace214b8b228a1297a4c2",
...         "f9dbfafc3af3400954975da24eb325e326960a25b87fffe23eef3e7ed2fb610e",
... ]
>>> tree = MerkleTree(len(hex_hashes))
>>> tree.nodes[4] = [bytes.fromhex(h) for h in hex_hashes]
>>> tree.nodes[3] = merkle_parent_level(tree.nodes[4])
>>> tree.nodes[2] = merkle_parent_level(tree.nodes[3])
>>> tree.nodes[1] = merkle_parent_level(tree.nodes[2])
>>> tree.nodes[0] = merkle_parent_level(tree.nodes[1])
>>> print(tree)
*597c4baf.*
6382df3f..., 87cf8fa3...
3ba6c080..., 8e894862..., 7ab01bb6..., 3df760ac...
272945ec..., 9a38d037..., 4a64abd9..., ec7c95e1..., 3b67006c..., 850683df..., \
d40d268b..., 8636b7a3...
9745f717..., 5573c8ed..., 82a02ecb..., 507ccae5..., a7a4aec2..., bb626766..., \
ea6d7ac1..., 45774386..., 76880292..., b1ae7f15..., 9b74f89f..., b3a92b5b..., \
b5c0b915..., c9d52c5c..., c555bc5f..., f9dbfafc...
```

This fills the tree and gets us the Merkle root. However, the message from the network may not be giving us all of the leaves. The message might contain some internal nodes as well. We need a cleverer way to fill the tree.

Tree traversal is going to be the way we do this. We can do a depth-first traversal and only fill in the nodes that we can calculate. To traverse, we need to keep track of where exactly in the tree we are. The properties `self.current_depth` and `self.current_index` do this.

We need methods to traverse the Merkle tree. We'll also include other useful methods:

```
class MerkleTree:
...
    def up(self):
        self.current_depth -= 1
        self.current_index //= 2

    def left(self):
        self.current_depth += 1
        self.current_index *= 2

    def right(self):
        self.current_depth += 1
        self.current_index = self.current_index * 2 + 1

    def root(self):
        return self.nodes[0][0]

    def set_current_node(self, value):        ❶
        self.nodes[self.current_depth][self.current_index] = value

    def get_current_node(self):
```

```
            return self.nodes[self.current_depth][self.current_index]

    def get_left_node(self):
        return self.nodes[self.current_depth + 1][self.current_index * 2]

    def get_right_node(self):
        return self.nodes[self.current_depth + 1][self.current_index * 2 + 1]

    def is_leaf(self):  ❷
        return self.current_depth == self.max_depth

    def right_exists(self):  ❸
        return len(self.nodes[self.current_depth + 1]) > \
            self.current_index * 2 + 1
```

❶ We want the ability to set the current node in the tree to some value.

❷ We want to know if we are a leaf node.

❸ In certain situations, we won't have a right child because we may be at the furthest-right node of a level whose child level has an odd number of items.

We have Merkle tree traversal methods left, right, and up. Let's use these methods to populate the tree via depth-first traversal:

```
>>> from merkleblock import MerkleTree
>>> from helper import merkle_parent
>>> hex_hashes = [
...     "9745f7173ef14ee4155722d1cbf13304339fd00d900b759c6f9d58579b5765fb",
...     "5573c8ede34936c29cdfdfe743f7f5fdfbd4f54ba0705259e62f39917065cb9b",
...     "82a02ecbb6623b4274dfcab82b336dc017a27136e08521091e443e62582e8f05",
...     "507ccae5ed9b340363a0e6d765af148be9cb1c8766ccc922f83e4ae681658308",
...     "a7a4aec28e7162e1e9ef33dfa30f0bc0526e6cf4b11a576f6c5de58593898330",
...     "bb6267664bd833fd9fc82582853ab144fece26b7a8a5bf328f8a059445b59add",
...     "ea6d7ac1ee77fbacee58fc717b990c4fcccf1b19af43103c090f601677fd8836",
...     "457743861de496c429912558a106b810b0507975a49773228aa788df40730d41",
...     "7688029288efc9e9a0011c960a6ed9e5466581abf3e3a6c26ee317461add619a",
...     "b1ae7f15836cb2286cdd4e2c37bf9bb7da0a2846d06867a429f654b2e7f383c9",
...     "9b74f89fa3f93e71ff2c241f32945d877281a6a50a6bf94adac002980aafe5ab",
...     "b3a92b5b255019bdaf754875633c2de9fec2ab03e6b8ce669d07cb5b18804638",
...     "b5c0b915312b9bdaedd2b86aa2d0f8feffc73a2d37668fd9010179261e25e263",
...     "c9d52c5cb1e557b92c84c52e7c4bfbce859408bedffc8a5560fd6e35e10b8800",
...     "c555bc5fc3bc096df0a0c9532f07640bfb76bfe4fc1ace214b8b228a1297a4c2",
...     "f9dbfafc3af3400954975da24eb325e326960a25b87fffe23eef3e7ed2fb610e",
... ]
>>> tree = MerkleTree(len(hex_hashes))
>>> tree.nodes[4] = [bytes.fromhex(h) for h in hex_hashes]
>>> while tree.root() is None:  ❶
...     if tree.is_leaf():  ❷
...         tree.up()
...     else:
```

```
...             left_hash = tree.get_left_node()
...             right_hash = tree.get_right_node()
...             if left_hash is None:  ❸
...                 tree.left()
...             elif right_hash is None:  ❹
...                 tree.right()
...             else:  ❺
...                 tree.set_current_node(merkle_parent(left_hash, right_hash))
...                 tree.up()
>>> print(tree)
597c4baf...
6382df3f..., 87cf8fa3...
3ba6c080..., 8e894862..., 7ab01bb6..., 3df760ac...
272945ec..., 9a38d037..., 4a64abd9..., ec7c95e1..., 3b67006c..., 850683df..., \
d40d268b..., 8636b7a3...
9745f717..., 5573c8ed..., 82a02ecb..., 507ccae5..., a7a4aec2..., bb626766..., \
ea6d7ac1..., 45774386..., 76880292..., b1ae7f15..., 9b74f89f..., b3a92b5b..., \
b5c0b915..., c9d52c5c..., c555bc5f..., f9dbfafc...
```

❶ We traverse until we calculate the Merkle root. Each time through the loop, we are at a particular node.

❷ If we are at a leaf node, we already have that hash, so we don't need to do anything but go back up.

❸ If we don't have the left hash, then we calculate the value first before calculating the current node's hash.

❹ If we don't have the right hash, we calculate the value before calculating the current node's hash. Note that we already have the left one due to the depth-first traversal.

❺ We have both the left and the right hash, so we calculate the Merkle parent value and set that to the current node. Once set, we can go back up.

This code will only work when the number of leaves is a power of two, as edge cases where there are an odd number of nodes on a level are not handled.

We handle the case where the parent is the parent of the rightmost node on a level with an odd number of nodes:

```
>>> from merkleblock import MerkleTree
>>> from helper import merkle_parent
>>> hex_hashes = [
...     "9745f7173ef14ee4155722d1cbf13304339fd00d900b759c6f9d58579b5765fb",
...     "5573c8ede34936c29cdfdfe743f7f5fdfbd4f54ba0705259e62f39917065cb9b",
...     "82a02ecbb6623b4274dfcab82b336dc017a27136e08521091e443e62582e8f05",
...     "507ccae5ed9b340363a0e6d765af148be9cb1c8766ccc922f83e4ae681658308",
...     "a7a4aec28e7162e1e9ef33dfa30f0bc0526e6cf4b11a576f6c5de58593898330",
...     "bb6267664bd833fd9fc82582853ab144fece26b7a8a5bf328f8a059445b59add",
```

```
...         "ea6d7ac1ee77fbacee58fc717b990c4fcccf1b19af43103c090f601677fd8836",
...         "457743861de496c429912558a106b810b0507975a49773228aa788df40730d41",
...         "7688029288efc9e9a0011c960a6ed9e5466581abf3e3a6c26ee317461add619a",
...         "b1ae7f15836cb2286cdd4e2c37bf9bb7da0a2846d06867a429f654b2e7f383c9",
...         "9b74f89fa3f93e71ff2c241f32945d877281a6a50a6bf94adac002980aafe5ab",
...         "b3a92b5b255019bdaf754875633c2de9fec2ab03e6b8ce669d07cb5b18804638",
...         "b5c0b915312b9bdaedd2b86aa2d0f8feffc73a2d37668fd9010179261e25e263",
...         "c9d52c5cb1e557b92c84c52e7c4bfbce859408bedffc8a5560fd6e35e10b8800",
...         "c555bc5fc3bc096df0a0c9532f07640bfb76bfe4fc1ace214b8b228a1297a4c2",
...         "f9dbfafc3af3400954975da24eb325e326960a25b87fffe23eef3e7ed2fb610e",
...         "38faf8c811988dff0a7e6080b1771c97bcc0801c64d9068cffb85e6e7aacaf51",
... ]
>>> tree = MerkleTree(len(hex_hashes))
>>> tree.nodes[5] = [bytes.fromhex(h) for h in hex_hashes]
>>> while tree.root() is None:
...     if tree.is_leaf():
...         tree.up()
...     else:
...         left_hash = tree.get_left_node()
...         if left_hash is None:          ❶
...             tree.left()
...         elif tree.right_exists():       ❷
...             right_hash = tree.get_right_node()
...             if right_hash is None:      ❸
...                 tree.right()
...             else:                       ❹
...                 tree.set_current_node(merkle_parent(left_hash, right_hash))
...                 tree.up()
...         else:                           ❺
...             tree.set_current_node(merkle_parent(left_hash, left_hash))
...             tree.up()
>>> print(tree)
0a313864...
597c4baf..., 6f8a8190...
6382df3f..., 87cf8fa3..., 5647f416...
3ba6c080..., 8e894862..., 7ab01bb6..., 3df760ac..., 28e93b98...
272945ec..., 9a38d037..., 4a64abd9..., ec7c95e1..., 3b67006c..., 850683df..., \
d40d268b..., 8636b7a3..., ce26d40b...
9745f717..., 5573c8ed..., 82a02ecb..., 507ccae5..., a7a4aec2..., bb626766..., \
ea6d7ac1..., 45774386..., 76880292..., b1ae7f15..., 9b74f89f..., b3a92b5b..., \
b5c0b915..., c9d52c5c..., c555bc5f..., f9dbfafc..., 38faf8c8...
```

❶ If we don't have the left node's value, we traverse to the left node, since all internal nodes are guaranteed a left child.

❷ We check first if this node has a right child. This is true unless this node happens to be the rightmost node and the child level has an odd number of nodes.

❸ If we don't have the right node's value, we traverse to that node.

❹ If we have both the left and the right node's values, we calculate the current node's value using `merkle_parent`.

❺ We have the left node's value, but the right child doesn't exist. This is the rightmost node of this level, so we combine the left value twice.

We can now traverse the tree for the number of leaves that aren't powers of two.

The merkleblock Command

The full node communicating a Merkle block sends all the information needed to verify that the interesting transaction is in the Merkle tree. The `merkleblock` network command is what communicates this information; it looks like Figure 11-6.

```
00000020df3b053dc46f162a9b00c7f0d5124e2676d47bbe7c5d0793a500000000000000ef445fef2
ed495c275892206ca533e7411907971013ab83e3b47bd0d692d14d4dc7c835b67d8001ac157e670bf
0d00000aba412a0d1480e370173072c9562becffe87aa661c1e4a6dbc305d38ec5dc088a7cf92e645
8aca7b32edae818f9c2c98c37e06bf72ae0ce80649a38655ee1e27d34d9421d940b16732f24b94023
e9d572a7f9ab8023434a4feb532d2adfc8c2c2158785d1bd04eb99df2e86c54bc13e1398628972174
00def5d72c280222c4cbaee7261831e1550dbb8fa82853e9fe506fc5fda3f7b919d8fe74b6282f927
63cef8e625f977af7c8619c32a369b832bc2d051ecd9c73c51e76370ceabd4f25097c256597fa898d
404ed53425de608ac6bfe426f6e2bb457f1c554866eb69dcb8d6bf6f880e9a59b3cd053e6c7060eea
caacf4dac6697dac20e4bd3f38a2ea2543d1ab7953e3430790a9f81e1c67f5b58c825acf46bd02848
384eebe9af917274cdfbb1a28a5d58a23a17977def0de10d644258d9c54f886d47d293a411cb62261
03b55635

                - 00000020 - version, 4 bytes, LE
                - df3b...00 - previous block, 32 bytes, LE
                - ef44...d4 - Merkle root, 32 bytes, LE
                - dc7c835b - timestamp, 4 bytes, LE
                - 67d8001a - bits, 4 bytes
                - c157e670 - nonce, 4 bytes
                - bf0d0000 - number of total transactions, 4 bytes, LE
                - 0a - number of hashes, varint
                - ba41...61 - hashes, 32 bytes * number of hashes
                - 03b55635 - flag bits
```

Figure 11-6. Parsed merkleblock

The first six fields are exactly the same as the block header from Chapter 9. The last four fields are the proof of inclusion.

The number of transactions field indicates how many leaves this particular Merkle tree will have. This allows a light client to construct an empty Merkle tree. The hashes field holds the blue and green boxes from Figure 11-5. Since the number of hashes in the hashes field is not fixed, it's prefixed with how many there are. Last, the flags field gives information about where the hashes go within the Merkle tree. The flags are parsed using `bytes_to_bits_field` to convert them to a list of bits (1's and 0's):

```
def bytes_to_bit_field(some_bytes):
    flag_bits = []
    for byte in some_bytes:
        for _ in range(8):
            flag_bits.append(byte & 1)
            byte >>= 1
    return flag_bits
```

The ordering for the bytes is a bit strange, but it's meant to be easy to convert into the flag bits needed to reconstruct the Merkle root.

Exercise 6

Write the `parse` method for `MerkleBlock`.

Using Flag Bits and Hashes

The flag bits inform where the hashes go using depth-first ordering.

The rules for the flag bits are:

1. If the node's value is given in the hashes field (blue box in Figure 11-7), the flag bit is 0.

2. If the node is an internal node and the value is to be calculated by the light client (dotted outline in Figure 11-7), the flag bit is 1.

3. If the node is a leaf node and is a transaction of interest (green box in Figure 11-7), the flag is 1 and the node's value is also given in the hashes field. These are the items proven to be included in the Merkle tree.

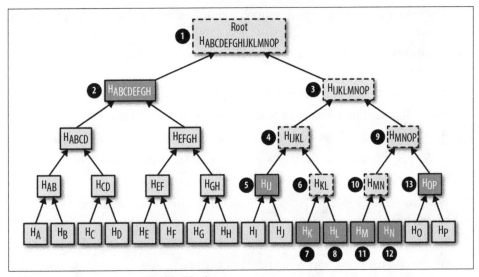

Figure 11-7. Processing a Merkle block

Given the tree from Figure 11-7:

- The flag bit is 1 for the root node (1), since that hash is calculated by the light client.
- The left child, $H_{ABCDEFGH}$ (2), is included in the hashes field, so the flag is 0.
- From here, we traverse to $H_{IJKLMNOP}$ (3) instead of H_{ABCD} or H_{EFGH} since $H_{ABCDEFGH}$ represents both those nodes and we don't need them.
- The right child, $H_{IJKLMNOP}$, is also calculated, so it has a flag bit of 1.
- To calculate $H_{IJKLMNOP}$, we need the values for H_{IJKL} and H_{MNOP} (9). The next node in depth-first order is the left child, H_{IJKL} (4), which is where we traverse to next.
- H_{IJKL} is an internal node that's calculated, so the flag bit is 1.
- From here, we traverse to its left child, H_{IJ} (5). We will be traversing to H_{KL} (6) when we come back to this node.
- H_{IJ} is next in depth-first ordering; its hash is included in the hashes list and the flag is 0.
- H_{KL} is an internal, calculated node, so the flag is 1.
- H_K (7) is a leaf node whose presence in the block is being proved, so the flag is 1.
- H_L (8) is a node whose value is included in the hashes field, so the flag is 0.
- We traverse up to H_{KL}, whose value can now be calculated since H_K and H_L are known.

- We traverse up to H_{IJKL}, whose value can now be calculated since H_{IJ} and H_{KL} are known.
- We traverse up to $H_{IJKLMNOP}$, whose value we can't calculate yet since we haven't been to H_{MNOP}.
- We traverse to H_{MNOP}, which is another internal node, so the flag is 1.
- H_{MN} (10) is another internal node that's calculated, so the flag is 1.
- H_M (11) is a node whose value is included in the hashes field, so the flag is 0.
- H_N (12) is of interest, so the flag is 1 and its value is in the hashes field.
- We traverse up to H_{MN}, whose value can now be calculated.
- We traverse up again to H_{MNOP}, whose value cannot be calculated because we haven't been to H_{OP} yet.
- H_{OP} (13) is given, so the flag is 1 and its hash is the final hash in the hashes field.
- We traverse to H_{MNOP}, which can now be calculated.
- We traverse to $H_{IJKLMNOP}$, which can now be calculated.
- Finally, we traverse to $H_{ABCDEFGHIJKLMNOP}$, which is the Merkle root, and calculate it!

The flag bits for nodes (1) through (13) are:

```
1, 0, 1, 1, 0, 1, 1, 0, 1, 1, 0, 1, 0
```

There should be seven hashes in the hashes field, in this order:

- $H_{ABCDEFGH}$
- H_{IJ}
- H_K
- H_L
- H_M
- H_N
- H_{OP}

Notice that every letter is represented in the hashes, A to P. This information is sufficient to prove that H_K and H_N (the green boxes in Figure 11-7) are included in the block.

As you can see from Figure 11-7, the flag bits are given in depth-first order. Anytime we're given a hash, as with $H_{ABCDEFGH}$, we skip its children and continue. In the case of $H_{ABCDEFGH}$, we traverse to $H_{IJKLMNOP}$ instead of H_{ABCD}. Flag bits are a clever mechanism to encode which nodes have which hash value.

We can now populate the Merkle tree and calculate the root, given the appropriate flag bits and hashes:

```
class MerkleTree:
...
    def populate_tree(self, flag_bits, hashes):
        while self.root() is None:  ❶
            if self.is_leaf():  ❷
                flag_bits.pop(0)  ❸
                self.set_current_node(hashes.pop(0))  ❹
                self.up()
            else:
                left_hash = self.get_left_node()
                if left_hash is None:  ❺
                    if flag_bits.pop(0) == 0:  ❻
                        self.set_current_node(hashes.pop(0))
                        self.up()
                    else:
                        self.left()  ❼
                elif self.right_exists():  ❽
                    right_hash = self.get_right_node()
                    if right_hash is None:  ❾
                        self.right()
                    else:  ❿
                        self.set_current_node(merkle_parent(left_hash,
                        right_hash))
                        self.up()
                else:  ⓫
                    self.set_current_node(merkle_parent(left_hash, left_hash))
                    self.up()
        if len(hashes) != 0:  ⓬
            raise RuntimeError('hashes not all consumed {}'.format(len(hashes)))
        for flag_bit in flag_bits:  ⓭
            if flag_bit != 0:
                raise RuntimeError('flag bits not all consumed')
```

❶ The point of populating this Merkle tree is to calculate the root. Each loop iteration processes one node until the root is calculated.

❷ For leaf nodes, we are always given the hash.

❸ `flag_bits.pop(0)` is a way in Python to dequeue the next flag bit. We may want to keep track of which hashes are of interest to us by looking at the flag bit, but for now, we don't do this.

❹ `hashes.pop(0)` is how we get the next hash from the hashes field. We need to set the current node to that hash.

⑤ If we don't have the left child value, there are two possibilities. This node's value may be in the hashes field, or it might need calculation.

⑥ The next flag bit tells us whether we need to calculate this node or not. If the flag bit is 0, the next hash in the hashes field is this node's value. If the flag bit is 1, we need to calculate the left (and possibly the right) node's value.

⑦ We are guaranteed that there's a left child, so we traverse to that node and get its value.

⑧ We check that the right node exists.

⑨ We have the left hash, but not the right. We traverse to the right node to get its value.

⑩ We have both the left and the right node's values, so we calculate their Merkle parent to get the current node's value.

⑪ We have the left node's value, but the right does not exist. In this case, according to Merkle tree rules, we calculate the Merkle parent of the left node twice.

⑫ All hashes must be consumed or we got bad data.

⑬ All flag bits must be consumed or we got bad data.

Exercise 7

Write the `is_valid` method for `MerkleBlock`.

Conclusion

Simplified payment verification is useful but not without some significant downsides. The full details are outside the scope of this book, but despite the programming being pretty straightforward, most light wallets do not use SPV and instead trust data from the wallet vendor servers. The main drawback of SPV is that the nodes you are connecting to know something about the transactions you are interested in. That is, you lose some privacy by using SPV. This will be covered in more detail in Chapter 12 as we make Bloom filters to tell nodes what transactions we are interested in.

CHAPTER 12

Bloom Filters

In Chapter 11 we learned how to validate a Merkle block. A full node can provide a proof of inclusion for transactions of interest through the merkleblock command. But how does the full node know which transactions are of interest?

A light client could tell the full node its addresses (or ScriptPubKeys). The full node can check for transactions that are relevant to these addresses, but that would be compromising the light client's privacy. A light client wouldn't want to reveal, for example, that it has 1,000 BTC to a full node. Privacy leaks are security leaks, and in Bitcoin, it's generally a good idea to not leak any privacy whenever possible.

One solution is for the light client to tell the full node enough information to create a *superset* of all transactions of interest. To create this superset, we use what's called a *Bloom filter*.

What Is a Bloom Filter?

A Bloom filter is a filter for all possible transactions. Full nodes run transactions through a Bloom filter and send merkleblock commands for transactions that make it through.

Suppose there are 50 total transactions. There is one transaction a light client is interested in. The light client wants to "hide" the transaction among a group of five transactions. This requires a function that groups the 50 transactions into 10 different buckets, and the full node can then send a single bucket of transactions, in a manner of speaking. This grouping would have to be *deterministic*—that is, be the same each time. How can this be accomplished?

The solution is to use a hash function to get a deterministic number and modulo to organize transactions into buckets.

A Bloom filter is a computer science structure that can be used on any data in a set, so suppose that we have one item, "hello world", that we want to create a Bloom filter for. We need a hash function, so we'll use one we already have: hash256. The process of figuring out what bucket our item goes into looks like this:

```
>>> from helper import hash256
>>> bit_field_size = 10  ❶
>>> bit_field = [0] * bit_field_size
>>> h = hash256(b'hello world')  ❷
>>> bit = int.from_bytes(h, 'big') % bit_field_size  ❸
>>> bit_field[bit] = 1  ❹
>>> print(bit_field)
[0, 0, 0, 0, 0, 0, 0, 0, 0, 1]
```

❶ Our `bit_field` is the list of "buckets," and we want there to be 10.

❷ We hash the item with hash256.

❸ We interpret this as a big-endian integer and modulo by 10 to determine the bucket this item belongs to.

❹ We indicate the bucket we want in the Bloom filter.

Conceptually, what we just did looks like Figure 12-1.

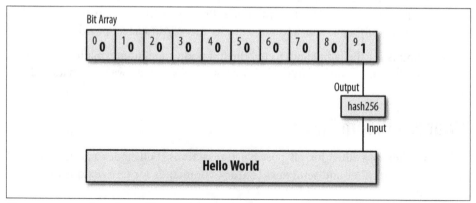

Figure 12-1. 10-bit Bloom filter with one element

Our Bloom filter consists of:

1. The size of the bit field

2. The hash function used (and how we converted that to a number)

3. The bit field, which indicates the bucket we're interested in

This works great for a single item, so it would work for a single address/ScriptPub-Key/transaction ID of interest. What do we do when we're interested in more than one item?

We can run a second item through the same filter and set that bit to 1 as well. The full node can then send multiple buckets of transactions instead of a single bucket. Let's create a Bloom filter with two items, "hello world" and "goodbye", using the following code:

```
>>> from helper import hash256
>>> bit_field_size = 10
>>> bit_field = [0] * bit_field_size
>>> for item in (b'hello world', b'goodbye'):  ❶
...     h = hash256(item)
...     bit = int.from_bytes(h, 'big') % bit_field_size
...     bit_field[bit] = 1
>>> print(bit_field)
[0, 0, 1, 0, 0, 0, 0, 0, 0, 1]
```

❶ We are creating a filter for two items here, but this can be extended to many more.

Figure 12-2 shows what this looks like conceptually.

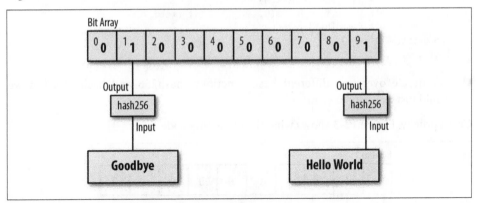

Figure 12-2. 10-bit Bloom filter with two elements

If the space of all possible items is 50, 10 items on average will make it through this filter instead of the 5 when we only had 1 item of interest, because 2 buckets are returned, not 1.

Exercise 1

Calculate the Bloom Filter for "hello world" and "goodbye" using the hash160 hash function over a bit field of 10.

Going a Step Further

Suppose that the space of all items is 1 million and we want bucket sizes to still be 5. We would need a Bloom filter that's 1,000,000 / 5 = 200,000 bits long. Each bucket would have on average 5 items and we would get 5 times the number of items we're interested in, 20% of which would be items of interest. 200,000 bits is 25,000 bytes and is a lot to transmit. Can we do better?

A Bloom filter using multiple hash functions can shorten the bit field considerably. If we use 5 hash functions over a bit field of 32, we have 32!/(27!5!) ~ 200,000 possible 5-bit combinations in that 32-bit field. Of 1 million possible items, 5 items on average should have that 5-bit combination. Instead of transmitting 25K bytes, we can transmit just 32 bits, or 4 bytes!

Here's what that would look like. For simplicity, we stick to the same 10-bit field but still have two items of interest:

```
>>> from helper import hash256, hash160
>>> bit_field_size = 10
>>> bit_field = [0] * bit_field_size
>>> for item in (b'hello world', b'goodbye'):
...     for hash_function in (hash256, hash160):  ❶
...         h = hash_function(item)
...         bit = int.from_bytes(h, 'big') % bit_field_size
...         bit_field[bit] = 1
>>> print(bit_field)
[1, 1, 1, 0, 0, 0, 0, 0, 0, 1]
```

❶ We iterate over two different hash functions (hash256 and hash160), but we could just as easily have more.

Conceptually, Figure 12-3 shows what the preceding code does.

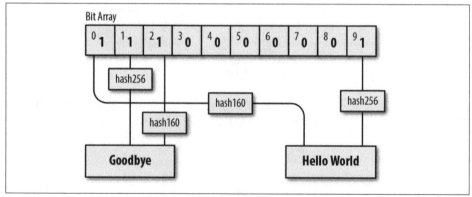

Figure 12-3. 10-bit Bloom filter with two elements and two hash functions

A Bloom filter can be optimized by changing the number of hash functions and bit field size to get a desirable false-positive rate.

BIP0037 Bloom Filters

BIP0037 specifies Bloom filters in network communication. The information contained in a Bloom filter is:

1. The size of the bit field, or how many buckets there are. The size is specified in bytes (8 bits per byte) and rounded up if necessary.
2. The number of hash functions.
3. A "tweak" to be able to change the Bloom filter slightly if it hits too many items.
4. The bit field that results from running the Bloom filter over the items of interest.

While we could define lots of hash functions (sha512, keccak384, ripemd160, blake256, etc.), in practice, we use a single hash function with a different seed. This allows the implementation to be simpler.

The hash function we use is called *murmur3*. Unlike sha256, murmur3 is not cryptographically secure, but it is much faster. The task of filtering and getting a deterministic, evenly distributed modulo does not require cryptographic security but benefits from speed, so murmur3 is the appropriate tool for the job. The seed formula is defined this way:

```
i*0xfba4c795 + tweak
```

`fba4c795` is a constant for Bitcoin Bloom filters. `i` is 0 for the first hash function, 1 for the second, 2 for the third, and so on. The `tweak` is a bit of entropy that can be added if the results of of one tweak are not satisfactory. The hash functions and the size of the bit field are used to calculate the bit field, which then gets transmitted:

```
>>> from helper import murmur3          ❶
>>> from bloomfilter import BIP37_CONSTANT   ❷
>>> field_size = 2
>>> num_functions = 2
>>> tweak = 42
>>> bit_field_size = field_size * 8
>>> bit_field = [0] * bit_field_size
>>> for phrase in (b'hello world', b'goodbye'):   ❸
...     for i in range(num_functions):     ❹
...         seed = i * BIP37_CONSTANT + tweak    ❺
...         h = murmur3(phrase, seed=seed)     ❻
...         bit = h % bit_field_size
...         bit_field[bit] = 1
>>> print(bit_field)
[0, 0, 0, 0, 0, 1, 1, 0, 0, 1, 1, 0, 0, 0, 0, 0]
```

❶ murmur3 is implemented in pure Python in *helper.py*.

❷ BIP37_CONSTANT is the fba4c795 number specified in BIP0037.

❸ We iterate over some items of interest.

❹ We use two hash functions.

❺ This is the seed formula.

❻ murmur3 returns a number, so we don't have to do a conversion to an integer.

This 2-byte Bloom filter has 4 bits set to 1 out of 16, so the probability of any random item passing through this filter is $1/4 \times 1/4 = 1/16$. If the space of all items numbers 160, a client will receive 10 items on average, 2 of which will be interesting.

We can start coding a BloomFilter class now:

```
class BloomFilter:

    def __init__(self, size, function_count, tweak):
        self.size = size
        self.bit_field = [0] * (size * 8)
        self.function_count = function_count
        self.tweak = tweak
```

Exercise 2

Given a Bloom Filter with size=10, function_count=5, tweak=99, what are the bytes that are set after adding these items? (Use bit_field_to_bytes to convert to bytes.)

- b'Hello World'
- b'Goodbye!'

Exercise 3

Write the add method for BloomFilter.

Loading a Bloom Filter

Once a light client has created a Bloom filter, it needs to let the full node know the details of the filter so the full node can send proofs of inclusion. The first thing a light client must do is set the optional relay flag in the version message (see Chapter 10) to 0. This tells the full node not to send transaction messages unless they match a Bloom filter or they have been specifically requested. After the relay flag, a light client then communicates to the full node the Bloom filter itself. The command to set the Bloom filter is called `filterload`. The payload looks like Figure 12-4.

```
0a4000600a08000001094005000000063000000000

- 0a4000600a080000010940 - Bit field, variable field
- 05000000 - Hash count, 4 bytes, little-endian
- 63000000 - Tweak, 4 bytes, little-endian
- 00 - Matched item flag
```

Figure 12-4. Parsed filterload

The elements of a Bloom filter are encoded into bytes. The bit field, hash function count, and tweak are encoded in this message. The last field, matched item flag, is a way of asking the full node to add any matched transactions to the Bloom filter.

Exercise 4

Write the `filterload` method for the `BloomFilter` class.

Getting Merkle Blocks

There is one more command that a light client needs: Merkle block information about transactions of interest from the full node. The `getdata` command is what communicates blocks and transactions. The specific type of data that a light client will want from a full node is something called a *filtered block*. A filtered block is asking for transactions that pass through the Bloom filter in the form of Merkle blocks. In other words, the light client can ask for Merkle blocks whose transactions of interest match the Bloom filter.

Figure 12-5 depicts the payload for `getdata`.

```
020300000030eb2540c41025690160a1014c577061596e32e426b712c7ca000
0000000000000300000001049847939585b0652fba793661c361223446b6fc410
89b8be00000000000000

        - 02 - Number of data items
        - 03000000 - Type of data item (tx, block, filtered
                    block, compact block), little-endian
        - 30...00 - Hash identifier
```

Figure 12-5. Parsed getdata

The number of items as a varint specifies how many items we want. Each item has a type. A type value of 1 is a transaction (Chapter 5), 2 is a normal block (Chapter 9), 3 is a Merkle block (Chapter 11), and 4 is a compact block (not covered in this book).

We can create this message in *network.py*:

```
class GetDataMessage:
    command = b'getdata'

    def __init__(self):
        self.data = []      ❶

    def add_data(self, data_type, identifier):
        self.data.append((data_type, identifier))      ❷
```

❶ We store the items we want.

❷ We add items to the message using the add_data method.

Exercise 5

Write the serialize method for the GetDataMessage class.

Getting Transactions of Interest

A light client that loads a Bloom filter with a full node will get all the information needed to prove that transactions of interest are included in particular blocks:

```
>>> from bloomfilter import BloomFilter
>>> from helper import decode_base58
>>> from merkleblock import MerkleBlock
>>> from network import FILTERED_BLOCK_DATA_TYPE, GetHeadersMessage, GetDataMe\
ssage, HeadersMessage, SimpleNode
>>> from tx import Tx
>>> last_block_hex = '00000000000538d5c2246336644f9a4956551afb44ba47278759ec55\
ea912e19'
>>> address = 'mwJn1YPMq7y5F8J3LkC5Hxg9PHyZ5K4cFv'
>>> h160 = decode_base58(address)
>>> node = SimpleNode('testnet.programmingbitcoin.com', testnet=True, logging=\
False)
>>> bf = BloomFilter(size=30, function_count=5, tweak=90210)      ❶
>>> bf.add(h160)      ❷
>>> node.handshake()
>>> node.send(bf.filterload())      ❸
>>> start_block = bytes.fromhex(last_block_hex)
>>> getheaders = GetHeadersMessage(start_block=start_block)
>>> node.send(getheaders)      ❹
>>> headers = node.wait_for(HeadersMessage)
>>> getdata = GetDataMessage()      ❺
>>> for b in headers.blocks:
...     if not b.check_pow():
...         raise RuntimeError('proof of work is invalid')
...     getdata.add_data(FILTERED_BLOCK_DATA_TYPE, b.hash())      ❻
>>> node.send(getdata)      ❼
```

```
>>> found = False
>>> while not found:
...     message = node.wait_for(MerkleBlock, Tx)  ❽
...     if message.command == b'merkleblock':
...         if not message.is_valid():  ❾
...             raise RuntimeError('invalid merkle proof')
...     else:
...         for i, tx_out in enumerate(message.tx_outs):
...             if tx_out.script_pubkey.address(testnet=True) == address:  ❿
...                 print('found: {}:{}'.format(message.id(), i))
...                 found = True
...                 break
found: e3930e1e566ca9b75d53b0eb9acb7607f547e1182d1d22bd4b661cfe18dcddf1:0
```

❶ We are creating a Bloom filter that's 30 bytes and uses 5 hash functions and a particularly popular '90s tweak.

❷ We filter for the address above.

❸ We send the `filterload` command from the Bloom filter we made.

❹ We get the block headers after `last_block_hex`.

❺ We create a getdata message for Merkle blocks that may have transactions of interest.

❻ We request a Merkle block proving transactions of interest to us are included. Most blocks will probably be complete misses.

❼ The getdata message asks for 2,000 Merkle blocks after the block defined by `last_block_hex`.

❽ We wait for the `merkleblock` command, which proves inclusion, and the `tx` command, which gives us the transaction of interest.

❾ We check that the Merkle block proves transaction inclusion.

❿ We're looking for UTXOs for `address`, and we print to screen if we find one.

What we've done is look at 2,000 blocks after a particular block for UTXOs corresponding to a particular address. This is without the use of any block explorer, which preserves, to some degree, our privacy.

Exercise 6

Get the current testnet block ID, send yourself some testnet coins, find the UTXO corresponding to the testnet coins *without using a block explorer*, create a transaction using that UTXO as an input, and broadcast the tx message on the testnet network.

Conclusion

In this chapter, we created everything necessary to connect peer to peer as a light client and ask for and receive the UTXOs necessary to construct a transaction, all while preserving some privacy by using a Bloom filter.

We now turn to Segwit, which is a new type of transaction that was activated in 2017.

CHAPTER 13

Segwit

Segwit stands for "segregated witness" and is a backward-compatible upgrade or "soft fork" that activated on the Bitcoin network in August 2017. While the activation was controversial, the features of this technology require some explanation. In this chapter, we'll explore how Segwit works, why it's backward compatible, and what Segwit enables.

As a brief overview, Segwit incorporated a multitude of changes:

- Block size increase
- Transaction malleability fix
- Segwit versioning for clear upgrade paths
- Quadratic hashing fix
- Offline wallet fee calculation security

It's not entirely obvious what Segwit is without looking at how it's implemented. We'll start by examining the most basic type of Segwit transaction, pay-to-witness-pubkey-hash.

Pay-to-Witness-Pubkey-Hash (p2wpkh)

Pay-to-witness-pubkey-hash (p2wpkh) is one of four types of scripts defined by Segwit in BIP0141 and BIP0143. This is a smart contract that acts a lot like pay-to-pubkey-hash and is named similarly for that reason. The main change from p2pkh is that the data for the ScriptSig is now in the witness field. The rearrangement is to fix transaction malleability.

Transaction Malleability

Transaction malleability is the ability to change the transaction's ID without altering the transaction's meaning. Mt. Gox CEO Mark Karpeles cited transaction malleability as the reason why his exchange was not allowing withdrawals back in 2013.

Malleability of the ID is an important consideration when creating payment channels, which are the atomic unit of the Lightning Network. A malleable transaction ID makes the safe creation of payment channel transactions much more difficult.

The reason why transaction malleability is a problem at all is because the transaction ID is calculated from the entire transaction. The ID of the transaction is the hash256 of the transaction. Most of the fields in a transaction cannot be changed without invalidating the transaction's signature (and thus the transaction itself), so from a malleability standpoint, these fields are not a problem.

The one field that does allow for some manipulation without invalidating the signature is the ScriptSig field on each input. The ScriptSig is emptied before creating the signature hash (see Chapter 7), so it's possible to change the ScriptSig without invalidating the signature. Also, as we learned in Chapter 3, signatures contain a random component. This means that two different ScriptSigs can essentially mean the same thing but be different byte-wise.

This makes the ScriptSig field *malleable*—that is, able to be changed without changing the meaning—and means that the entire transaction, and the transaction ID, are malleable. A malleable transaction ID means that any *dependent* transactions (that is, any transaction spending one of the malleable transaction's outputs) cannot be constructed in such a way as to guarantee validity. The previous transaction hash is uncertain, so the dependent transaction's transaction input field cannot be guaranteed to be valid.

This is not usually a problem as once a transaction enters the blockchain, the transaction ID is fixed and no longer malleable (at least without finding a proof-of-work!). However, with payment channels, there are dependent transactions created *before* the funding transaction is added to the blockchain.

Fixing Malleability

Transaction malleability is fixed by emptying the ScriptSig field and putting the data in another field that's not used for ID calculation. For p2wpkh, the signature and pubkey are the items from ScriptSig, so those get moved to the witness field, which is not used for ID calculation. This way, the transaction ID stays stable as the malleability vector disappears. The witness field, and the whole Segwit serialization of a transaction, is only sent to nodes that ask for it. In other words, old nodes that haven't upgraded to Segwit don't receive the witness field and don't verify the pubkey and signature.

If this sounds familiar, it should. This is similar to how p2sh works (Chapter 8) in that newer nodes do additional validation that older nodes do not, and is the basis for why Segwit is a soft fork (backward-compatible upgrade) and not a hard fork (backward-incompatible upgrade).

p2wpkh Transactions

To understand Segwit, it helps to look at what a transaction looks like when sent to an old node (Figure 13-1) versus a new node (Figure 13-2).

```
010000000115e180dc28a2327e687facc33f10f2a20da717e5548406f7ae8b4c811072f8560100000
000ffffffff0100b4f505000000001976a9141d7cd6c75c2e86f4cbf98eaed221b30bd9a0b92888ac
00000000

                - 01000000 - version
                - 01 - # of inputs
                - 15e1...56 - previous tx hash
                - 01000000 - previous tx index
                - 00 - ScriptSig
                - ffffffff - sequence
                - 01 - # of outputs
                - 00b4...00 - output amounts
                - 1976...ac - ScriptPubKey
                - 00000000 - locktime
```

Figure 13-1. Pay-to-witness-pubkey-hash (p2wpkh) as seen by pre-BIP0141 software

```
010000000000010115e180dc28a2327e687facc33f10f2a20da717e5548406f7ae8b4c811072f856010
0000000ffffffff0100b4f505000000001976a9141d7cd6c75c2e86f4cbf98eaed221b30bd9a0b928
88ac02483045022100df7b7e5cda14ddf91290e02ea10786e03eb11ee36ec02dd862fe9a326bbcb7f
d02203f5b4496b667e6e281cc654a2da9e4f08660c620a1051337fa8965f727eb19190121038262a6
c6cec93c2d3ecd6c6072efea86d02ff8e3328bbd0242b20af3425990ac00000000

                - 01000000 - version
                - 00 - Segwit marker
                - 01 - Segwit flag
                - 01 - # of inputs
                - 15e1...56 - previous tx hash
                - 01000000 - previous tx index
                - 00 - ScriptSig
                - ffffffff - sequence
                - 01 - # of outputs
                - 00b4...00 - output amounts
                - 1976...ac - ScriptPubKey
                - 0248...ac - witness
                - 00000000 - locktime
```

Figure 13-2. Pay-to-witness-pubkey-hash (p2wpkh) as seen by post-BIP0141 software

The difference between these two serializations is that the latter transaction (Segwit serialization) has the marker, flag, and witness fields. Otherwise, the two transactions look similar. The reason the transaction ID is not malleable is because the first serialization is used for calculating the transaction ID.

The witness field in p2wpkh has the signature and pubkey as its two elements. These will be used for validation for upgraded nodes only.

The ScriptPubKey for p2wpkh is OP_0 *<20-byte hash>*. The ScriptSig, as seen in both serializations, is empty. The combined script is shown in Figure 13-3.

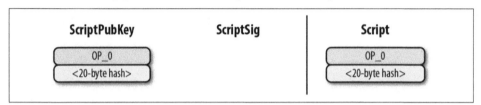

Figure 13-3. Pay-to-witness-pubkey-hash (p2wpkh) ScriptPubKey

The processing of the combined script starts like Figure 13-4.

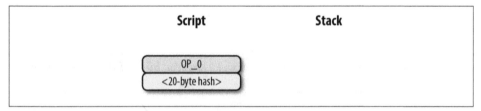

Figure 13-4. p2wpkh start

OP_0 pushes a 0 to the stack (Figure 13-5).

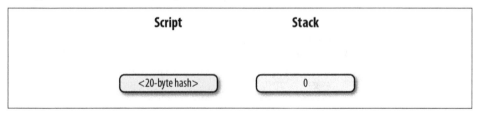

Figure 13-5. p2wpkh step 1

The 20-byte hash is an element, so it's pushed to the stack (Figure 13-6).

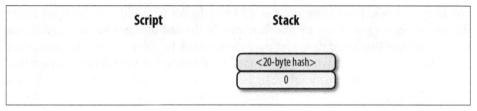

Figure 13-6. p2wpkh step 2

At this point, older nodes will stop as there are no more Script commands to be processed. Since the top element is nonzero, this will be counted as a valid script. This is very similar to p2sh (Chapter 8) in that older nodes cannot validate further. Newer nodes, however, have a special Segwit rule much like the special rule for p2sh (see Chapter 8). Recall that with p2sh, the exact script sequence of *<RedeemScript>* OP_HASH160 *<hash>* OP_EQUAL triggers a special rule.

In the case of p2wpkh, the script sequence is OP_0 *<20-byte hash>*. When that script sequence is encountered, the pubkey and signature from the witness field and the 20-byte hash are added to the command set in exactly the same sequence as with p2pkh, namely *<signature>* *<pubkey>* OP_DUP OP_HASH160 *<20-byte hash>* OP_EQUALVERIFY OP_CHECKSIG. Figure 13-7 shows the state that is encountered next.

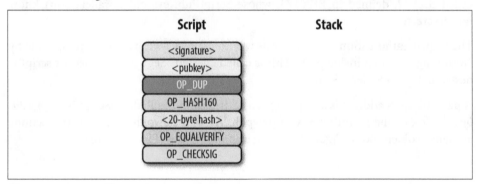

Figure 13-7. p2wpkh step 3

The rest of the processing of p2wpkh is the same as the processing of p2pkh, as seen in Chapter 6. The end state is a single 1 on the stack if and only if the 20-byte hash is the hash160 of the pubkey and the signature is valid (Figure 13-8).

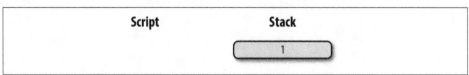

Figure 13-8. p2wpkh step 4

For an older node, processing stops at *<20-byte hash>* 0, as older nodes don't know the special Segwit rule. Only upgraded nodes do the rest of the validation, much like with p2sh. Note that less data is sent over the network to older nodes. Also, nodes are given the option of not having to download (and hence not verify) transactions that are *x* blocks old if they don't want to. In a sense, the signature has been witnessed by a bunch of people and a node can choose to trust that this is valid instead of validating directly if it so chooses.

Note also that this is a special rule for Segwit version 0. Segwit version 1 can have a completely different processing path. *<20-byte hash>* 1 could be the special script sequence that triggers a different rule. Upgrades of Segwit can introduce Schnorr signatures, Graftroot, or even a different scripting system altogether, like Simplicity. Segwit gives us a clear upgrade path. Software that understands how to validate Segwit version X will validate such transactions, but software that isn't aware of Segwit version X simply processes only up to the point of the special rule.

p2sh-p2wpkh

p2wpkh is great, but unfortunately, this is a new type of script and older wallets cannot send bitcoins to p2wpkh ScriptPubKeys. p2wpkh uses a new address format called Bech32, defined in BIP0173, whose ScriptPubKeys older wallets don't know how to create.

The Segwit authors found an ingenious way to make Segwit backward compatible by "wrapping" p2wpkh inside p2sh. This is called "nested" Segwit as the Segwit script is nested in a p2sh RedeemScript.

A p2sh-p2wpkh address is a normal p2sh address, but the RedeemScript is OP_0 *<20-byte hash>*, or the ScriptPubKey of p2wpkh. As with p2wpkh, different transactions are sent to older nodes (Figure 13-9) versus newer nodes (Figure 13-10).

```
0100000001712e5b4e97ab549d50ca60a4f5968b2225215e9fab82dae4720078711406972f0000000
017160014848202fc47fb475289652fbd1912cc853ecb0096feffffff0232360000000000001976a9
14121ae7a2d55d2f0102ccc117cbcb70041b0e037f88ac10270000000000001976a914ec0be509516
51261765cfa71d7bd41c7b9245bb388ac075a0700
```

```
      - 01000000 - version
      - 01 - # of inputs
      - 712e...2f - previous tx hash
      - 00000000 - previous tx index
      - 1716...96 - ScriptSig
      - feffffff - sequence
      - 02 - # of outputs
      - 3236...00 - output amounts
      - 1976...ac - ScriptPubKey
      - 075a0700 - locktime
```

Figure 13-9. Pay-to-script-hash-pay-to-witness-pubkey-hash (p2sh-p2wpkh) to pre-BIP0141 software

```
010000000000101712e5b4e97ab549d50ca60a4f5968b2225215e9fab82dae4720078711406972f000
0000017160014848202fc47fb475289652fbd1912cc853ecb0096feffffff023236000000000000019
76a914121ae7a2d55d2f0102ccc117cbcb70041b0e037f88ac10270000000000001976a914ec0be50
951651261765cfa71d7bd41c7b9245bb388ac024830450221009263c7de80c297d5b21aba846cf6f0
a970e1d339568167d1e4c1355c7711bc1602202c9312b8d32fd9c7acc54c46cab50eb7255ce3c0122
14c41fe1ad91bccb16a13012102ebdf6fc448431a2bd6380f912a0fa6ca291ca3340e79b6f0c1fdaf
f73cf54061075a0700
```

```
      - 01000000 - version
      - 00 - Segwit marker
      - 01 - Segwit flag
      - 01 - # of inputs
      - 712e...2f - previous tx hash
      - 00000000 - previous tx index
      - 1716...96 - ScriptSig
      - feffffff - sequence
      - 02 - # of outputs
      - 3236...00 - output amounts
      - 1976...ac - ScriptPubKey
      - 0248...61 - witness
      - 075a0700 - locktime
```

Figure 13-10. p2sh-p2wpkh to post-BIP0141 software

The difference from p2wpkh is that the ScriptSig is no longer empty. The ScriptSig has a RedeemScript, which is equal to the ScriptPubkey in p2wpkh. As this is a p2sh script, the ScriptPubKey is the same as in any other p2sh script. The combined script looks like Figure 13-11.

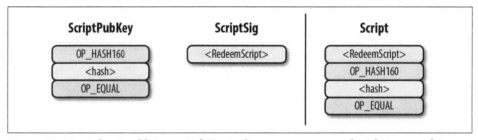

Figure 13-11. p2sh-p2wpkh ScriptPubKey is the same as a normal p2sh ScriptPubKey

We start the script evaluation like in Figure 13-12.

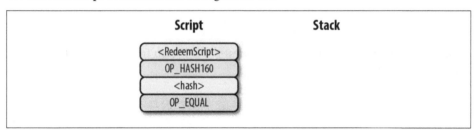

Figure 13-12. p2sh-p2wpkh start

Notice that the commands to be processed are exactly what triggers the p2sh special rule. The RedeemScript goes on the stack (Figure 13-13).

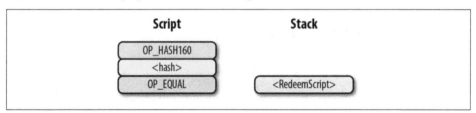

Figure 13-13. p2sh-p2wpkh step 1

The OP_HASH160 will return the RedeemScript's hash (Figure 13-14).

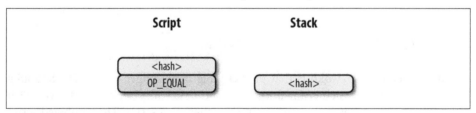

Figure 13-14. p2sh-p2wpkh step 2

The hash will go on the stack, and we then get to OP_EQUAL (Figure 13-15).

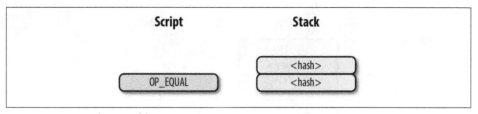

Figure 13-15. p2sh-p2wpkh step 3

At this point, if the hashes are equal, pre-BIP0016 nodes will simply mark the input as valid, as they are unaware of the p2sh validation rules. However, post-BIP0016 nodes recognize the special script sequence for p2sh, so the RedeemScript will then be evaluated as Script commands. The RedeemScript is OP_0 *<20-byte hash>*, which is the same as the ScriptPubKey for p2wpkh. This makes the script state look like Figure 13-16.

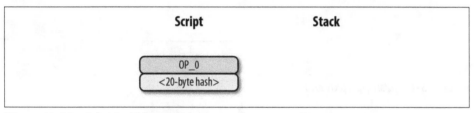

Figure 13-16. p2sh-p2wpkh step 4

This should look familiar, as this is the state that p2wpkh starts with. After OP_0 and the 20-byte hash we are left with Figure 13-17.

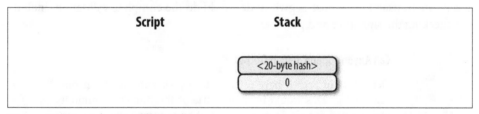

Figure 13-17. p2sh-p2wpkh step 5

At this point, pre-Segwit nodes will mark this input as valid as they are unaware of the Segwit validation rules. However, post-Segwit nodes will recognize the special script sequence for p2wpkh. The signature and pubkey from the witness field along with the 20-byte hash will add the p2pkh commands (Figure 13-18).

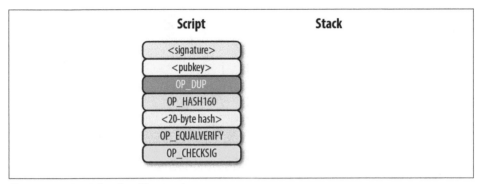

Figure 13-18. p2sh-p2wpkh step 6

The rest of the processing is the same as p2pkh (Chapter 6). Assuming the signature and pubkey are valid, we are left with Figure 13-19.

Figure 13-19. p2sh-p2wpkh end

As you can see, a p2sh-p2wpkh transaction is backward compatible all the way to before BIP0016. A pre-BIP0016 node would consider the script valid once the RedeemScripts were equal, and a post-BIP0016, pre-Segwit node would consider the script valid at the 20-byte hash. Both would not do the full validation and would accept the transaction. A post-Segwit node would do the complete validation, including checking the signature and pubkey.

Can Anyone Spend Segwit Outputs?

Detractors of Segwit have referred to Segwit outputs as "anyone-can-spend." This would have been true if the Bitcoin community had rejected Segwit. In other words, if an economically significant part of the Bitcoin community had refused to do the Segwit validation and actively split from the network by accepting transactions that were not Segwit-valid, the outputs would have been anyone-can-spend. However, due to a variety of economic incentives, Segwit was activated on the network, there was no network split, a lot of bitcoins are now locked in Segwit outputs, and Segwit transactions are validated per the soft-fork rules by the vast economic majority of nodes. We can now say confidently that the detractors were wrong.

Coding p2wpkh and p2sh-p2wpkh

The first change we're going to make is to the Tx class, where we need to mark whether the transaction is Segwit or not:

```
class Tx:
    command = b'tx'

    def __init__(self, version, tx_ins, tx_outs,
            locktime, testnet=False, segwit=False):
        self.version = version
        self.tx_ins = tx_ins
        self.tx_outs = tx_outs
        self.locktime = locktime
        self.testnet = testnet
        self.segwit = segwit
        self._hash_prevouts = None
        self._hash_sequence = None
        self._hash_outputs = None
```

Next, we change the `parse` method depending on the serialization we receive:

```
class Tx:
...
    @classmethod
    def parse(cls, s, testnet=False):
        s.read(4)  ❶
        if s.read(1) == b'\x00':  ❷
            parse_method = cls.parse_segwit
        else:
            parse_method = cls.parse_legacy
        s.seek(-5, 1)  ❸
        return parse_method(s, testnet=testnet)

    @classmethod
    def parse_legacy(cls, s, testnet=False):
        version = little_endian_to_int(s.read(4))  ❹
        num_inputs = read_varint(s)
        inputs = []
        for _ in range(num_inputs):
            inputs.append(TxIn.parse(s))
        num_outputs = read_varint(s)
        outputs = []
        for _ in range(num_outputs):
            outputs.append(TxOut.parse(s))
        locktime = little_endian_to_int(s.read(4))
        return cls(version, inputs, outputs, locktime,
                    testnet=testnet, segwit=False)
```

❶ To determine whether we have a Segwit transaction or not, we look at the fifth byte. The first four are the version, the fifth is the Segwit marker.

❷ The fifth byte being 0 is how we tell that this transaction is Segwit (this is not foolproof, but it's what we're going to use). We use different parsers depending on whether it's Segwit.

❸ We put the stream back to the position before we examined the first 5 bytes.

❹ We've moved the old `parse` method to `parse_legacy`.

Here's a parser for the Segwit serialization:

```python
class Tx:
...
    @classmethod
    def parse_segwit(cls, s, testnet=False):
        version = little_endian_to_int(s.read(4))
        marker = s.read(2)
        if marker != b'\x00\x01':    ❶
            raise RuntimeError('Not a segwit transaction {}'.format(marker))
        num_inputs = read_varint(s)
        inputs = []
        for _ in range(num_inputs):
            inputs.append(TxIn.parse(s))
        num_outputs = read_varint(s)
        outputs = []
        for _ in range(num_outputs):
            outputs.append(TxOut.parse(s))
        for tx_in in inputs:    ❷
            num_items = read_varint(s)
            items = []
            for _ in range(num_items):
                item_len = read_varint(s)
                if item_len == 0:
                    items.append(0)
                else:
                    items.append(s.read(item_len))
            tx_in.witness = items
        locktime = little_endian_to_int(s.read(4))
        return cls(version, inputs, outputs, locktime,
                    testnet=testnet, segwit=True)
```

❶ There are two new fields; one of them is the Segwit marker.

❷ The second new field is witness, which contains items for each input.

We now code the corresponding changes to the serialization methods:

```python
class Tx:
...
    def serialize(self):
        if self.segwit:
            return self.serialize_segwit()
```

```
            else:
                return self.serialize_legacy()

    def serialize_legacy(self):   ❶
        result = int_to_little_endian(self.version, 4)
        result += encode_varint(len(self.tx_ins))
        for tx_in in self.tx_ins:
            result += tx_in.serialize()
        result += encode_varint(len(self.tx_outs))
        for tx_out in self.tx_outs:
            result += tx_out.serialize()
        result += int_to_little_endian(self.locktime, 4)
        return result

    def serialize_segwit(self):
        result = int_to_little_endian(self.version, 4)
        result += b'\x00\x01'   ❷
        result += encode_varint(len(self.tx_ins))
        for tx_in in self.tx_ins:
            result += tx_in.serialize()
        result += encode_varint(len(self.tx_outs))
        for tx_out in self.tx_outs:
            result += tx_out.serialize()
        for tx_in in self.tx_ins:   ❸
            result += int_to_little_endian(len(tx_in.witness), 1)
            for item in tx_in.witness:
                if type(item) == int:
                    result += int_to_little_endian(item, 1)
                else:
                    result += encode_varint(len(item)) + item
        result += int_to_little_endian(self.locktime, 4)
        return result
```

❶ What used to be called `serialize` is now `serialize_legacy`.

❷ The Segwit serialization adds the markers.

❸ The witness is serialized at the end.

We also have to change the `hash` method to use the legacy serialization, even for Segwit transactions, as that will keep the transaction ID stable:

```
class Tx:
...
    def hash(self):
        '''Binary hash of the legacy serialization'''
        return hash256(self.serialize_legacy())[::-1]
```

The `verify_input` method requires a different `z` for Segwit transactions. The Segwit transaction signature hash calculation is specified in BIP0143. In addition, the witness field is passed through to the script evaluation engine:

```
class Tx:
...
    def verify_input(self, input_index):
        tx_in = self.tx_ins[input_index]
        script_pubkey = tx_in.script_pubkey(testnet=self.testnet)
        if script_pubkey.is_p2sh_script_pubkey():
            command = tx_in.script_sig.commands[-1]
            raw_redeem = int_to_little_endian(len(command), 1) + command
            redeem_script = Script.parse(BytesIO(raw_redeem))
            if redeem_script.is_p2wpkh_script_pubkey():      ❶
                z = self.sig_hash_bip143(input_index, redeem_script)   ❷
                witness = tx_in.witness
            else:
                z = self.sig_hash(input_index, redeem_script)
                witness = None
        else:
            if script_pubkey.is_p2wpkh_script_pubkey():      ❸
                z = self.sig_hash_bip143(input_index)   ❷
                witness = tx_in.witness
            else:
                z = self.sig_hash(input_index)
                witness = None
        combined_script = tx_in.script_sig + tx_in.script_pubkey(self.testnet)
        return combined_script.evaluate(z, witness)   ❹
```

❶ This handles the p2sh-p2wpkh case.

❷ The BIP0143 signature hash generation code is in *tx.py* of this chapter's code.

❸ This handles the p2wpkh case.

❹ The witness passes through to the evaluation engine so that p2wpkh can construct the right commands.

We also define what a p2wpkh script looks like in *script.py*:

```
def p2wpkh_script(h160):
    '''Takes a hash160 and returns the p2wpkh ScriptPubKey'''
    return Script([0x00, h160])   ❶
...
    def is_p2wpkh_script_pubkey(self):      ❷
        return len(self.cmds) == 2 and self.cmds[0] == 0x00 \
            and type(self.cmds[1]) == bytes and len(self.cmds[1]) == 20
```

❶ This is OP_0 *<20-byte-hash>*.

❷ This checks if the current script is a p2wpkh ScriptPubKey.

Last, we need to implement the special rule in the `evaluate` method.

```
class Script:
    ...
    def evaluate(self, z, witness):
        ...
        while len(commands) > 0:
            ...
            else:
                stack.append(command)
                ...
                if len(stack) == 2 and stack[0] == b'' and len(stack[1]) == 20:  ❶
                    h160 = stack.pop()
                    stack.pop()
                    cmds.extend(witness)
                    cmds.extend(p2pkh_script(h160).cmds)
```

❶ This is where we execute witness program version 0 for p2wpkh. We make a p2pkh combined script from the 20-byte hash, signature, and pubkey and evaluate.

Pay-to-Witness-Script-Hash (p2wsh)

While p2wpkh takes care of a major use case, we need something more flexible if we want more complicated (e.g., multisig) scripts. This is where pay-to-witness-script-hash (p2wsh) comes in. p2wsh is like p2sh, but with all the ScriptSig data in the witness field instead.

As with p2wpkh, we send different data to pre-BIP0141 software (Figure 13-20) versus post-BIP0141 software (Figure 13-21).

```
0100000001593a2db37b841b2a46f4e9bb63fe9c1012da3ab7fe30b9f9c974242778b5af898000000
0000ffffffff01806fb307000000001976a914bbef244bcad13cffb68b5cef3017c7423675552288a
c00000000

    - 01000000 - version
    - 01 - # of inputs
    - 593a...98 - previous tx hash
    - 00000000 - previous tx index
    - 00 - ScriptSig
    - ffffffff - sequence
    - 01 - # of outputs
    - 806f...00 - output amounts
    - 1976...ac - ScriptPubKey
    - 00000000 - locktime
```

Figure 13-20. Pay-to-witness-script-hash as seen by pre-BIP0141 software

```
01000000000101593a2db37b841b2a46f4e9bb63fe9c1012da3ab7fe30b9f9c974242778b5af89800
00000000ffffffff01806fb307000000001976a914bbef244bcad13cffb68b5cef3017c7423675552
288ac040047304402203cdcaf02a44e37e409646e8a506724e9e1394b890cb52429ea65bac4cc2403
f1022024b934297bcd0c21f22cee0e48751c8b184cc3a0d704cae2684e14858550af7d01483045022
100feb4e1530c13e72226dc912dcd257df90d81ae22dbddb5a3c2f6d86f81d47c8e022069889ddb76
388fa7948aaa018b2480ac36132009bb9cfade82b651e88b4b137a01695221026ccfb8061f235cc11
0697c0bfb3afb99d82c886672f6b9b5393b25a434c0cbf32103befa190c0c22e2f53720b1be9476dc
f11917da4665c44c9c71c3a2d28a933c352102be46dc245f58085743b1cc37c82f0d63a960efa43b5
336534275fc469b49f4ac53ae00000000
```

- 01000000 - version
- **00 - Segwit marker**
- 01 - Segwit flag
- 01 - # of inputs
- 593a...98 - previous tx hash
- 00000000 - previous tx index
- 00 - ScriptSig
- ffffffff - sequence
- 01 - # of outputs
- 806f...00 - output amounts
- 1976...ac - ScriptPubKey
- 0400…ae - witness
- 00000000 - locktime

Figure 13-21. Pay-to-witness-script-hash as seen by post-BIP0141 software

The ScriptPubKey for p2wsh script is OP_0 <*32-byte hash*>. This sequence triggers another special rule. The ScriptSig, as with p2wpkh, is empty. When p2wsh outputs are being spent, the combined script looks like Figure 13-22.

Figure 13-22. Pay-to-witness-script-hash (p2wsh) ScriptPubKey

The processing of this script starts similarly to p2wpkh (Figures 13-23 and 13-24).

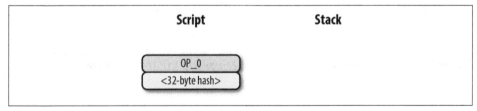

Figure 13-23. p2sh start

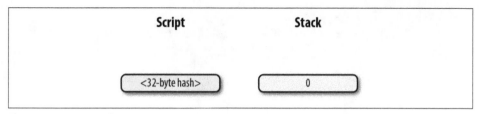

Figure 13-24. p2wsh step 1

The 32-byte hash is an element, so it is pushed to the stack (Figure 13-25).

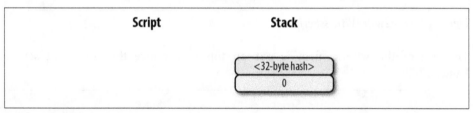

Figure 13-25. p2wsh step 2

As with p2wpkh, older nodes will stop here because there are no more Script commands to be processed. Newer nodes will recognize the special sequence and do additional validation by looking at the witness field.

The witness field for p2wsh in our case is a 2-of-3 multisig (Figure 13-26).

```
040047304402203cdcaf02a44e37e409646e8a506724e9e1394b890cb52429ea65bac4cc2403f1022
024b934297bcd0c21f22cee0e48751c8b184cc3a0d704cae2684e14858550af7d01483045022100fe
b4e1530c13e72226dc912dcd257df90d81ae22dbddb5a3c2f6d86f81d47c8e022069889ddb76388fa
7948aaa018b2480ac36132009bb9cfade82b651e88b4b137a01695221026ccfb8061f235cc110697c
0bfb3afb99d82c886672f6b9b5393b25a434c0cbf32103befa190c0c22e2f53720b1be9476dcf1191
7da4665c44c9c71c3a2d28a933c352102be46dc245f58085743b1cc37c82f0d63a960efa43b533653
4275fc469b49f4ac53ae

                - 04 - Number of witness elements
                - 00 - OP_0
                - 47 - Length of <signaturex>
                - 3044...01 - <signaturex>
                - 3045...01 - <signaturex>
                - 69 - Length of WitnessScript
                - 5221...ae - <WitnessScript>
```

Figure 13-26. p2wsh witness

The last item of the witness is called the *WitnessScript* and must sha256 to the 32-byte hash from the ScriptPubKey. Note this is sha256, not hash256. Once the WitnessScript is validated by having the same hash value, it is interpreted as script commands and put into the command set. The WitnessScript looks like Figure 13-27.

```
5221026ccfb8061f235cc110697c0bfb3afb99d82c886672f6b9b5393b25a434c0cbf32103befa190
c0c22e2f53720b1be9476dcf11917da4665c44c9c71c3a2d28a933c352102be46dc245f58085743b1
cc37c82f0d63a960efa43b5336534275fc469b49f4ac53ae
```

- 52 - OP_2
- 21 - Length of <pubkeyx>
- 026c…f3 - <pubkeyx>
- 03be…35 - <pubkeyx>
- 02be…53 - <pubkeyx>
- 53 - OP_3
- ae - OP_CHECKMULTISIG

Figure 13-27. p2wsh WitnessScript

The rest of the witness field is put on top to produce the command set in Figure 13-28.

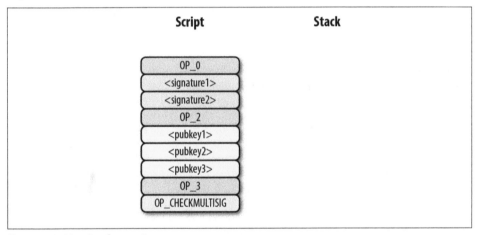

Figure 13-28. p2wsh step 3

As you can see, this is a 2-of-3 multisig much like what was explored in Chapter 8 (Figure 13-29).

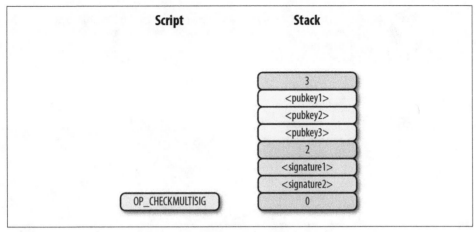

Figure 13-29. p2wsh step 4

If the signatures are valid, we end like Figure 13-30.

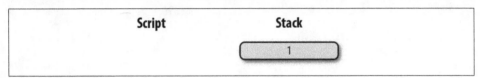

Figure 13-30. p2wsh step 5

The WitnessScript is very similar to the RedeemScript in that the sha256 of the serialization is addressed in the ScriptPubKey, but only revealed when the output is being spent. Once the sha256 of the WitnessScript is found to be the same as the 32-byte hash, the WitnessScript is interpreted as script commands and added to the command set. The rest of the witness field is then added to the command set as well, producing the final set of commands to be evaluated. p2wsh is particularly important, as unmalleable multisig transactions are required for creating bidirectional payment channels for the Lightning Network.

p2sh-p2wsh

Like p2sh-p2wpkh, p2sh-p2wsh is a way to make p2wsh backward compatible. Again, different transactions are sent to older nodes (Figure 13-31) versus newer nodes (Figure 13-32).

```
0100000001708256c5896fb3f00ef37601f8e30c5b460dbcd1fca1cd7199f9b56fc4ecd5400
00000023220020615ae01ed1bc1ffaad54da31d7805d0bb55b52dfd3941114330368c1bbf69
b4cffffffff01603edb0300000000160014bbef244bcad13cffb68b5cef3017c74236755522
00000000

              - 01000000 - version
              - 01 - # of inputs
              - 7082...54 - previous tx hash
              - 00000000 - previous tx index
              - 2322...4c - ScriptSig
              - ffffffff - sequence
              - 01 - # of outputs
              - 603e...00 - output amounts
              - 1600...22 - ScriptPubKey
              - 00000000 - locktime
```

Figure 13-31. Pay-to-script-hash-pay-to-witness-script-hash (p2sh-p2wsh) to pre-BIP0141 software

```
010000000000101708256c5896fb3f00ef37601f8e30c5b460dbcd1fca1cd7199f9b56fc4ecd540000
000023220020615ae01ed1bc1ffaad54da31d7805d0bb55b52dfd3941114330368c1bbf69b4cffffff
fff01603edb0300000000160014bbef244bcad13cffb68b5cef3017c742367555220400473044022 0
010d2854b86b90b7c33661ca25f9d9f15c24b88c5c4992630f77ff004b998fb802204106fc3ec8481
fa98e07b7e78809ac91b6ccaf60bf4d3f729c5a75899bb664a501473044022046d66321c6766abcb1
366a793f9bfd0e11e0b080354f18188588961ea76c5ad002207262381a0661d66f5c39825202524c4
5f29d500c6476176cd910b1691176858701695221026ccfb8061f235cc110697c0bfb3afb99d82c88
6672f6b9b5393b25a434c0cbf32103befa190c0c22e2f53720b1be9476dcf11917da4665c44c9c71c
3a2d28a933c352102be46dc245f58085743b1cc37c82f0d63a960efa43b5336534275fc469b49f4ac
53ae00000000

              - 01000000 - version
              - 00 - Segwit marker
              - 01 - Segwit flag
              - 01 - # of inputs
              - 7082...54 - previous tx hash
              - 00000000 - previous tx index
              - 2322...4c - ScriptSig
              - ffffffff - sequence
              - 01 - # of outputs
              - 603e...00 - output amounts
              - 1600...22 - ScriptPubKey
              - 0400...ae - witness
              - 00000000 - locktime
```

Figure 13-32. p2sh-p2wsh to post-BIP0141 software

As with p2sh-p2wpkh, the ScriptPubKey is indistinguishable from any other p2sh address and the ScriptSig is only the RedeemScript (Figure 13-33).

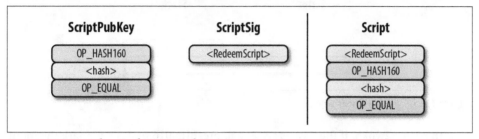

Figure 13-33. p2sh-p2wsh ScriptPubKey

We start the p2sh-p2wsh script evaluation in exactly the same way that p2sh-p2wpkh script evaluation starts (Figure 13-34).

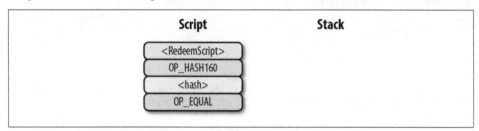

Figure 13-34. p2sh-p2wsh start

The RedeemScript is pushed to the stack (Figure 13-35).

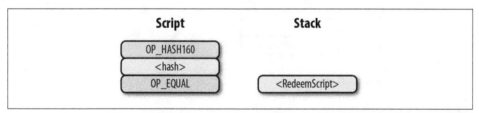

Figure 13-35. p2sh-p2wsh step 1

The OP_HASH160 will return the RedeemScript's hash (Figure 13-36).

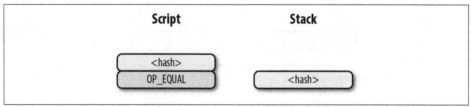

Figure 13-36. p2sh-p2wsh step 2

The hash is pushed to the stack, and we then get to OP_EQUAL (Figure 13-37).

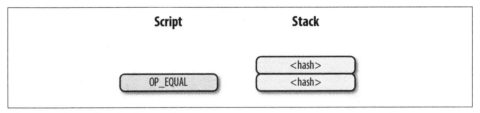

Figure 13-37. p2sh-p2wsh step 3

As with p2sh-p2wpkh, if the hashes are equal, pre-BIP0016 nodes will mark the input as valid as they are unaware of the p2sh validation rules. However, post-BIP0016 nodes will recognize the special script sequence for p2sh, so the RedeemScript will be interpreted as new script commands. The RedeemScript is OP_0 *32-byte hash*, which is the same as the ScriptPubKey for p2wsh (Figure 13-38).

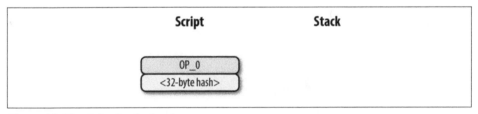

Figure 13-38. p2sh-p2wsh RedeemScript

This makes the script state look like Figure 13-39.

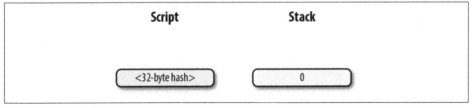

Figure 13-39. p2sh-p2wsh step 4

Of course, this is the exact same starting state as for p2wsh (Figure 13-40).

Figure 13-40. p2sh-p2wsh step 5

The 32-byte hash is an element, so it is pushed to the stack (Figure 13-41).

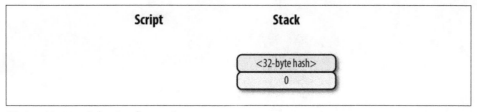

Script	Stack
	`<32-byte hash>`
	`0`

Figure 13-41. p2sh-p2wsh step 6

At this point, pre-Segwit nodes will mark this input as valid, as they are unaware of the Segwit validation rules. However, post-Segwit nodes will recognize the special script sequence for p2wsh. The witness field (Figure 13-42) contains the Witness-Script (Figure 13-43). The sha256 of the WitnessScript is checked against the 32-byte hash, and if they're equal the WitnessScript is interpreted as script commands and put into the command set (Figure 13-44).

```
040047304402200010d2854b86b90b7c33661ca25f9d9f15c24b88c5c4992630f77ff004
b998fb802204106fc3ec8481fa98e07b7e78809ac91b6ccaf60bf4d3f729c5a75899bb6
64a501473044022046d66321c6766abcb1366a793f9bfd0e11e0b080354f18188588961
ea76c5ad002207262381a0661d66f5c39825202524c45f29d500c6476176cd910b16911
76858701695221026ccfb8061f235cc110697c0bfb3afb99d82c886672f6b9b5393b25a
434c0cbf32103befa190c0c22e2f53720b1be9476dcf11917da4665c44c9c71c3a2d28a
933c352102be46dc245f58085743b1cc37c82f0d63a960efa43b5336534275fc469b49f
4ac53ae

        - 04 - Number of witness elements
        - 00 - OP_0
        - 47 - Length of <signaturex>
        - 3044...01 - <signaturex>
        - 3044...01 - <signaturex>
        - 69 - Length of WitnessScript
        - 5221...ae - <WitnessScript>
```

Figure 13-42. p2sh-p2wsh witness

```
5221026ccfb8061f235cc110697c0bfb3afb99d82c886672f6b9b5393b25a434c0cbf32103befa190
c0c22e2f53720b1be9476dcf11917da4665c44c9c71c3a2d28a933c352102be46dc245f58085743b1
cc37c82f0d63a960efa43b5336534275fc469b49f4ac53ae

        - 52 - OP_2
        - 21 - Length of <pubkeyx>
        - 026c_f3 - <pubkeyx>
        - 03be_35 - <pubkeyx>
        - 02be_53 - <pubkeyx>
        - 53 - OP_3
        - ae - OP_CHECKMULTISIG
```

Figure 13-43. p2sh-p2wsh WitnessScript

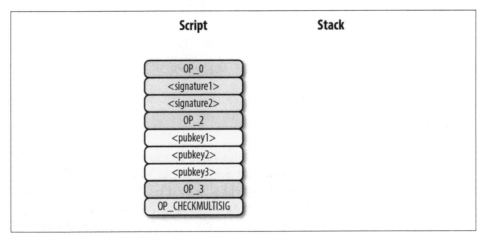

Figure 13-44. p2sh-p2wsh step 7

As you can see, this is a 2-of-3 multisig as in Chapter 8. If the signatures are valid, we end like Figure 13-45.

Figure 13-45. p2sh-p2wsh end

This makes p2wsh backward compatible, allowing older wallets to send to p2sh ScriptPubKeys that they can handle.

Coding p2wsh and p2sh-p2wsh

The parsing and serialization are exactly the same as before. The main changes have to do with `verify_input` in *tx.py* and `evaluate` in *script.py*:

```
class Tx:
...
    def verify_input(self, input_index):
        tx_in = self.tx_ins[input_index]
        script_pubkey = tx_in.script_pubkey(testnet=self.testnet)
        if script_pubkey.is_p2sh_script_pubkey():
            command = tx_in.script_sig.commands[-1]
            raw_redeem = int_to_little_endian(len(command), 1) + command
            redeem_script = Script.parse(BytesIO(raw_redeem))
            if redeem_script.is_p2wpkh_script_pubkey():
                z = self.sig_hash_bip143(input_index, redeem_script)
                witness = tx_in.witness
            elif redeem_script.is_p2wsh_script_pubkey():  ❶
```

```
                command = tx_in.witness[-1]
                raw_witness = encode_varint(len(command)) + command
                witness_script = Script.parse(BytesIO(raw_witness))
                z = self.sig_hash_bip143(input_index,
                                         witness_script=witness_script)
                witness = tx_in.witness
            else:
                z = self.sig_hash(input_index, redeem_script)
                witness = None
        else:
            if script_pubkey.is_p2wpkh_script_pubkey():
                z = self.sig_hash_bip143(input_index)
                witness = tx_in.witness
            elif script_pubkey.is_p2wsh_script_pubkey():    ❷
                command = tx_in.witness[-1]
                raw_witness = encode_varint(len(command)) + command
                witness_script = Script.parse(BytesIO(raw_witness))
                z = self.sig_hash_bip143(input_index,
                                         witness_script=witness_script)
                witness = tx_in.witness
            else:
                z = self.sig_hash(input_index)
                witness = None
        combined_script = tx_in.script_sig + tx_in.script_pubkey(self.testnet)
        return combined_script.evaluate(z, witness)
```

❶ This takes care of p2sh-p2wsh.

❷ This takes care of p2wsh.

Next, we code a way to identify p2wsh in *script.py*:

```
def p2wsh_script(h256):
    '''Takes a hash160 and returns the p2wsh ScriptPubKey'''
    return Script([0x00, h256])    ❶
...
class Script:
...
    def is_p2wsh_script_pubkey(self):
        return len(self.cmds) == 2 and self.cmds[0] == 0x00 \
            and type(self.cmds[1]) == bytes and len(self.cmds[1]) == 32
```

❶ OP_0 *<32-byte script>* is what we expect.

Last, we handle the special rule for p2wsh:

```
class Script:
...
    def evaluate(self, z, witness):
...
        while len(commands) > 0:
...
```

```
    else:
        stack.append(command)
        ...
    if len(stack) == 2 and stack[0] == b'' and len(stack[1]) == 32:
        s256 = stack.pop()   ❶
        stack.pop()   ❷
        cmds.extend(witness[:-1])   ❸
        witness_script = witness[-1]   ❹
        if s256 != sha256(witness_script):   ❺
            print('bad sha256 {} vs {}'.format
                (s256.hex(), sha256(witness_script).hex()))
            return False
        stream = BytesIO(encode_varint(len(witness_script))
            + witness_script)
        witness_script_cmds = Script.parse(stream).cmds   ❻
        cmds.extend(witness_script_cmds)
```

❶ The top element is the sha256 hash of the WitnessScript.

❷ The second element is the witness version, 0.

❸ Everything but the WitnessScript is added to the command set.

❹ The WitnessScript is the last item of the witness field.

❺ The WitnessScript must hash to the sha256 that was in the stack.

❻ We parse the WitnessScript and add it to the command set.

Other Improvements

Segwit also fixes the quadratic hashing problem through a different calculation of the
signature hash. A lot of the calculations for the signature hash, *z*, can be reused
instead of requiring a new hash256 hash for each input. The signature hash calculation is detailed in BIP0143 and can be seen in *code-ch13/tx.py*.

Another improvement is that by policy, uncompressed SEC pubkeys are now forbid-
den; only compressed SEC pubkeys are used for Segwit, saving space.

Conclusion

The chapter covered the details of Segwit as a taste of what's now possible. Chapter 14
discusses the next steps that you can take on your Bitcoin developer journey.

Advanced Topics and Next Steps

If you've made it this far, congratulations! You've learned a lot about Bitcoin's inner workings, and hopefully you are inspired to learn a lot more. This book has only scratched the surface. In this chapter, we'll go through some other topics you might want to explore, how to bootstrap your career as a Bitcoin developer, and ways to contribute to the community.

Suggested Topics to Study Next

Wallets

Creating a wallet is a challenging task because securing private keys is very difficult. That said, there are a bunch of standards for creating wallets that can help.

Hierarchical Deterministic Wallets

For privacy purposes, reusing addresses is very bad (see Chapter 7). That means we need to create lots of addresses. Unfortunately, storing a different secret for each address generated can become a security and backup problem. How do you back them all up in a secure way? Do you generate a ton of secrets and then back them up? What if you run out of secrets? How do you back them up again? What system can you use to ensure that the backups are current?

To combat this problem, Armory, an early Bitcoin wallet, first implemented *deterministic* wallets. The idea of a deterministic wallet is that you can generate one seed and create lots and lots of different addresses with that one seed. The Armory-style deterministic wallets were great, except people wanted some grouping of addresses—so, the *hierarchical deterministic* (HD) wallet standard, BIP0032, was born. BIP0032 wallets have multiple layers and keys, each with a unique derivation path. The specifications and test vectors are defined in the BIP0032 standard, so implementing your own HD wallet on testnet is a great way to learn.

Additionally, BIP0044 defines what each layer of the BIP0032 hierarchy can mean and the best practices for using a single HD seed to store coins from a lot of different cryptocurrencies. Implementing BIP0044 can also be a way to understand the HD wallet infrastructure a lot better. While many wallets (Trezor, Coinomi, etc.) implement both BIP0032 and BIP0044, some wallets ignore BIP0044 altogether and use their own BIP0032 hierarchy (Electrum and Edge being two examples).

Mnemonic Seeds

Writing down and transcribing a 256-bit seed is a pain, and fraught with errors. To combat this, BIP0039 describes a way to encode the seed into a bunch of English words. There are 2,048 possible words, or 2^{11}, which means that each word encodes 11 bits of the seed. The standard defines exactly how the mnemonic backup gets translated to a BIP0032 seed. BIP0039 along with BIP0032 and BIP0044 is how most wallets implement backup and restoration. Writing a testnet wallet that implements BIP0039 is another good way to get a taste for Bitcoin development.

Payment Channels and Lightning Network

Payment channels are the atomic unit of the Lightning Network, and learning how they work is a good next step. There are many ways to implement payment channels, but the BOLT standard is the specification that lightning nodes use. The specifications are in progress as of this writing and are available at *https://github.com/lightning network/lightning-rfc/*.

Contributing

A large part of the Bitcoin ethic is contributing back to the community. The main way you can do that is through open source projects. There are almost too many to list, but here's a sample:

Bitcoin Core (https://github.com/bitcoin/bitcoin)
　　The reference client

Libbitcoin (https://github.com/libbitcoin/libbitcoin)
　　An alternate implementation of Bitcoin in C++

btcd (https://github.com/btcsuite/btcd)
　　A Golang-based implementation of Bitcoin

Bcoin (https://github.com/bcoin-org/bcoin)
　　A JavaScript-based implementation of Bitcoin, maintained by purse.io

pycoin (https://github.com/richardkiss/pycoin)
  A Python library for Bitcoin

BitcoinJ (https://github.com/bitcoinj/bitcoinj)
  A Java library for Bitcoin

BitcoinJS (https://github.com/bitcoinjs/bitcoinjs-lib)
  A JavaScript library for Bitcoin

BTCPay (https://github.com/btcpayserver/btcpayserver)
  A Bitcoin payment processing engine written in C#

Contributing can be very beneficial for a lot of reasons, including future employment opportunities, learning, getting good business ideas, and so on.

Suggested Next Projects

If at this point you're still wondering what projects would be beneficial for you, what follows are some suggestions.

Testnet Wallet

It's hard to understate the importance of security in Bitcoin. Writing a wallet even on testnet will help you understand the various considerations that go into creating a wallet. UI, backups, address books, and transaction histories are just some of the things that you have to deal with when creating a wallet. As this is the most popular application of Bitcoin, creating a wallet will give you a lot of insight into users' needs.

Block Explorer

A more ambitious project would be to write your own block explorer. The key to making your own block explorer is to store the blockchain data in an easy-to-access fashion. Using a traditional database like Postgres or MySQL may be useful here. As Bitcoin Core does not have address indexes, adding one will make it possible for you to allow lookups of UTXOs and past transactions by address, which is what most users desire.

Web Shop

A Bitcoin-based shop is another project that helps you learn. This is particularly appropriate for web developers as they typically know how to create a web application. A web application with a Bitcoin backend can be a powerful way to avoid third-party dependencies for payment. Once again, it's advised that you start on testnet and use the cryptographically secure libraries that are available to hook up the plumbing for payments.

Utility Library

A utility library like the one built in this book is another great way to learn more about Bitcoin. Writing the BIP0143 serialization for the signature hash of Segwit, for example, can be instructive in getting used to protocol programming. Porting the code from this book to another language would also be a great learning tool.

Finding a Job

If you are interested in getting into this industry in more depth, there are lots of great opportunities for developers. The key to proving that you know something is to have a portfolio of projects that you've done on your own. Contributing to an existing open source project or making your own project will help you get noticed by companies. In addition, programming against the API of any particular company is a great way to get an interview!

Generally, local work is going to be a lot easier to get as companies don't like the risk profile of remote workers. Go to local meetups and network with people that you meet there, and the local Bitcoin jobs will be a lot easier to come by.

Similarly, remote work requires that you put yourself out there to be noticed. Besides open source contributions, go to conferences, network, and create technical content (YouTube videos, blog posts, etc.). These will help quite a bit in getting noticed and getting a remote job.

Conclusion

I'm excited that you've made it to the end. If you are so inclined, please send me notes about your progress, as I would love to hear from you! I can be reached at *jimmy@programmingblockchain.com*.

Solutions

Chapter 1: Finite Fields

Exercise 1

Write the corresponding method __ne__, which checks if two FieldElement objects are *not equal* to each other.

```
class FieldElement:
...
    def __ne__(self, other):
        # this should be the inverse of the == operator
        return not (self == other)
```

Exercise 2

Solve these problems in F_{57} (assume all +'s here are $+_f$ and –'s here are $-_f$):

- 44 + 33
- 9 – 29
- 17 + 42 + 49
- 52 – 30 – 38

```
>>> prime = 57
>>> print((44+33)%prime)
20
>>> print((9-29)%prime)
37
>>> print((17+42+49)%prime)
51
```

```
>>> print((52-30-38)%prime)
41
```

Exercise 3

Write the corresponding __sub__ method that defines the subtraction of two FieldElement objects.

```
class FieldElement:
...
    def __sub__(self, other):
        if self.prime != other.prime:
            raise TypeError('Cannot subtract two numbers in different Fields')
        # self.num and other.num are the actual values
        # self.prime is what we need to mod against
        num = (self.num - other.num) % self.prime
        # we return an element of the same class
        return self.__class__(num, self.prime)
```

Exercise 4

Solve the following equations in F_{97} (again, assume · and exponentiation are field versions):

- $95 \cdot 45 \cdot 31$
- $17 \cdot 13 \cdot 19 \cdot 44$
- $12^7 \cdot 77^{49}$

```
>>> prime = 97
>>> print(95*45*31 % prime)
23
>>> print(17*13*19*44 % prime)
68
>>> print(12**7*77**49 % prime)
63
```

Exercise 5

For $k = 1, 3, 7, 13, 18$, what is this set in F_{19}?

$$\{k \cdot 0, k \cdot 1, k \cdot 2, k \cdot 3, ... k \cdot 18\}$$

Do you notice anything about these sets?

```
>>> prime = 19
>>> for k in (1,3,7,13,18):
...     print([k*i % prime for i in range(prime)])
[0, 1, 2, 3, 4, 5, 6, 7, 8, 9, 10, 11, 12, 13, 14, 15, 16, 17, 18]
[0, 3, 6, 9, 12, 15, 18, 2, 5, 8, 11, 14, 17, 1, 4, 7, 10, 13, 16]
```

```
[0, 7, 14, 2, 9, 16, 4, 11, 18, 6, 13, 1, 8, 15, 3, 10, 17, 5, 12]
[0, 13, 7, 1, 14, 8, 2, 15, 9, 3, 16, 10, 4, 17, 11, 5, 18, 12, 6]
[0, 18, 17, 16, 15, 14, 13, 12, 11, 10, 9, 8, 7, 6, 5, 4, 3, 2, 1]
>>> for k in (1,3,7,13,18):
...     print(sorted([k*i % prime for i in range(prime)]))
[0, 1, 2, 3, 4, 5, 6, 7, 8, 9, 10, 11, 12, 13, 14, 15, 16, 17, 18]
[0, 1, 2, 3, 4, 5, 6, 7, 8, 9, 10, 11, 12, 13, 14, 15, 16, 17, 18]
[0, 1, 2, 3, 4, 5, 6, 7, 8, 9, 10, 11, 12, 13, 14, 15, 16, 17, 18]
[0, 1, 2, 3, 4, 5, 6, 7, 8, 9, 10, 11, 12, 13, 14, 15, 16, 17, 18]
[0, 1, 2, 3, 4, 5, 6, 7, 8, 9, 10, 11, 12, 13, 14, 15, 16, 17, 18]
```

When sorted, the results are always the same set.

Exercise 6

Write the corresponding __mul__ method that defines the multiplication of two finite field elements.

```
class FieldElement:
...
    def __mul__(self, other):
        if self.prime != other.prime:
            raise TypeError('Cannot multiply two numbers in different Fields')
        # self.num and other.num are the actual values
        # self.prime is what we need to mod against
        num = (self.num * other.num) % self.prime
        # we return an element of the same class
        return self.__class__(num, self.prime)
```

Exercise 7

For $p = 7, 11, 17, 31$, what is this set in F_p?

$$\{1^{(p-1)}, 2^{(p-1)}, 3^{(p-1)}, 4^{(p-1)}, ... (p-1)^{(p-1)}\}$$

```
>>> for prime in (7, 11, 17, 31):
...     print([pow(i, prime-1, prime) for i in range(1, prime)])
[1, 1, 1, 1, 1, 1]
[1, 1, 1, 1, 1, 1, 1, 1, 1, 1]
[1, 1, 1, 1, 1, 1, 1, 1, 1, 1, 1, 1, 1, 1, 1, 1]
[1, 1, 1, 1, 1, 1, 1, 1, 1, 1, 1, 1, 1, 1, 1, 1, 1, 1, 1, 1, 1, 1, 1, \
1, 1, 1, 1, 1, 1]
```

Exercise 8

Solve the following equations in F_{31}:

- $3 / 24$

- 17^{-3}

- $4^{-4} \cdot 11$

```
>>> prime = 31
>>> print(3*pow(24, prime-2, prime) % prime)
4
>>> print(pow(17, prime-4, prime))
29
>>> print(pow(4, prime-5, prime)*11 % prime)
13
```

Exercise 9

Write the corresponding __truediv__ method that defines the division of two field elements.

Note that in Python 3, division is separated into __truediv__ and __floordiv__. The first does normal division and the second does integer division.

```
class FieldElement:
...
    def __truediv__(self, other):
        if self.prime != other.prime:
            raise TypeError('Cannot divide two numbers in different Fields')
        # use Fermat's little theorem:
        # self.num**(p-1) % p == 1
        # this means:
        # 1/n == pow(n, p-2, p)
        # we return an element of the same class
        num = self.num * pow(other.num, self.prime - 2, self.prime) % self.prime
        return self.__class__(num, self.prime)
```

Chapter 2: Elliptic Curves

Exercise 1

Determine which of these points are on the curve $y^2 = x^3 + 5x + 7$:

(2,4), (−1,−1), (18,77), (5,7)

```
>>> def on_curve(x, y):
...     return y**2 == x**3 + 5*x + 7
>>> print(on_curve(2,4))
False
>>> print(on_curve(-1,-1))
True
>>> print(on_curve(18,77))
True
>>> print(on_curve(5,7))
False
```

Exercise 2

Write the __ne__ method for Point.

```
class Point:
    ...
    def __ne__(self, other):
        return not (self == other)
```

Exercise 3

Handle the case where the two points are additive inverses (that is, they have the same x but a different y, causing a vertical line). This should return the point at infinity.

```
class Point:
    ...
    if self.x == other.x and self.y != other.y:
        return self.__class__(None, None, self.a, self.b)
```

Exercise 4

For the curve $y^2 = x^3 + 5x + 7$, what is $(2,5) + (-1,-1)$?

```
>>> x1, y1 = 2, 5
>>> x2, y2 = -1, -1
>>> s = (y2 - y1) / (x2 - x1)
>>> x3 = s**2 - x1 - x2
>>> y3 = s * (x1 - x3) - y1
>>> print(x3, y3)
3.0 -7.0
```

Exercise 5

Write the __add__ method where $x_1 \neq x_2$.

```
class Point:
    ...
    def __add__(self, other):
        ...
        if self.x != other.x:
            s = (other.y - self.y) / (other.x - self.x)
            x = s**2 - self.x - other.x
            y = s * (self.x - x) - self.y
            return self.__class__(x, y, self.a, self.b)
```

Exercise 6

For the curve $y^2 = x^3 + 5x + 7$, what is $(-1,-1) + (-1,-1)$?

```
>>> a, x1, y1 = 5, -1, -1
>>> s = (3 * x1**2 + a) / (2 * y1)
>>> x3 = s**2 - 2*x1
```

```
>>> y3 = s*(x1-x3)-y1
>>> print(x3,y3)
18.0 77.0
```

Exercise 7

Write the __add__ method when $P_1 = P_2$.

```
class Point:
...
    def __add__(self, other):
    ...
    if self == other:
        s = (3 * self.x**2 + self.a) / (2 * self.y)
        x = s**2 - 2 * self.x
        y = s * (self.x - x) - self.y
        return self.__class__(x, y, self.a, self.b)
```

Chapter 3: Elliptic Curve Cryptography

Exercise 1

Evaluate whether these points are on the curve $y^2 = x^3 + 7$ over F_{223}:

(192,105), (17,56), (200,119), (1,193), (42,99)

```
>>> from ecc import FieldElement
>>> prime = 223
>>> a = FieldElement(0, prime)
>>> b = FieldElement(7, prime)
>>> def on_curve(x,y):
...     return y**2 == x**3 + a*x + b
>>> print(on_curve(FieldElement(192, prime), FieldElement(105, prime)))
True
>>> print(on_curve(FieldElement(17, prime), FieldElement(56, prime)))
True
>>> print(on_curve(FieldElement(200, prime), FieldElement(119, prime)))
False
>>> print(on_curve(FieldElement(1, prime), FieldElement(193, prime)))
True
>>> print(on_curve(FieldElement(42, prime), FieldElement(99, prime)))
False
```

Exercise 2

For the curve $y^2 = x^3 + 7$ over F_{223}, find:

- (170,142) + (60,139)
- (47,71) + (17,56)

- $(143,98) + (76,66)$

```
>>> from ecc import FieldElement, Point
>>> prime = 223
>>> a = FieldElement(0, prime)
>>> b = FieldElement(7, prime)
>>> p1 = Point(FieldElement(170, prime), FieldElement(142, prime), a, b)
>>> p2 = Point(FieldElement(60, prime), FieldElement(139, prime), a, b)
>>> print(p1+p2)
Point(220,181)_0_7 FieldElement(223)
>>> p1 = Point(FieldElement(47, prime), FieldElement(71, prime), a, b)
>>> p2 = Point(FieldElement(17, prime), FieldElement(56, prime), a, b)
>>> print(p1+p2)
Point(215,68)_0_7 FieldElement(223)
>>> p1 = Point(FieldElement(143, prime), FieldElement(98, prime), a, b)
>>> p2 = Point(FieldElement(76, prime), FieldElement(66, prime), a, b)
>>> print(p1+p2)
Point(47,71)_0_7 FieldElement(223)
```

Exercise 3

Extend ECCTest to test for the additions from the previous exercise. Call this
test_add.

```
def test_add(self):
    prime = 223
    a = FieldElement(0, prime)
    b = FieldElement(7, prime)
    additions = (
        (192, 105, 17, 56, 170, 142),
        (47, 71, 117, 141, 60, 139),
        (143, 98, 76, 66, 47, 71),
    )
    for x1_raw, y1_raw, x2_raw, y2_raw, x3_raw, y3_raw in additions:
        x1 = FieldElement(x1_raw, prime)
        y1 = FieldElement(y1_raw, prime)
        p1 = Point(x1, y1, a, b)
        x2 = FieldElement(x2_raw, prime)
        y2 = FieldElement(y2_raw, prime)
        p2 = Point(x2, y2, a, b)
        x3 = FieldElement(x3_raw, prime)
        y3 = FieldElement(y3_raw, prime)
        p3 = Point(x3, y3, a, b)
        self.assertEqual(p1 + p2, p3)
```

Exercise 4

For the curve $y^2 = x^3 + 7$ over F_{223}, find:

- $2 \cdot (192,105)$

- $2 \cdot (143,98)$

- $2 \cdot (47,71)$

- $4 \cdot (47,71)$

- $8 \cdot (47,71)$

- $21 \cdot (47,71)$

```
>>> from ecc import FieldElement, Point
>>> prime = 223
>>> a = FieldElement(0, prime)
>>> b = FieldElement(7, prime)
>>> x1 = FieldElement(num=192, prime=prime)
>>> y1 = FieldElement(num=105, prime=prime)
>>> p = Point(x1,y1,a,b)
>>> print(p+p)
Point(49,71)_0_7 FieldElement(223)
>>> x1 = FieldElement(num=143, prime=prime)
>>> y1 = FieldElement(num=98, prime=prime)
>>> p = Point(x1,y1,a,b)
>>> print(p+p)
Point(64,168)_0_7 FieldElement(223)
>>> x1 = FieldElement(num=47, prime=prime)
>>> y1 = FieldElement(num=71, prime=prime)
>>> p = Point(x1,y1,a,b)
>>> print(p+p)
Point(36,111)_0_7 FieldElement(223)
>>> print(p+p+p+p)
Point(194,51)_0_7 FieldElement(223)
>>> print(p+p+p+p+p+p+p+p)
Point(116,55)_0_7 FieldElement(223)
>>> print(p+p+p+p+p+p+p+p+p+p+p+p+p+p+p+p+p+p+p+p+p)
Point(infinity)
```

Exercise 5

For the curve $y^2 = x^3 + 7$ over F_{223}, find the order of the group generated by (15,86).

```
>>> prime = 223
>>> a = FieldElement(0, prime)
>>> b = FieldElement(7, prime)
>>> x = FieldElement(15, prime)
>>> y = FieldElement(86, prime)
>>> p = Point(x, y, a, b)
>>> inf = Point(None, None, a, b)
>>> product = p
>>> count = 1
>>> while product != inf:
...     product += p
...     count += 1
>>> print(count)
7
```

Exercise 6

Verify whether these signatures are valid:

```
P = (0x887387e452b8eacc4acfde10d9aaf7f6d9a0f975aabb10d006e4da568744d06c,
     0x61de6d95231cd89026e286df3b6ae4a894a3378e393e93a0f45b666329a0ae34)

# signature 1
z = 0xec208baa0fc1c19f708a9ca96fdeff3ac3f230bb4a7ba4aede4942ad003c0f60
r = 0xac8d1c87e51d0d441be8b3dd5b05c8795b48875dffe00b7ffcfac23010d3a395
s = 0x68342ceff8935ededd102dd876ffd6ba72d6a427a3edb13d26eb0781cb423c4

# signature 2
z = 0x7c076ff316692a3d7eb3c3bb0f8b1488cf72e1afcd929e29307032997a838a3d
r = 0xeff69ef2b1bd93a66ed5219add4fb51e11a840f404876325a1e8ffe0529a2c
s = 0xc7207fee197d27c618aea621406f6bf5ef6fca38681d82b2f06fddbdce6feab6
```

```
>>> from ecc import S256Point, N, G
>>> point = S256Point(
...        0x887387e452b8eacc4acfde10d9aaf7f6d9a0f975aabb10d006e4da568744d06c,
...        0x61de6d95231cd89026e286df3b6ae4a894a3378e393e93a0f45b666329a0ae34)
>>> z = 0xec208baa0fc1c19f708a9ca96fdeff3ac3f230bb4a7ba4aede4942ad003c0f60
>>> r = 0xac8d1c87e51d0d441be8b3dd5b05c8795b48875dffe00b7ffcfac23010d3a395
>>> s = 0x68342ceff8935ededd102dd876ffd6ba72d6a427a3edb13d26eb0781cb423c4
>>> u = z * pow(s, N-2, N) % N
>>> v = r * pow(s, N-2, N) % N
>>> print((u*G + v*point).x.num == r)
True
>>> z = 0x7c076ff316692a3d7eb3c3bb0f8b1488cf72e1afcd929e29307032997a838a3d
>>> r = 0xeff69ef2b1bd93a66ed5219add4fb51e11a840f404876325a1e8ffe0529a2c
>>> s = 0xc7207fee197d27c618aea621406f6bf5ef6fca38681d82b2f06fddbdce6feab6
>>> u = z * pow(s, N-2, N) % N
>>> v = r * pow(s, N-2, N) % N
>>> print((u*G + v*point).x.num == r)
True
```

Exercise 7

Sign the following message with the secret:

```
e = 12345
z = int.from_bytes(hash256('Programming Bitcoin!'), 'big')
```

```
>>> from ecc import S256Point, G, N
>>> from helper import hash256
>>> e = 12345
>>> z = int.from_bytes(hash256(b'Programming Bitcoin!'), 'big')
>>> k = 1234567890
>>> r = (k*G).x.num
>>> k_inv = pow(k, N-2, N)
>>> s = (z+r*e) * k_inv % N
>>> print(e*G)
S256Point(f01d6b9018ab421dd410404cb869072065522bf85734008f105cf385a023a80f, \
```

```
0eba29d0f0c5408ed681984dc525982abefccd9f7ff01dd26da4999cf3f6a295)
>>> print(hex(z))
0x969f6056aa26f7d2795fd013fe88868d09c9f6aed96965016e1936ae47060d48
>>> print(hex(r))
0x2b698a0f0a4041b77e63488ad48c23e8e8838dd1fb7520408b121697b782ef22
>>> print(hex(s))
0x1dbc63bfef4416705e602a7b564161167076d8b20990a0f26f316cff2cb0bc1a
```

Chapter 4: Serialization

Exercise 1

Find the uncompressed SEC format for the public key where the private key secrets are:

- 5,000
- $2,018^5$
- 0xdeadbeef12345

```
>>> from ecc import PrivateKey
>>> priv = PrivateKey(5000)
>>> print(priv.point.sec(compressed=False).hex())
04ffe558e388852f0120e46af2d1b370f85854a8eb0841811ece0e3e03d282d57c315dc72890a4\
f10a1481c031b03b351b0dc79901ca18a00cf009dbdb157a1d10
>>> priv = PrivateKey(2018**5)
>>> print(priv.point.sec(compressed=False).hex())
04027f3da1918455e03c46f659266a1bb5204e959db7364d2f473bdf8f0a13cc9dff87647fd023\
c13b4a4994f17691895806e1b40b57f4fd22581a4f46851f3b06
>>> priv = PrivateKey(0xdeadbeef12345)
>>> print(priv.point.sec(compressed=False).hex())
04d90cd625ee87dd38656dd95cf79f65f60f7273b67d3096e68bd81e4f5342691f842efa762fd5\
9961d0e99803c61edba8b3e3f7dc3a341836f97733aebf987121
```

Exercise 2

Find the compressed SEC format for the public key where the private key secrets are:

- 5,001
- $2,019^5$
- 0xdeadbeef54321

```
>>> from ecc import PrivateKey
>>> priv = PrivateKey(5001)
>>> print(priv.point.sec(compressed=True).hex())
0357a4f368868a8a6d572991e484e664810ff14c05c0fa023275251151fe0e53d1
>>> priv = PrivateKey(2019**5)
>>> print(priv.point.sec(compressed=True).hex())
```

```
02933ec2d2b111b92737ec12f1c5d20f3233a0ad21cd8b36d0bca7a0cfa5cb8701
>>> priv = PrivateKey(0xdeadbeef54321)
>>> print(priv.point.sec(compressed=True).hex())
0296be5b1292f6c856b3c5654e886fc13511462059089cdf9c479623bfcbe77690
```

Exercise 3

Find the DER format for a signature whose r and s values are:

r = 0x37206a0610995c58074999cb9767b87af4c4978db68c06e8e6e81d282047a7c6

s = 0x8ca63759c1157ebeaec0d03cecca119fc9a75bf8e6d0fa65c841c8e2738cdaec

```
>>> from ecc import Signature
>>> r = 0x37206a0610995c58074999cb9767b87af4c4978db68c06e8e6e81d282047a7c6
>>> s = 0x8ca63759c1157ebeaec0d03cecca119fc9a75bf8e6d0fa65c841c8e2738cdaec
>>> sig = Signature(r,s)
>>> print(sig.der().hex())
3045022037206a0610995c58074999cb9767b87af4c4978db68c06e8e6e81d282047a7c6022100\
8ca63759c1157ebeaec0d03cecca119fc9a75bf8e6d0fa65c841c8e2738cdaec
```

Exercise 4

Convert the following hex values to binary and then to Base58:

- 7c076ff316692a3d7eb3c3bb0f8b1488cf72e1afcd929e29307032997a838a3d

- eff69ef2b1bd93a66ed5219add4fb51e11a840f404876325a1e8ffe0529a2c

- c7207fee197d27c618aea621406f6bf5ef6fca38681d82b2f06fddbdce6feab6

```
>>> from helper import encode_base58
>>> h = '7c076ff316692a3d7eb3c3bb0f8b1488cf72e1afcd929e29307032997a838a3d'
>>> print(encode_base58(bytes.fromhex(h)))
9MA8fRQrT4u8Zj8ZRd6MAiiyaxb2Y1CMpvVkHQu5hVM6
>>> h = 'eff69ef2b1bd93a66ed5219add4fb51e11a840f404876325a1e8ffe0529a2c'
>>> print(encode_base58(bytes.fromhex(h)))
4fE3H2E6XMp4SsxtwinF7w9a34ooUrwWe4WsW1458Pd
>>> h = 'c7207fee197d27c618aea621406f6bf5ef6fca38681d82b2f06fddbdce6feab6'
>>> print(encode_base58(bytes.fromhex(h)))
EQJsjkd6JaGwxrjEhfeqPenqHwrBmPQZjJGNSCHBkcF7
```

Exercise 5

Find the addresses corresponding to the public keys whose private key secrets are:

- 5002 (use uncompressed SEC on testnet)
- 2020^5 (use compressed SEC on testnet)
- 0x12345deadbeef (use compressed SEC on mainnet)

```
>>> from ecc import PrivateKey
>>> priv = PrivateKey(5002)
>>> print(priv.point.address(compressed=False, testnet=True))
mmTPbXQFxboEtNRkwfh6K51jvdtHLxGeMA
>>> priv = PrivateKey(2020**5)
>>> print(priv.point.address(compressed=True, testnet=True))
mopVkxp8UhXqRYbCYJsbeE1h1fiF64jcoH
>>> priv = PrivateKey(0x12345deadbeef)
>>> print(priv.point.address(compressed=True, testnet=False))
1F1Pn2y6pDb68E5nYJJeba4TLg2U7B6KF1
```

Exercise 6

Find the WIF for the private key whose secrets are:

- 5003 (compressed, testnet)
- 2021^5 (uncompressed, testnet)
- 0x54321deadbeef (compressed, mainnet)

```
>>> from ecc import PrivateKey
>>> priv = PrivateKey(5003)
>>> print(priv.wif(compressed=True, testnet=True))
cMahea7zqjxrtgAbB7LSGbcQUr1uX1ojuat9jZodMN8rFTv2sfUK
>>> priv = PrivateKey(2021**5)
>>> print(priv.wif(compressed=False, testnet=True))
91avARGdfge8E4tZfYLoxeJ5sGBdNJQH4kvjpWAxgzczjbCwxic
>>> priv = PrivateKey(0x54321deadbeef)
>>> print(priv.wif(compressed=True, testnet=False))
KwDiBf89QgGbjEhKnhXJuH7LrciVrZi3qYjgiuQJv1h8Ytr2S53a
```

Exercise 7

Write a function `little_endian_to_int` that takes Python bytes, interprets those bytes in little-endian, and returns the number.

```
def little_endian_to_int(b):
    '''little_endian_to_int takes byte sequence as a little-endian number.
    Returns an integer'''
    return int.from_bytes(b, 'little')
```

Exercise 8

Write a function `int_to_little_endian` that does the reverse of the last exercise.

```
def int_to_little_endian(n, length):
    '''endian_to_little_endian takes an integer and returns the little-endian
    byte sequence of length'''
    return n.to_bytes(length, 'little')
```

Exercise 9

Create a testnet address for yourself using a long secret that only you know. This is important as there are bots on testnet trying to steal testnet coins. Make sure you write this secret down somewhere! You will be using it later to sign transactions.

```
>>> from ecc import PrivateKey
>>> from helper import hash256, little_endian_to_int
>>> passphrase = b'jimmy@programmingblockchain.com my secret'
>>> secret = little_endian_to_int(hash256(passphrase))
>>> priv = PrivateKey(secret)
>>> print(priv.point.address(testnet=True))
mft9LRNtaBNtpkknB8xgm17UvPedZ4ecYL
```

Chapter 5: Transactions

Exercise 1

Write the version parsing part of the parse method that we've defined. To do this properly, you'll have to convert 4 bytes into a little-endian integer.

```
class Tx:
...
@classmethod
def parse(cls, s, testnet=False):
    version = little_endian_to_int(s.read(4))
    return cls(version, None, None, None, testnet=testnet)
```

Exercise 2

Write the inputs parsing part of the parse method in Tx and the parse method for TxIn.

```
class Tx:
...
    @classmethod
    def parse(cls, s, testnet=False):
        version = little_endian_to_int(s.read(4))
        num_inputs = read_varint(s)
        inputs = []
        for _ in range(num_inputs):
            inputs.append(TxIn.parse(s))
        return cls(version, inputs, None, None, testnet=testnet)
...

class TxIn:
...
    @classmethod
    def parse(cls, s):
        '''Takes a byte stream and parses the tx_input at the start.
```

```
            Returns a TxIn object.
            '''
            prev_tx = s.read(32)[::-1]
            prev_index = little_endian_to_int(s.read(4))
            script_sig = Script.parse(s)
            sequence = little_endian_to_int(s.read(4))
            return cls(prev_tx, prev_index, script_sig, sequence)
```

Exercise 3

Write the outputs parsing part of the parse method in Tx and the parse method for TxOut.

```
class Tx:
...
class Tx:
...
    @classmethod
    def parse(cls, s, testnet=False):
        version = little_endian_to_int(s.read(4))
        num_inputs = read_varint(s)
        inputs = []
        for _ in range(num_inputs):
            inputs.append(TxIn.parse(s))
        num_outputs = read_varint(s)
        outputs = []
        for _ in range(num_outputs):
            outputs.append(TxOut.parse(s))
        return cls(version, inputs, outputs, None, testnet=testnet)
...

class TxOut:
...
    @classmethod
    def parse(cls, s):
        '''Takes a byte stream and parses the tx_output at the start.
        Returns a TxOut object.
        '''
        amount = little_endian_to_int(s.read(8))
        script_pubkey = Script.parse(s)
        return cls(amount, script_pubkey)
```

Exercise 4

Write the locktime parsing part of the parse method in Tx.

```
class Tx:
...
    @classmethod
    def parse(cls, s, testnet=False):
        version = little_endian_to_int(s.read(4))
        num_inputs = read_varint(s)
```

```
inputs = []
for _ in range(num_inputs):
    inputs.append(TxIn.parse(s))
num_outputs = read_varint(s)
outputs = []
for _ in range(num_outputs):
    outputs.append(TxOut.parse(s))
locktime = little_endian_to_int(s.read(4))
return cls(version, inputs, outputs, locktime, testnet=testnet)
```

Exercise 5

What are the ScriptSig of the second input, the ScriptPubKey of the first output, and the amount of the second output for this transaction?

```
010000000456919960ac691763688d3d3bcea9ad6ecaf875df5339e148a1fc61c6ed7a069e0100
00006a47304402204585bcdef85e6b1c6af5c2669d4830ff86e42dd205c0e089bc2a821657e951
c002201024a10366077f87d6bce1f7100ad8cfa8a064b39d4e8fe4ea13a7b71aa8180f012102f0
da57e85eec2934a82a585ea337ce2f4998b50ae699dd79f5880e253dafafb7fefffffffeb8f51f4
038dc17e6313cf831d4f02281c2a468bde0fafd37f1bf882729e7fd3000000006a473044022078
99531a52d59a6de200179928ca900254a36b8dff8bb75f5f5d71b1cdc26125022008b422690b84
61cb52c3cc30330b23d574351872b7c361e9aae3649071c1a7160121035d5c93d9ac96881f19ba
1f686f15f009ded7c62efe85a872e6a19b43c15a2937fefffffff567bf40595119d1bb8a3037c35
6efd56170b64cbcc160fb028fa10704b45d775000000006a47304402204c7c7818424c7f7911da
6cddc59655a70af1cb5eaf17c69dadbfc74ffa0b662f02207599e08bc8023693ad4e9527dc42c3
4210f7a7d1d1ddfc8492b654a11e7620a0012102158b46fbdff65d0172b7989aec8850aa0dae49
abfb84c81ae6e5b251a58ace5cfefffffffd63a5e6c16e620f86f375925b21cabaf736c779f88fd
04dcad51d26690f7f345010000006a47304402200633ea0d3314bea0d95b3cd8dadb2ef79ea833
1ffe1e61f762c0f6daea0fabde022029f23b3e9c30f080446150b23852028751635dcee2be669c
2a1686a4b5edf304012103ffd6f4a67e94aba353a00882e563ff2722eb4cff0ad6006e86ee20df
e7520d55fefffffff0251430f00000000001976a914ab0c0b2e98b1ab6dbf67d4750b0a56244948
a87988ac005a6202000000001976a9143c82d7df364eb6c75be8c80df2b3eda8db57397088ac46
430600
```

```
>>> from io import BytesIO
>>> from tx import Tx
>>> hex_transaction = '010000000456919960ac691763688d3d3bcea9ad6ecaf875df5339e\
148a1fc61c6ed7a069e010000006a47304402204585bcdef85e6b1c6af5c2669d4830ff86e42dd\
205c0e089bc2a821657e951c002201024a10366077f87d6bce1f7100ad8cfa8a064b39d4e8fe4e\
a13a7b71aa8180f012102f0da57e85eec2934a82a585ea337ce2f4998b50ae699dd79f5880e253\
dafafb7fefffffffeb8f51f4038dc17e6313cf831d4f02281c2a468bde0fafd37f1bf882729e7fd\
3000000006a47304402207899531a52d59a6de200179928ca900254a36b8dff8bb75f5f5d71b1c\
dc26125022008b422690b8461cb52c3cc30330b23d574351872b7c361e9aae3649071c1a716012\
1035d5c93d9ac96881f19ba1f686f15f009ded7c62efe85a872e6a19b43c15a2937fefffffff567\
bf40595119d1bb8a3037c356efd56170b64cbcc160fb028fa10704b45d775000000006a4730440\
2204c7c7818424c7f7911da6cddc59655a70af1cb5eaf17c69dadbfc74ffa0b662f02207599e08\
bc8023693ad4e9527dc42c34210f7a7d1d1ddfc8492b654a11e7620a0012102158b46fbdff65d0\
172b7989aec8850aa0dae49abfb84c81ae6e5b251a58ace5cfefffffffd63a5e6c16e620f86f375\
925b21cabaf736c779f88fd04dcad51d26690f7f345010000006a47304402200633ea0d3314bea\
0d95b3cd8dadb2ef79ea8331ffe1e61f762c0f6daea0fabde022029f23b3e9c30f080446150b23\
852028751635dcee2be669c2a1686a4b5edf304012103ffd6f4a67e94aba353a00882e563ff272\
2eb4cff0ad6006e86ee20dfe7520d55fefffffff0251430f0000000000019761a914ab0c0b2e98b1a\
```

```
b6dbf67d4750b0a56244948a87988ac005a6202000000001976a9143c82d7df364eb6c75be8c80\
df2b3eda8db57397088ac46430600'
>>> stream = BytesIO(bytes.fromhex(hex_transaction))
>>> tx_obj = Tx.parse(stream)
>>> print(tx_obj.tx_ins[1].script_sig)
304402207899531a52d59a6de200179928ca900254a36b8dff8bb75f5f5d71b1cdc26125022008\
b422690b8461cb52c3cc30330b23d574351872b7c361e9aae3649071c1a71601 035d5c93d9ac9\
6881f19ba1f686f15f009ded7c62efe85a872e6a19b43c15a2937
>>> print(tx_obj.tx_outs[0].script_pubkey)
OP_DUP OP_HASH160 ab0c0b2e98b1ab6dbf67d4750b0a56244948a879 \
OP_EQUALVERIFY OP_CHECKSIG
>>> print(tx_obj.tx_outs[1].amount)
40000000
```

Exercise 6

Write the fee method for the Tx class.

```
class Tx:
...
    def fee(self, testnet=False):
        input_sum, output_sum = 0, 0
        for tx_in in self.tx_ins:
            input_sum += tx_in.value(testnet=testnet)
        for tx_out in self.tx_outs:
            output_sum += tx_out.amount
        return input_sum - output_sum
```

Chapter 6: Script

Exercise 1

Write the op_hash160 function.

```
def op_hash160(stack):
    if len(stack) < 1:
        return False
    element = stack.pop()
    h160 = hash160(element)
    stack.append(h160)
    return True
```

Exercise 2

Write the op_checksig function in *op.py*.

```
def op_checksig(stack, z):
    if len(stack) < 2:
        return False
    sec_pubkey = stack.pop()
    der_signature = stack.pop()[:-1]
```

```
try:
    point = S256Point.parse(sec_pubkey)
    sig = Signature.parse(der_signature)
except (ValueError, SyntaxError) as e:
    return False
if point.verify(z, sig):
    stack.append(encode_num(1))
else:
    stack.append(encode_num(0))
return True
```

Exercise 3

Create a ScriptSig that can unlock this ScriptPubKey:

767695935687

Note that OP_MUL multiplies the top two elements of the stack.

- 56 = OP_6

- 76 = OP_DUP

- 87 = OP_EQUAL

- 93 = OP_ADD

- 95 = OP_MUL

```
>>> from script import Script
>>> script_pubkey = Script([0x76, 0x76, 0x95, 0x93, 0x56, 0x87])
>>> script_sig = Script([0x52])
>>> combined_script = script_sig + script_pubkey
>>> print(combined_script.evaluate(0))
True
```

OP_2 or 52 will satisfy the equation $x^2 + x - 6 = 0$.

Exercise 4

Figure out what this script is doing:

6e879169a77ca787

- 69 = OP_VERIFY

- 6e = OP_2DUP

- 7c = OP_SWAP

- 87 = OP_EQUAL

- 91 = OP_NOT

- a7 = OP_SHA1

Use the `Script.parse` method and look up what various opcodes do at *https://en.bitcoin.it/wiki/Script*.

```
>>> from script import Script
>>> script_pubkey = Script([0x6e, 0x87, 0x91, 0x69, 0xa7, 0x7c, 0xa7, 0x87])
>>> c1 = '255044462d312e330a25e2e3cfd30a0a0a312030206f626a0a3c3c2f576964746820\
32203020522f4865696768742033203020522f547970652034203020522f537562747970652035\
203020522f46696c74657220362036203020522f436f6c6f7253706163652037203020522f4c656e67\
7468203820203020522f42697473506572436f6d706f6e6574420383e3e0a73747265616d0d0affd8\
fffe00245348412d312069732064656164212121212121852fec092339759c39b1a1c63c4c97e1ff\
fe017f46dc93a6b67e013b029aaa1db2560b45ca67d688c7f84b8c4c791fe02b3df614f86db169\
0901c56b45c1530afedfb76038e972722fe7ad728f0e4904e046c230570fe9d41398abe12ef5bc\
942be33542a4802d98b5d70f2a332ec37fac3514e74ddc0f2cc1a874cd0c78305a215664613097\
89606bd0bf3f98cda8044629a1'
>>> c2 = '255044462d312e330a25e2e3cfd30a0a0a312030206f626a0a3c3c2f576964746820\
32203020522f4865696768742033203020522f547970652034203020522f537562747970652035\
203020522f46696c74657220362036203020522f436f6c6f7253706163652037203020522f4c656e67\
7468203820203020522f42697473506572436f6d706f6e6574420383e3e0a73747265616d0d0affd8\
fffe00245348412d312069732064656164212121212121852fec092339759c39b1a1c63c4c97e1ff\
fe017346dc9166b67e118f029ab621b2560ff9ca67cca8c7f85ba84c79030c2b3de218f86db3a9\
0901d5df45c14f26fedfb3dc38e96ac22fe7bd728f0e45bce046d23c570feb141398bb552ef5a0\
a82be331fea48037b8b5d71f0e332edf93ac3500eb4ddc0decc1a864790c782c76215660dd3097\
91d06bd0af3f98cda4bc4629b1'
>>> collision1 = bytes.fromhex(c1)  ❶
>>> collision2 = bytes.fromhex(c2)
>>> script_sig = Script([collision1, collision2])
>>> combined_script = script_sig + script_pubkey
>>> print(combined_script.evaluate(0))
True
```

❶ collision1 and collision2 are from the SHA-1 preimages that Google found to collide (*http://bit.ly/2HZF3om*).

This is looking for a SHA-1 collision. The only way to satisfy this script is to give x and y such that x≠y but sha1(x)=sha1(y).

Chapter 7: Transaction Creation and Validation

Exercise 1

Write the `sig_hash` method for the Tx class.

```
class Tx:
...
    def sig_hash(self, input_index):
        s = int_to_little_endian(self.version, 4)
        s += encode_varint(len(self.tx_ins))
        for i, tx_in in enumerate(self.tx_ins):
```

```
            if i == input_index:
                s += TxIn(
                    prev_tx=tx_in.prev_tx,
                    prev_index=tx_in.prev_index,
                    script_sig=tx_in.script_pubkey(self.testnet),
                    sequence=tx_in.sequence,
                ).serialize()
            else:
                s += TxIn(
                    prev_tx=tx_in.prev_tx,
                    prev_index=tx_in.prev_index,
                    sequence=tx_in.sequence,
                ).serialize()
    s += encode_varint(len(self.tx_outs))
    for tx_out in self.tx_outs:
        s += tx_out.serialize()
    s += int_to_little_endian(self.locktime, 4)
    s += int_to_little_endian(SIGHASH_ALL, 4)
    h256 = hash256(s)
    return int.from_bytes(h256, 'big')
```

Exercise 2

Write the `verify_input` method for the Tx class. You will want to use the
`TxIn.script_pubkey`, `Tx.sig_hash`, and `Script.evaluate` methods.

```
class Tx:
...
    def verify_input(self, input_index):
        tx_in = self.tx_ins[input_index]
        script_pubkey = tx_in.script_pubkey(testnet=self.testnet)
        z = self.sig_hash(input_index)
        combined = tx_in.script_sig + script_pubkey
        return combined.evaluate(z)
```

Exercise 3

Write the `sign_input` method for the Tx class.

```
class Tx:
...
    def sign_input(self, input_index, private_key):
        z = self.sig_hash(input_index)
        der = private_key.sign(z).der()
        sig = der + SIGHASH_ALL.to_bytes(1, 'big')
        sec = private_key.point.sec()
        self.tx_ins[input_index].script_sig = Script([sig, sec])
        return self.verify_input(input_index)
```

Exercise 4

Create a testnet transaction that sends 60% of a single UTXO to
mwJn1YPMq7y5F8J3LkC5Hxg9PHyZ5K4cFv. The remaining amount minus fees should
go back to your own change address. This should be a one-input, two-output
transaction.

You can broadcast the transaction at *https://blockstream.info/testnet/tx/push.*

```
>>> from ecc import PrivateKey
>>> from helper import decode_base58, SIGHASH_ALL
>>> from script import p2pkh_script, Script
>>> from tx import TxIn, TxOut, Tx
>>> prev_tx = bytes.fromhex('75a1c4bc671f55f626dda1074c7725991e6f68b8fcefcfca7\
b64405ca3b45f1c')
>>> prev_index = 1
>>> target_address = 'miKegze5FQNCnGw6PKyqUbYUeBa4x2hFeM'
>>> target_amount = 0.01
>>> change_address = 'mzx5YhAH9kNHtcN481u6WkjeHjYtVeKVh2'
>>> change_amount = 0.009
>>> secret = 8675309
>>> priv = PrivateKey(secret=secret)
>>> tx_ins = []
>>> tx_ins.append(TxIn(prev_tx, prev_index))
>>> tx_outs = []
>>> h160 = decode_base58(target_address)
>>> script_pubkey = p2pkh_script(h160)
>>> target_satoshis = int(target_amount*100000000)
>>> tx_outs.append(TxOut(target_satoshis, script_pubkey))
>>> h160 = decode_base58(change_address)
>>> script_pubkey = p2pkh_script(h160)
>>> change_satoshis = int(change_amount*100000000)
>>> tx_outs.append(TxOut(change_satoshis, script_pubkey))
>>> tx_obj = Tx(1, tx_ins, tx_outs, 0, testnet=True)
>>> print(tx_obj.sign_input(0, priv))
True
>>> print(tx_obj.serialize().hex())
01000000011c5fb4a35c40647bcacfeffcb8686f1e9925774c07a1dd26f6551f67bcc4a1750100\
00006b483045022100a08ebb92422b3599a2d2fcdaa11f8f807a66ccf33e7f4a9ff0a3c51f1b1e\
c5dd02205ed21dfede5925362b8d9833e908646c54be7ac6664e31650159e8f69b6ca539012103\
935581e52c354cd2f484fe8ed83af7a3097005b2f9c60bff71d35bd795f54b67ffffffff024042\
0f00000000001976a9141ec51b3654c1f1d0f4929d11a1f702937eaf50c888ac9fbb0d00000000\
001976a914d52ad7ca9b3d096a38e752c2018e6fbc40cdf26f88ac00000000
```

Exercise 5

Advanced: Get some more testnet coins from a testnet faucet and create a two-input,
one-output transaction. One input should be from the faucet, the other should be
from the previous exercise; the output can be your own address.

You can broadcast the transaction at *https://blockstream.info/testnet/tx/push.*

```
>>> from ecc import PrivateKey
>>> from helper import decode_base58, SIGHASH_ALL
>>> from script import p2pkh_script, Script
>>> from tx import TxIn, TxOut, Tx
>>> prev_tx_1 = bytes.fromhex('11d05ce707c1120248370d1cbf5561d22c4f83aeba04367\
92c82e0bd57fe2a2f')
>>> prev_index_1 = 1
>>> prev_tx_2 = bytes.fromhex('51f61f77bd061b9a0da60d4bedaaf1b1fad0c11e65fdc74\
4797ee22d20b03d15')
>>> prev_index_2 = 1
>>> target_address = 'mwJn1YPMq7y5F8J3LkC5Hxg9PHyZ5K4cFv'
>>> target_amount = 0.0429
>>> secret = 8675309
>>> priv = PrivateKey(secret=secret)
>>> tx_ins = []
>>> tx_ins.append(TxIn(prev_tx_1, prev_index_1))
>>> tx_ins.append(TxIn(prev_tx_2, prev_index_2))
>>> tx_outs = []
>>> h160 = decode_base58(target_address)
>>> script_pubkey = p2pkh_script(h160)
>>> target_satoshis = int(target_amount*100000000)
>>> tx_outs.append(TxOut(target_satoshis, script_pubkey))
>>> tx_obj = Tx(1, tx_ins, tx_outs, 0, testnet=True)
>>> print(tx_obj.sign_input(0, priv))
True
>>> print(tx_obj.sign_input(1, priv))
True
>>> print(tx_obj.serialize().hex())
01000000022f2afe57bde0822c793604baae834f2cd26155bf1c0d37480212c107e75cd0110100\
00006a47304402204cc5fe11b2b025f8fc9f6073b5e3942883bbba266b71751068badeb8f11f03\
64022070178363f5dea4149581a4b9b9dbad91ec1fd990e3fa14f9de3ccb421fa5b26901210393\
5581e52c354cd2f484fe8ed83af7a3097005b2f9c60bff71d35bd795f54b67ffffffff153db020\
2de27e7944c7fd651ec1d0fab1f1aaed4b0da60d9a1b06bd771ff651010000006b483045022100\
b7a938d4679aa7271f0d32d83b61a85eb0180cf1261d44feaad23dfd9799dafb02205ff2f366dd\
d9555f7146861a8298b7636be8b292090a224c5dc84268480d8be1012103935581e52c354cd2f4\
84fe8ed83af7a3097005b2f9c60bff71d35bd795f54b67ffffffff01d0754100000000001976a9\
14ad346f8eb57dee9a37981716e498120ae80e44f788ac00000000
```

Chapter 8: Pay to Script Hash

Exercise 1

Write the op_checkmultisig function of *op.py*.

```
def op_checkmultisig(stack, z):
    if len(stack) < 1:
        return False
    n = decode_num(stack.pop())
    if len(stack) < n + 1:
        return False
    sec_pubkeys = []
```

```
for _ in range(n):
    sec_pubkeys.append(stack.pop())
m = decode_num(stack.pop())
if len(stack) < m + 1:
    return False
der_signatures = []
for _ in range(m):
    der_signatures.append(stack.pop()[:-1])
stack.pop()
try:
    points = [S256Point.parse(sec) for sec in sec_pubkeys]
    sigs = [Signature.parse(der) for der in der_signatures]
    for sig in sigs:
        if len(points) == 0:
            return False
        while points:
            point = points.pop(0)
            if point.verify(z, sig):
                break
    stack.append(encode_num(1))
except (ValueError, SyntaxError):
    return False
return True
```

Exercise 2

Write the h160_to_p2pkh_address function that converts a 20-byte hash160 into a p2pkh address.

```
def h160_to_p2pkh_address(h160, testnet=False):
    if testnet:
        prefix = b'\x6f'
    else:
        prefix = b'\x00'
    return encode_base58_checksum(prefix + h160)
```

Exercise 3

Write the h160_to_p2sh_address function that converts a 20-byte hash160 into a p2sh address.

```
def h160_to_p2sh_address(h160, testnet=False):
    if testnet:
        prefix = b'\xc4'
    else:
        prefix = b'\x05'
    return encode_base58_checksum(prefix + h160)
```

Exercise 4

Validate the second signature from the preceding transaction.

```
>>> from io import BytesIO
>>> from ecc import S256Point, Signature
>>> from helper import hash256, int_to_little_endian
>>> from script import Script
>>> from tx import Tx, SIGHASH_ALL
>>> hex_tx = '0100000001868278ed6ddfb6c1ed3ad5f8181eb0c7a385aa0836f01d5e4789e6\
bd304d87221a000000db00483045022100dc92655fe37036f47756db8102e0d7d5e28b3beb83a8\
fef4f5dc0559bddfb94e02205a36d4e4e6c7fcd16658c50783e00c341609977aed3ad00937bf4e\
e942a8993701483045022100da6bee3c93766232079a01639d07fa869598749729ae323eab8eef\
53577d611b02207bef15429dcadce2121ea07f233115c6f09034c0be68db99980b9a6c5e754022\
01475221022626e955ea6ea6d98850c994f9107b036b1334f18ca8830bfff1295d21cfdb702103\
b287eaf122eea69030a0e9feed096bed8045c8b98bec453e1ffac7fbdbd4bb7152aefffffffff04\
d3b11400000000001976a914904a49878c0adfc3aa05de7afad2cc15f483a56a88ac7f40090000\
0000001976a914418327e3f3dda4cf5b9089325a4b95abdfa0334088ac722c0c00000000001976\
a914ba35042cfe9fc66fd35ac2224eebdafd1028ad2788acdc4ace020000000017a91474d691da\
1574e6b3c192ecfb52cc8984ee7b6c568700000000'
>>> hex_sec = '03b287eaf122eea69030a0e9feed096bed8045c8b98bec453e1ffac7fbdbd4b\
b71'
>>> hex_der = '3045022100da6bee3c93766232079a01639d07fa869598749729ae323eab8ee\
f53577d611b02207bef15429dcadce2121ea07f233115c6f09034c0be68db99980b9a6c5e75402\
2'
>>> hex_redeem_script = '475221022626e955ea6ea6d98850c994f9107b036b1334f18ca88\
30bfff1295d21cfdb702103b287eaf122eea69030a0e9feed096bed8045c8b98bec453e1ffac7f\
bdbd4bb7152ae'
>>> sec = bytes.fromhex(hex_sec)
>>> der = bytes.fromhex(hex_der)
>>> redeem_script = Script.parse(BytesIO(bytes.fromhex(hex_redeem_script)))
>>> stream = BytesIO(bytes.fromhex(hex_tx))
>>> tx_obj = Tx.parse(stream)
>>> s = int_to_little_endian(tx_obj.version, 4)
>>> s += encode_varint(len(tx_obj.tx_ins))
>>> i = tx_obj.tx_ins[0]
>>> s += TxIn(i.prev_tx, i.prev_index, redeem_script, i.sequence).serialize()
>>> s += encode_varint(len(tx_obj.tx_outs))
>>> for tx_out in tx_obj.tx_outs:
...     s += tx_out.serialize()
>>> s += int_to_little_endian(tx_obj.locktime, 4)
>>> s += int_to_little_endian(SIGHASH_ALL, 4)
>>> z = int.from_bytes(hash256(s), 'big')
>>> point = S256Point.parse(sec)
>>> sig = Signature.parse(der)
>>> print(point.verify(z, sig))
True
```

Exercise 5

Modify the `sig_hash` and `verify_input` methods to be able to verify p2sh transactions.

```
class Tx:
...
    def sig_hash(self, input_index, redeem_script=None):
        '''Returns the integer representation of the hash that needs to get
        signed for index input_index'''
        s = int_to_little_endian(self.version, 4)
        s += encode_varint(len(self.tx_ins))
        for i, tx_in in enumerate(self.tx_ins):
            if i == input_index:
                if redeem_script:
                    script_sig = redeem_script
                else:
                    script_sig = tx_in.script_pubkey(self.testnet)
            else:
                script_sig = None
            s += TxIn(
                prev_tx=tx_in.prev_tx,
                prev_index=tx_in.prev_index,
                script_sig=script_sig,
                sequence=tx_in.sequence,
            ).serialize()
        s += encode_varint(len(self.tx_outs))
        for tx_out in self.tx_outs:
            s += tx_out.serialize()
        s += int_to_little_endian(self.locktime, 4)
        s += int_to_little_endian(SIGHASH_ALL, 4)
        h256 = hash256(s)
        return int.from_bytes(h256, 'big')


    def verify_input(self, input_index):
        tx_in = self.tx_ins[input_index]
        script_pubkey = tx_in.script_pubkey(testnet=self.testnet)
        if script_pubkey.is_p2sh_script_pubkey():
            cmd = tx_in.script_sig.cmds[-1]
            raw_redeem = encode_varint(len(cmd)) + cmd
            redeem_script = Script.parse(BytesIO(raw_redeem))
        else:
            redeem_script = None
        z = self.sig_hash(input_index, redeem_script)
        combined = tx_in.script_sig + script_pubkey
        return combined.evaluate(z)
```

Chapter 9: Blocks

Exercise 1

Write the `is_coinbase` method of the Tx class.

```
class Tx:
...
    def is_coinbase(self):
        if len(self.tx_ins) != 1:
            return False
        first_input = self.tx_ins[0]
        if first_input.prev_tx != b'\x00' * 32:
            return False
        if first_input.prev_index != 0xffffffff:
            return False
        return True
```

Exercise 2

Write the `coinbase_height` method for the Tx class.

```
class Tx:
...
    def coinbase_height(self):
        if not self.is_coinbase():
            return None
        element = self.tx_ins[0].script_sig.cmds[0]
        return little_endian_to_int(element)
```

Exercise 3

Write the `parse` method for `Block`.

```
class Block:
...
    @classmethod
    def parse(cls, s):
        version = little_endian_to_int(s.read(4))
        prev_block = s.read(32)[::-1]
        merkle_root = s.read(32)[::-1]
        timestamp = little_endian_to_int(s.read(4))
        bits = s.read(4)
        nonce = s.read(4)
        return cls(version, prev_block, merkle_root, timestamp, bits, nonce)
```

Exercise 4

Write the `serialize` method for `Block`.

```
class Block:
...
    def serialize(self):
        result = int_to_little_endian(self.version, 4)
        result += self.prev_block[::-1]
        result += self.merkle_root[::-1]
        result += int_to_little_endian(self.timestamp, 4)
        result += self.bits
        result += self.nonce
        return result
```

Exercise 5

Write the hash method for `Block`.

```
class Block:
...
    def hash(self):
        s = self.serialize()
        sha = hash256(s)
        return sha[::-1]
```

Exercise 6

Write the `bip9` method for the `Block` class.

```
class Block:
...
    def bip9(self):
        return self.version >> 29 == 0b001
```

Exercise 7

Write the `bip91` method for the `Block` class.

```
class Block:
...
    def bip91(self):
        return self.version >> 4 & 1 == 1
```

Exercise 8

Write the `bip141` method for the `Block` class.

```
class Block:
...
```

```
def bip141(self):
    return self.version >> 1 & 1 == 1
```

Exercise 9

Write the `bits_to_target` function in *helper.py*.

```
def bits_to_target(bits):
    exponent = bits[-1]
    coefficient = little_endian_to_int(bits[:-1])
    return coefficient * 256**(exponent - 3)
```

Exercise 10

Write the `difficulty` method for `Block`.

```
class Block:
...
    def difficulty(self):
        lowest = 0xffff * 256**(0x1d - 3)
        return lowest / self.target()
```

Exercise 11

Write the `check_pow` method for `Block`.

```
class Block:
...
    def check_pow(self):
        sha = hash256(self.serialize())
        proof = little_endian_to_int(sha)
        return proof < self.target()
```

Exercise 12

Calculate the new bits given the first and last blocks of this 2,016-block difficulty adjustment period:

- Block 471744:

  ```
  000000203471101bbda3fe307664b3283a9ef0e97d9a38a7eacd88000000000000000000
  10c8aba8479bbaa5e0848152fd3c2289ca50e1c3e58c9a4faaafbdf5803c5448ddb84559
  7e8b0118e43a81d3
  ```

- Block 473759:

  ```
  02000020f1472d9db4b563c35f97c428ac903f23b7fc055d1cfc2600000000000000000000
  b3f449fcbe1bc4cfbcb8283a0d2c037f961a3fdf2b8bedc144973735eea707e126425859
  7e8b0118e5f00474
  ```

```
>>> from io import BytesIO
>>> from block import Block
```

```
>>> from helper import TWO_WEEKS
>>> from helper import target_to_bits
>>> block1_hex = '000000203471101bbda3fe307664b3283a9ef0e97d9a38a7eacd88000000\
00000000000010c8aba8479bbaa5e0848152fd3c2289ca50e1c3e58c9a4faaafbdf5803c5448dd\
b845597e8b0118e43a81d3'
>>> block2_hex = '02000020f1472d9db4b563c35f97c428ac903f23b7fc055d1cfc26000000\
000000000000b3f449fcbe1bc4cfbcb8283a0d2c037f961a3fdf2b8bedc144973735eea707e126\
4258597e8b0118e5f00474'
>>> last_block = Block.parse(BytesIO(bytes.fromhex(block1_hex)))
>>> first_block = Block.parse(BytesIO(bytes.fromhex(block2_hex)))
>>> time_differential = last_block.timestamp - first_block.timestamp
>>> if time_differential > TWO_WEEKS * 4:
...     time_differential = TWO_WEEKS * 4
>>> if time_differential < TWO_WEEKS // 4:
...     time_differential = TWO_WEEKS // 4
>>> new_target = last_block.target() * time_differential // TWO_WEEKS
>>> new_bits = target_to_bits(new_target)
>>> print(new_bits.hex())
80df6217
```

Exercise 13

Write the `calculate_new_bits` function in *helper.py*.

```
def calculate_new_bits(previous_bits, time_differential):
    if time_differential > TWO_WEEKS * 4:
        time_differential = TWO_WEEKS * 4
    if time_differential < TWO_WEEKS // 4:
        time_differential = TWO_WEEKS // 4
    new_target = bits_to_target(previous_bits) * time_differential // TWO_WEEKS
    return target_to_bits(new_target)
```

Chapter 10: Networking

Exercise 1

Write the `parse` method for `NetworkEnvelope`.

```
@classmethod
def parse(cls, s, testnet=False):
    magic = s.read(4)
    if magic == b'':
        raise IOError('Connection reset!')
    if testnet:
        expected_magic = TESTNET_NETWORK_MAGIC
    else:
        expected_magic = NETWORK_MAGIC
    if magic != expected_magic:
        raise SyntaxError('magic is not right {} vs {}'.format(magic.hex(),
            expected_magic.hex()))
    command = s.read(12)
```

```
        command = command.strip(b'\x00')
        payload_length = little_endian_to_int(s.read(4))
        checksum = s.read(4)
        payload = s.read(payload_length)
        calculated_checksum = hash256(payload)[:4]
        if calculated_checksum != checksum:
            raise IOError('checksum does not match')
        return cls(command, payload, testnet=testnet)
```

Exercise 2

Determine what this network message is:

f9beb4d976657261636b000000000000000000005df6e0e2

```
class NetworkEnvelope:
...
    >>> from network import NetworkEnvelope
    >>> from io import BytesIO
    >>> message_hex = 'f9beb4d976657261636b000000000000000000005df6e0e2'
    >>> stream = BytesIO(bytes.fromhex(message_hex))
    >>> envelope = NetworkEnvelope.parse(stream)
    >>> print(envelope.command)
    b'verack'
    >>> print(envelope.payload)
    b''
```

Exercise 3

Write the serialize method for NetworkEnvelope.

```
class NetworkEnvelope:
...
    def serialize(self):
        result = self.magic
        result += self.command + b'\x00' * (12 - len(self.command))
        result += int_to_little_endian(len(self.payload), 4)
        result += hash256(self.payload)[:4]
        result += self.payload
        return result
```

Exercise 4

Write the serialize method for VersionMessage.

```
class VersionMessage:
...
    def serialize(self):
        result = int_to_little_endian(self.version, 4)
        result += int_to_little_endian(self.services, 8)
        result += int_to_little_endian(self.timestamp, 8)
        result += int_to_little_endian(self.receiver_services, 8)
        result += b'\x00' * 10 + b'\xff\xff' + self.receiver_ip
```

```
result += self.receiver_port.to_bytes(2, 'big')
result += int_to_little_endian(self.sender_services, 8)
result += b'\x00' * 10 + b'\xff\xff' + self.sender_ip
result += self.sender_port.to_bytes(2, 'big')
result += self.nonce
result += encode_varint(len(self.user_agent))
result += self.user_agent
result += int_to_little_endian(self.latest_block, 4)
if self.relay:
    result += b'\x01'
else:
    result += b'\x00'
return result
```

Exercise 5

Write the handshake method for SimpleNode.

```
class SimpleNode:
...
    def handshake(self):
        version = VersionMessage()
        self.send(version)
        self.wait_for(VerAckMessage)
```

Exercise 6

Write the serialize method for GetHeadersMessage.

```
class GetHeadersMessage:
...
    def serialize(self):
        result = int_to_little_endian(self.version, 4)
        result += encode_varint(self.num_hashes)
        result += self.start_block[::-1]
        result += self.end_block[::-1]
        return result
```

Chapter 11: Simplified Payment Verification

Exercise 1

Write the merkle_parent function.

```
def merkle_parent(hash1, hash2):
    '''Takes the binary hashes and calculates the hash256'''
    return hash256(hash1 + hash2)
```

Exercise 2

Write the `merkle_parent_level` function.

```
def merkle_parent_level(hashes):
    '''Takes a list of binary hashes and returns a list that's half
    the length'''
    if len(hashes) == 1:
        raise RuntimeError('Cannot take a parent level with only 1 item')
    if len(hashes) % 2 == 1:
        hashes.append(hashes[-1])
    parent_level = []
    for i in range(0, len(hashes), 2):
        parent = merkle_parent(hashes[i], hashes[i + 1])
        parent_level.append(parent)
    return parent_level
```

Exercise 3

Write the `merkle_root` function.

```
def merkle_root(hashes):
    '''Takes a list of binary hashes and returns the merkle root
    '''
    current_level = hashes
    while len(current_level) > 1:
        current_level = merkle_parent_level(current_level)
    return current_level[0]
```

Exercise 4

Write the `validate_merkle_root` method for `Block`.

```
class Block:
...
    def validate_merkle_root(self):
        hashes = [h[::-1] for h in self.tx_hashes]
        root = merkle_root(hashes)
        return root[::-1] == self.merkle_root
```

Exercise 5

Create an empty Merkle Tree with 27 items and print each level.

```
>>> import math
>>> total = 27
>>> max_depth = math.ceil(math.log(total, 2))
>>> merkle_tree = []
>>> for depth in range(max_depth + 1):
...     num_items = math.ceil(total / 2**(max_depth - depth))
...     level_hashes = [None] * num_items
...     merkle_tree.append(level_hashes)
```

```
>>> for level in merkle_tree:
...     print(level)
[None]
[None, None]
[None, None, None, None]
[None, None, None, None, None, None, None]
[None, None, None, None, None, None, None, None, None, None, None, None, None,\
 None]
[None, None, None, None, None, None, None, None, None, None, None, None, None,\
 None, None, None, None, None, None, None, None, None, None, None, None, None,\
 None]
```

Exercise 6

Write the parse method for MerkleBlock.

```
class MerkleBlock:
...
    @classmethod
    def parse(cls, s):
        version = little_endian_to_int(s.read(4))
        prev_block = s.read(32)[::-1]
        merkle_root = s.read(32)[::-1]
        timestamp = little_endian_to_int(s.read(4))
        bits = s.read(4)
        nonce = s.read(4)
        total = little_endian_to_int(s.read(4))
        num_hashes = read_varint(s)
        hashes = []
        for _ in range(num_hashes):
            hashes.append(s.read(32)[::-1])
        flags_length = read_varint(s)
        flags = s.read(flags_length)
        return cls(version, prev_block, merkle_root, timestamp, bits,
                   nonce, total, hashes, flags)
```

Exercise 7

Write the is_valid method for MerkleBlock.

```
class MerkleBlock:
...
    def is_valid(self):
        flag_bits = bytes_to_bit_field(self.flags)
        hashes = [h[::-1] for h in self.hashes]
        merkle_tree = MerkleTree(self.total)
        merkle_tree.populate_tree(flag_bits, hashes)
        return merkle_tree.root()[::-1] == self.merkle_root
```

Chapter 12: Bloom Filters

Exercise 1

Calculate the Bloom Filter for "hello world" and "goodbye" using the hash160 hash function over a bit field of 10.

```
>>> from helper import hash160
>>> bit_field_size = 10
>>> bit_field = [0] * bit_field_size
>>> for item in (b'hello world', b'goodbye'):
...     h = hash160(item)
...     bit = int.from_bytes(h, 'big') % bit_field_size
...     bit_field[bit] = 1
>>> print(bit_field)
[1, 1, 0, 0, 0, 0, 0, 0, 0, 0]
```

Exercise 2

Given a Bloom Filter with size=10, function_count=5, tweak=99, what are the bytes that are set after adding these items? (Use bit_field_to_bytes to convert to bytes.)

- b'Hello World'
- b'Goodbye!'

```
>>> from bloomfilter import BloomFilter, BIP37_CONSTANT
>>> from helper import bit_field_to_bytes, murmur3
>>> field_size = 10
>>> function_count = 5
>>> tweak = 99
>>> items = (b'Hello World', b'Goodbye!')
>>> bit_field_size = field_size * 8
>>> bit_field = [0] * bit_field_size
>>> for item in items:
...     for i in range(function_count):
...         seed = i * BIP37_CONSTANT + tweak
...         h = murmur3(item, seed=seed)
...         bit = h % bit_field_size
...         bit_field[bit] = 1
>>> print(bit_field_to_bytes(bit_field).hex())
4000600a080000010940
```

Exercise 3

Write the add method for BloomFilter.

```
class BloomFilter:
...
    def add(self, item):
```

```
        for i in range(self.function_count):
            seed = i * BIP37_CONSTANT + self.tweak
            h = murmur3(item, seed=seed)
            bit = h % (self.size * 8)
            self.bit_field[bit] = 1
```

Exercise 4

Write the `filterload` method for the `BloomFilter` class.

```
class BloomFilter:
...
    def filterload(self, flag=1):
        payload = encode_varint(self.size)
        payload += self.filter_bytes()
        payload += int_to_little_endian(self.function_count, 4)
        payload += int_to_little_endian(self.tweak, 4)
        payload += int_to_little_endian(flag, 1)
        return GenericMessage(b'filterload', payload)
```

Exercise 5

Write the `serialize` method for the `GetDataMessage` class.

```
class GetDataMessage:
...
    def serialize(self):
        result = encode_varint(len(self.data))
        for data_type, identifier in self.data:
            result += int_to_little_endian(data_type, 4)
            result += identifier[::-1]
        return result
```

Exercise 6

Get the current testnet block ID, send yourself some testnet coins, find the UTXO corresponding to the testnet coins *without using a block explorer*, create a transaction using that UTXO as an input, and broadcast the tx message on the testnet network.

```
>>> import time
>>> from block import Block
>>> from bloomfilter import BloomFilter
>>> from ecc import PrivateKey
>>> from helper import (
...     decode_base58,
...     encode_varint,
...     hash256,
...     little_endian_to_int,
...     read_varint,
... )
>>> from merkleblock import MerkleBlock
>>> from network import (
```

```
...         GetDataMessage,
...         GetHeadersMessage,
...         HeadersMessage,
...         NetworkEnvelope,
...         SimpleNode,
...         TX_DATA_TYPE,
...         FILTERED_BLOCK_DATA_TYPE,
... )
>>> from script import p2pkh_script, Script
>>> from tx import Tx, TxIn, TxOut
>>> last_block_hex = '00000000000000a03f9432ac63813c6710bfe41712ac5ef6faab093f\
e2917636'
>>> secret = little_endian_to_int(hash256(b'Jimmy Song'))
>>> private_key = PrivateKey(secret=secret)
>>> addr = private_key.point.address(testnet=True)
>>> h160 = decode_base58(addr)
>>> target_address = 'mwJn1YPMq7y5F8J3LkC5Hxg9PHyZ5K4cFv'
>>> target_h160 = decode_base58(target_address)
>>> target_script = p2pkh_script(target_h160)
>>> fee = 5000  # fee in satoshis
>>> # connect to testnet.programmingbitcoin.com in testnet mode
>>> node = SimpleNode('testnet.programmingbitcoin.com', testnet=True, logging=\
False)
>>> # Create a Bloom Filter of size 30 and 5 functions. Add a tweak.
>>> bf = BloomFilter(30, 5, 90210)
>>> # add the h160 to the Bloom Filter
>>> bf.add(h160)
>>> # complete the handshake
>>> node.handshake()
>>> # load the Bloom Filter with the filterload command
>>> node.send(bf.filterload())
>>> # set start block to last_block from above
>>> start_block = bytes.fromhex(last_block_hex)
>>> # send a getheaders message with the starting block
>>> getheaders = GetHeadersMessage(start_block=start_block)
>>> node.send(getheaders)
>>> # wait for the headers message
>>> headers = node.wait_for(HeadersMessage)
>>> # store the last block as None
>>> last_block = None
>>> # initialize the GetDataMessage
>>> getdata = GetDataMessage()
>>> # loop through the blocks in the headers
>>> for b in headers.blocks:
...     # check that the proof of work on the block is valid
...     if not b.check_pow():
...         raise RuntimeError('proof of work is invalid')
...     # check that this block's prev_block is the last block
...     if last_block is not None and b.prev_block != last_block:
...         raise RuntimeError('chain broken')
...     # add a new item to the getdata message
...     # should be FILTERED_BLOCK_DATA_TYPE and block hash
```

```
...         getdata.add_data(FILTERED_BLOCK_DATA_TYPE, b.hash())
...         # set the last block to the current hash
...         last_block = b.hash()
>>> # send the getdata message
>>> node.send(getdata)
>>> # initialize prev_tx, prev_index, and prev_amount to None
>>> prev_tx, prev_index, prev_amount = None, None, None
>>> # loop while prev_tx is None
>>> while prev_tx is None:
...     # wait for the merkleblock or tx commands
...     message = node.wait_for(MerkleBlock, Tx)
...     # if we have the merkleblock command
...     if message.command == b'merkleblock':
...         # check that the MerkleBlock is valid
...         if not message.is_valid():
...             raise RuntimeError('invalid merkle proof')
...     # else we have the tx command
...     else:
...         # set the tx's testnet to be True
...         message.testnet = True
...         # loop through the tx outs
...         for i, tx_out in enumerate(message.tx_outs):
...             # if our output has the same address as our address we found it
...             if tx_out.script_pubkey.address(testnet=True) == addr:
...                 # we found our utxo; set prev_tx, prev_index, and tx
...                 prev_tx = message.hash()
...                 prev_index = i
...                 prev_amount = tx_out.amount
...                 print('found: {}:{}'.format(prev_tx.hex(), prev_index))
found: b2cddd41d18d00910f88c31aa58c6816a190b8fc30fe7c665e1cd2ec60efdf3f:7
>>> # create the TxIn
>>> tx_in = TxIn(prev_tx, prev_index)
>>> # calculate the output amount (previous amount minus the fee)
>>> output_amount = prev_amount - fee
>>> # create a new TxOut to the target script with the output amount
>>> tx_out = TxOut(output_amount, target_script)
>>> # create a new transaction with the one input and one output
>>> tx_obj = Tx(1, [tx_in], [tx_out], 0, testnet=True)
>>> # sign the only input of the transaction
>>> print(tx_obj.sign_input(0, private_key))
True
>>> # serialize and hex to see what it looks like
>>> print(tx_obj.serialize().hex())
01000000013fdfef60ecd21c5e667cfe30fcb890a116688ca51ac3880f91008dd141ddcdb20700\
00006b483045022100ff77d2559261df5490ed00d231099c4b8ea867e6ccfe8e3e6d077313ed4f\
1428022033a1db8d69eb0dc376f89684d1ed1be75719888090388a16f1e8eedeb8067768012103\
dc585d46cfca73f3a75ba1ef0c5756a21c1924587480700c6eb64e3f75d22083ffffffff019334\
e500000000001976a914ad346f8eb57dee9a37981716e498120ae80e44f788ac00000000
>>> # send this signed transaction on the network
>>> node.send(tx_obj)
>>> # wait a sec so this message goes through with time.sleep(1)
>>> time.sleep(1)
```

```
>>> # now ask for this transaction from the other node
>>> # create a GetDataMessage
>>> getdata = GetDataMessage()
>>> # ask for our transaction by adding it to the message
>>> getdata.add_data(TX_DATA_TYPE, tx_obj.hash())
>>> # send the message
>>> node.send(getdata)
>>> # now wait for a Tx response
>>> received_tx = node.wait_for(Tx)
>>> # if the received tx has the same id as our tx, we are done!
>>> if received_tx.id() == tx_obj.id():
...     print('success!')
success!
```

Index

Symbols

% (modulo) operator, 5
* (multiplication) operator, 12
** operator, 12
+ (addition) operator, 10
== operator, 4
>> (right bit-shift) operator, 169
__add__ method, 9
__eq__ method, 4
__floordiv__ method, 15
__init__ method, 4
__mul__ method, 12
__ne__ method, 4
__pow__ method, 12, 16
__rmul__ method, 57
__sub__ method, 9
__truediv__ method, 15
∈ (element of) symbol, 8

A

acknowledgments, xxi-xxiii
addition (+) operator, 10
additive inverse, 2
address format, 83
addresses, reusing, 138, 247
amount field (outputs), 96
AntMiner S9, 171
Armory, 247
associativity, 32, 55
asymmetric problems, 51
attributions, xx

B

backup and restoration, 248

bare multisig, 143-149
Base58, 81-82
Base64, 81
Bech32 standard, 82
big-endian encoding, 74, 85
binary expansion, 57
binary trees, 197
BIP (Bitcoin Improvement Proposals)
  BIP0009, 168
  BIP0012, 155
  BIP0016, 150, 156, 229, 242
  BIP0032, 247
  BIP0034, 165
  BIP0037, 215
  BIP0039, 248
  BIP0044, 248
  BIP0065, 98, 168
  BIP0066, 168
  BIP0068, 168
  BIP0091, 168
  BIP0112, 90, 168
  BIP0113, 168, 169
  BIP0141, 168, 221, 235
  BIP0143, 135, 221, 233, 246, 250
  BIP0173, 82, 226
Bitcoin
  approach to learning, xiii
  developer of, xxi
  downloading and installation, xv-xviii
  open source projects, 248
  opportunities for developers, 250
  overview of components, 1
  prerequisites to learning, xiv
  suggested next projects, 249

About the Author

Jimmy Song is a developer with over 20 years' experience who started his career by reading the second edition of *Programming Perl*, published by the very same publisher as this book. He's been involved in way too many startups and got into Bitcoin full time in 2014. He's contributed to many different Bitcoin open source projects over the years, including Armory, Bitcoin Core, btcd, and pycoin.

If you ever meet Jimmy and want him to rant, ask him about Bitcoin, sound money, how fiat money makes everything worse, fasting, carnivory, powerlifting, raising children, or cowboy hats.

Colophon

The animal on the cover of *Programming Bitcoin* is a honey badger (*Mellivora capensis*), also known as a ratel. This mammal, despite its name, resembles a weasel or polecat more than a badger. It is found throughout Africa, the Indian subcontinent, and Southwest Asia. The honey badger is carnivorous, and has few predators because of its incredibly fierce nature when defending itself.

This animal gets its common name from its habit of raiding beehives to eat its favored food of honey (and bee larvae); it has a thick hide that minimizes the effect of bee stings. Honey badgers have a very diverse diet, however, which also includes snakes (including the venomous variety), rodents, insects, frogs, eggs, birds, fruit, roots, and plant bulbs. The honey badger has been seen chasing young lions away from kills, and is one of the few species to have been observed using tools.

The honey badger is a sturdy animal with a long body, a broad back, and a small flat head. Its legs are short and its feet are tipped with strong claws that make it an exceptional digger. The badger digs not only to unearth prey, but also to create a burrow for itself (around 3–10 feet long, on average). It has a gland at the base of its tail filled with a smelly secretion used to mark territory and warn away other animals. The skin at the back of the badger's neck is loose, which allows it to twist around and bite when it is being held.

The honey badger was the subject of a viral video in 2011, featuring comical narration over National Geographic footage of the animal's fearless behavior.

Many of the animals on O'Reilly covers are endangered; all of them are important to the world. To learn more about how you can help, go to *animals.oreilly.com*.

The cover illustration is by Karen Montgomery, based on a black and white engraving from *Natural History of Animals*. The cover fonts are Gilroy Semibold and Guardian Sans. The text font is Adobe Minion Pro; the heading font is Adobe Myriad Condensed; and the code font is Dalton Maag's Ubuntu Mono.